**Praise for Des Wilson's *Swimming with the Devilfish*
... *Under the Surface of Professional Poker:***

"... an enjoyable journey through the card-playing
world, colored equally by Wilson's impressive journalistic
background and his huge enthusiasm for the beautiful game"
—*The Guardian*

"Hugely enjoyable and highly informative"
—*Sunday Telegraph*

"The rich story of poker in Britain has never before been told.
This is what Wilson offers, revealingly and compellingly, in a
labor of love driven at a cracking pace ... an action-packed
read"—*The Observer*

"[Wilson] is brilliant at explaining the finer points of the game,
various hands and the psychological insights needed to be a
top player ... the book shines an awful lot of light on the
game"—*Daily Mirror*

"A book that finally puts Britain on the literary poker map"
—*Poker Player*

"It's gripping, revelatory and often very funny ...
a compulsive read from cover to cover"—*Poker Europa*

"Des Wilson has come up with a true classic of poker
literature ... a delightful, thoughtful and enjoyable read"
—PokerNews.com

Ghosts
at the Table

Riverboat Gamblers, Texas Rounders,
Internet Gamers, and
the Living Legends Who
Made **Poker** What It Is Today

Des Wilson

Da Capo Press
A Member of the Perseus Books Group

Cataloging-in-Publication Data for this book is available from the Library of Con-
gress.

First Da Capo Press edition 2008
First published in Great Britain by Mainstream Publishing Company, 2007
ISBN-13: 978-0-306-81628-4

Published by Da Capo Press
A Member of the Perseus Books Group
http://www.dacapopress.com

Da Capo Press books are available at special discounts for bulk purchase in the
U.S. by corporations, institutions, and other organizations. For more information,
please contact the Special Markets Department at the Perseus Books Group, 2300
Chestnut Street, Suite 200, Philadelphia, PA 19103, or call (800) 255-1514, or e-
mail special.markets@perseusbooks.com.

1 2 3 4 5 6 7 8 9

Contents

Contents

Preface
The four ages of poker

Poker is about people more than cards. Top players have been known to win a hand without even looking at their cards— they just *know* that if they make *this* bet at *this* moment with *this* opponent they will win, because their opponent will, in effect, walk away. This book, too, is about poker people, rather than cards. It's the *players* . . . the baseball-cap kid with dreams of wealth and glory, and the world-weary old pro bent on sur- vival and a bankroll saved for another day . . . the high-stakes professional gambler and the dime-and-dollar amateur . . . the honest man for whom the game's the thing, and the cheat and hustler to whom taking the money, by fair means or foul, is all that matters . . . it's these poker *people* who give the game its special aura. And it's the game's mythology—endur- ing stories of characters and confrontations from the past—that gives it a romance all of its own.

That does not mean this is a love story—far from it. Poker is fascinating and fun, but, at the professional or semi- professional level, it can be brutal. Poker players can be color- ful, companionable, even generous away from the table—but when they're in the game they're killers. They have to be, otherwise they should not be there. Sports stars get paid whether they win or lose; business leaders and politicians get paid whether they succeed or fail—but not poker players: if they win they have money, if they lose they don't. The only way a poker player can win is to take someone else's money— that's the scorecard. No room for sentiment here.

There's truth in the old saying that games like Texas hold'em take a moment to learn and a lifetime to master. Be in no doubt, poker *is* a game of skill. It calls for discipline and patience, for courage and a sense of timing, for psychological insight and cool and careful decision making under pressure, for practice and study, and for intellectual and physical stamina. Luck helps—of course it does—but you need the ability and experience to get to where the luck matters. In Jesse May's memorable phrase, "the trick to poker is mastering the luck" . . . and then, when you've done that, when you've mastered both the game and the luck, and when you've got the big stack, when you're dominating the table, when you're *the man*, it's about the exercise of power—about domination, exploitation, manipulation of the weak. Oh yes, poker mirrors life.*

On this journey from poker's past to its present I have not turned a blind eye to its less savory days and personalities. My story will not please everyone in the game. Yet it *should* because the game is greater than its coarser moments and players. It is no coincidence that poker has become so popular. Its great players are both fearless and exceptionally gifted. Its history is full of characters and color and competitive moments to compare with any recreational activity you can name. Away from the professional or semi-professional card rooms it is also enjoyed by millions and millions all over the world, in their homes, local clubs and pubs. It's both tough and uncompromising *and* companionable and enjoyable.

This history of poker does not rely just on previous writings and/or interviews. Wherever possible I have gone back to the places where it happened, to sniff the air and duck into the dark alleys where the game was played in its more dangerous days. My aim has been to set today's game in the context of its past. You have to drive for hour after hour after hour "fadin' the white line" in Texas to understand how hard the lives of the

---

*See *A simple guide to Texas hold'em* (p. 326) *for definitions and rules of the game.*

road gamblers were . . . you have to go to Deadwood and Tombstone to fully understand the nature of those who lived and fought and played poker there in the days of the Wild West—and I have done that and much more.

Why has poker become so hugely popular? Partly because it works on television . . . partly because the Internet has made it a game one can play alone at home . . . partly because of the huge sums now spent promoting it, and the equally huge sums that can be won. Partly, too, it's because it is such an endlessly fascinating game. But, all that said, I believe the key to its popularity is its history. The players, even the youngest, *know* it comes from the back alley, the gangsters' den, the Western saloon. They *know* there was a time when there were guns in the game . . . they *know* that there are ghosts at the table. And that's what makes it special. Poker's history is always there, hovering over every hand, not least because some of the greatest names in its history are still alive, still competing and seemingly destined to play until the day they're carried from the card room, their last hand dealt.

Poker's history is, above all, about the unique combination of guts, nerve, shrewdness, ruthlessness and survivability that have seen these extraordinary characters eventually come, with the game itself, out of the shadows and into the sunlight.

Ghosts at the Table is not an exhaustive history of poker. My aim has been to identify its special characters and the stories that matter, and, above all, to answer some of the game's unanswered questions and solve some of its mysteries. This is a game shrouded in mythology. Perhaps it's because fact merges with fiction, we hear so many versions of the more famous stories. Perhaps because it has been illegal in so many places for so long, poker is short on records and statistics. Perhaps because poker players live for the moment—this hand, this game—they lack curiosity about what happened when and why. Whatever the reason, what should be simple questions— like where and when did Texas hold'em begin?—prove extraordinarily difficult to answer. But I believe I have got as close as it's possible to get.

I have built my story around what I have identified as the four ages of poker:

First, *old frontier poker* . . . the poker of the riverboats and the Western gaming halls of the nineteenth century. In poker parlance, this was the game *pre-flop*.

Second, *the poker of the road gamblers* in Texas and other Southern states in the mid-twentieth century . . . without them the game would never have become what it is today. In poker parlance, *the flop*.

Third, *the rise of poker in Las Vegas* and, from there, throughout the world at the end of the twentieth century and the beginning of the twenty-first, *the turn*.

And fourth, *the poker explosion* of the last decade, *the river*.

What will come next? Poker will, I suspect, continue to grow, worldwide, because it has proved its resilience and because a lifetime is not enough for anyone to beat it. I also suspect it will become cleaner, and more respectable, and the rough edges will be knocked off it.

The danger is that as the last of the Texan road gamblers die away and the bright young guys with their caps and shades and minds like calculators take over, poker's amazing history will be forgotten.

Hopefully this book will help to stop that happening.

If so, the journey we now begin will have been more than worthwhile.

The first age of poker

Fact or fiction on the frontier?

. . . an investigation into the mythology of poker's past

one

Aces and eights
. . . death in Deadwood

I wake at five in the morning and look out the window. It's snowing in Deadwood. With no one around, and Main Street completely white, it looks like a ghost town. I'm reminded of the disconcerting warning I received when I checked in at the Bullock Hotel that there is, in fact, a ghost in the building.

Seth Bullock came to Deadwood in 1876 in the same week Wild Bill Hickok was killed. He and his partner, Sol Star, opened a hardware store. Seth eventually became the county's first sheriff and Sol its mayor. When the store burned down, they replaced it with this atmospheric old hotel. In a way their store, Star Bullock Hardware, marked the beginning and end of respectability in Deadwood; turn left as you came out the door and you were on your way to the more reputable end of Main Street, with its banks and brokers, its stores and livery stables; turn right and you almost immediately entered the Badlands, with its brothels, gambling halls, rowdy saloons, and opium houses.

This snowy morning, however, I'm more concerned about coming face to face with the ghost. This is no joke. There have been at least thirty sightings. Others have reported "a strong paranormal presence" in the rooms. The ghost is Seth himself. Apparently he gets irritated when he thinks the staff is shirking its duties: plates and glasses shake and even fly across the restaurant, things move, electrical appliances switch themselves on and off. An antique clock that has not worked for years suddenly chimes. Some claim they hear their name shouted by a male voice, or are tapped on the shoulder. There are reports of footsteps when there's no one there. And what worries me is that *my room*—the Roosevelt Room (apparently Seth was friendly with Theodore)—has been more affected than any other.

As soon as possible I'm out of it and walking down the street to where the Badlands once were. Under its blanket of snow, Main Street looks much as it must have in the winters of the 1870s. It's only a matter of seconds before I'm standing where Nuttall and Mann's Saloon No. 10 once was. A rough wooden sign tells the story: *Historic site—Saloon No. 10, where Wild Bill was shot, August 2, 1876.*

What, you may be wondering, is the relevance of this to poker? Well, for a start, Wild Bill is in poker's Hall of Fame— one of only thirty-three so honored. And I've come to find out why. Also, he was shot while playing poker, and possibly shot *because* of poker—specifically because of a game played the night before he died. And, of course, he is said to have been holding aces and eights—now universally known (and by the more superstitious feared) as the dead man's hand. But I'm not convinced. I have come to Deadwood with questions. Was he *really* holding aces and eights? How do we know this? And, if he was, what was the fifth card?

Deadwood itself is not short of folk who think they have the answers. The problem is, they're different answers. The only thing uniting them is that Wild Bill and his murder are good for business. While many old gold-rush places are now ghost towns, Deadwood is a survivor. With its population fallen from about 30,000 in its wild days to fewer than 2,500, Deadwood legalized gambling in 1989. This helped to preserve and restore the place, albeit paying the price of becoming a mini Las Vegas with eighty or so gambling joints and more than its fair share of saloons. Thus, it needs Wild Bill. It is Wild Bill who attracts two million gamblers a year from all over the northwest and beyond. Wild Bill is Deadwood's star. He's everywhere, alive and well and living on a T-shirt. He *has* to be alive in order that over the summer he can be shot daily outside Saloon No. 10.

There's money in Wild Bill and no one gets more of it than the re-created Saloon No. 10, now on the respectable end of Main Street and owned by the Keehn family. It organizes the daily murders and its walls are covered with pictures of Bill and his cohorts. As I play cards in its cozy card room, in a chair facing the door (of course), my every move is silently but, I feel, critically watched from the walls by Martha Jane Cannary (better known as Calamity Jane) . . . by the black former slave Nat Love (better known as Deadwood Dick) . . . and by Potato Creek Johnny, Buffalo Bill Cody, Colorado Charlie Utter, Seth Bullock, and, of course, Wild Bill himself.

Right in front of me is Poker Alice Tubbs, cigar clenched between her teeth. So daunting is her stare that after each hand I glance up in the hope of an approving nod. I should be so lucky! Unlike the others on the wall, Poker Alice came to Deadwood well after Wild Bill was killed. She was already a veteran of mining camps in Arizona, Colorado, and New Mexico, where she dealt cards and, it's alleged, ran at least one brothel (though she was a religious woman and, it is said, wouldn't let the girls work on Sundays). She was gutsy, as tough as they come. As a note in the local museum says: "She was familiar with cards, guns, and men, and could handle all three." It's claimed that she was a hell of a poker player and once won $6,000 in a game, a fortune in those days. She was once asked if she ever lost: "I've never seen anyone grow humpbacked carrying away the money they won from me," she replied. She always carried a gun and once shot a player in the arm at the poker table when he drew a knife on the gambler who became her second husband, W. G. Tubbs. She also once stood trial for killing a man but was acquitted. By sheer grit she lived to seventy-nine.

While trying to avoid her eye at Saloon No. 10, my attention is captured by five playing cards, carefully displayed in a glass case on the wall. There are two black aces and two black eights—and a nine of diamonds.

Nine of diamonds?

So Saloon No. 10 has taken a position on one of poker's enduring puzzles: what was the fifth card? A sign even offers me $250 if I'm dealt the hand. (As the *Gambling Times* once estimated the odds on this exact hand at 2,598,959 to one, I decide not to stay in town until I get it.)

We will come back to the fifth card, for I am moving too fast. There are facts to recall—about who Wild Bill was and what actually happened that fateful day. Deadwood has the answers . . . in its splendid Adams Museum . . . in an exhibition in the basement of the (old) Saloon No. 10 . . . and in countless books and pamphlets. Probably anyone in Deadwood could tell you about Wild Bill. This is what I learn:

James Butler Hickok was born in 1837. When you consider his legendary status, it's surprising to discover that he lived only thirty-nine years (in fact, a lot of the old West's most famous names died young—usually full of bullet holes). And when you consider how his name has forever been associated with Deadwood, it's also surprising to learn that he was actually there for only three weeks.

Joseph Rosa, perhaps the leading authority on Wild Bill, says he was physically impressive:

> He was over six feet tall, broad-shouldered, and narrow-hipped. He wore his auburn hair shoulder-length and had a straw-colored moustache. But his dominant feature was his blue-grey eyes; these became coldly implacable when aroused. Around his waist he wore a belt from which hung a matched set of ivory-handled Colt's Model 1851 Navy revolvers. He was rarely without them and was reputed never to miss.[1]

Rosa says Hickok's personality surprised many who met him for the first time, knowing only his reputation:

> Instead of the raw-boned desperado . . . he was courteous, soft-spoken, self-effacing and, generally knowledgeable . . . a man of courage and integrity.

Hickok left Illinois when he was nineteen and for a while drove a stagecoach on the Oregon and Santa Fe Trails before becoming a well-known Civil War scout. He also served General Custer. He later combined poker playing with being a much-admired and feared lawman in Kansas, notably in the cattle boomtowns of Hays, where he was acting sheriff for a time, and Abilene, where he was marshal. He was also a deputy US marshal in Kansas for three years.

His critics say he was unnecessarily violent, but an article in *City Life* in 1895 claims:

> He never wantonly took human life. It is true that in his exciting career on the borders of civilization he killed several men, but there is no instance on record where he shed blood except in defense of his own life or in the line of duty as a peace officer.

Another Deadwood historian, Thadd Turner, acknowledges that Hickok was "either well-liked, unconditionally feared, or misrepresented as a bad man and killer." Turner comes down on the positive side:

> Hickok provided valuable service in the Union Army during the Civil War, was a respected plainsman and frontiersman, reliable cavalry scout, and performed much-needed duties as a fearless lawman. These activities have been clearly documented. Wild Bill was a law-abiding and respectable citizen—he was one of the good guys.[2]

As Rosa says, if he had a passion, it was for gambling. One observer is quoted as saying Wild Bill "would rather indulge in poker than eat."

He was probably not as heroic as we've been led to believe, or as bad as his critics maintain. He became nationally famous as a result of an article in *Harper's* magazine in February of 1867. Written by Colonel George Ward Nichols, a serving officer in the Union Army, this colorful account of Wild Bill's exploits appears to be part fact, part fiction, although Nichols undoubtedly believed it all. Wild Bill himself possibly had some fun with his interviewer, but others, too, "helped" Nichols to create the extraordinary and heroic personality who emerged from the piece. Other magazine articles and "dime books" were to follow, and Wild Bill's reputation as a great fighter and frontiersman was established for all time.

One of his more famous gunfights, and one of the few not "in the line of duty," helped establish the kind of confrontation that became an essential scene in every Hollywood Western: hero and bad guy facing each other in the street, staring each other down, hands near their gun holsters, each knowing his life depends on outdrawing the other and shooting first and shooting straight. This is more or less what happened in July of 1865. Hickok became involved in a dispute with another gambler called Tutt over a debt. Hickok felt his honor had been impugned. The two emerged from opposite ends of the street in the early evening and, having walked toward each other, drew their guns and fired. Tutt missed; Hickok did not, and Tutt was killed. Hickok was subsequently arrested, but acquitted of the crime as it was judged to be self-defense.

His most tragic fight occurred some years later when in his capacity as lawman he attempted to disarm Phil Coe, a saloon owner in Abilene, with whom he had quarreled. Coe fired at him and Hickok killed him. As he did so, he caught sight of someone else brandishing a gun and instinctively fired, killing one of his best friends.

By the time he was thirty-nine, Wild Bill was already world-weary and his eyesight was going. The killing of his friend had also done much to knock the stuffing out of him as a fighter. He began to contemplate a quieter life. In Cheyenne in 1876 he fell in love with a widow, Agnes Lake Thatcher, and they were married on March 5 that year. He was at the time short of money and when his old friend and partner, Colorado Charlie Utter, told him that he and others were planning to take a wagon train to the Black Hills of South Dakota in search of gold, Hickok decided to join them. Most likely he hoped that the mining communities springing up in the Black Hills would create opportunities in law enforcement. On the way they were joined by Calamity Jane, who later claimed a relationship with Hickok and was to be buried beside his grave. By all accounts, their affair existed only in her imagination; Hickok had little to do with her.

The wagon train arrived in Deadwood on July 12, 1876, and Utter, Hickok, and the others found themselves in a lawless, violent boomtown. Surrounded by canvas tents and crudely constructed log cabins, the place teemed with gold miners and those who fed off them, with more arriving in the hundreds every day. Main Street was already emerging as a major business center for the Black Hills: banks, stores, and stables were opening daily, and saloons, gambling joints, and "houses of ill repute" were packed with hell-raising miners. Deadwood even had its own Chinatown, complete with opium dens.

Fortunately I don't have to depend on others' writings to picture the scene; photography had already been invented and I can see for myself from some striking images in the Adams Museum how the miners could hardly move on the street for the wagons with their supplies of food, construction and mining equipment, and other necessities for a city springing up from nowhere.

Charlie Utter and Hickok lived in tents in one of the many miners' camps within a relatively short walk of Main Street.

While Utter thrived in Deadwood, Hickok had difficulty settling. Deadwood in those days has been described as "the most lawless place on the frontier." For every miner, there was someone plotting to exploit his toil by cheating, manipulating, or robbing—even killing—him. Deadwood, it was said, saw a murder a day. The vicious criminal element needed someone of Hickok's law-upholding reputation like a hole in the head. They let it be known that if he were to seek to become a law officer, he would live his life in constant danger.

In fact, from the moment he arrived in Deadwood, Hickok had premonitions of death. He is reputed to have said to Utter: "Charlie, I feel this is going to be my last camp and I won't leave it alive." A newspaper later reported that he said to someone else: "I feel that my days are numbered, my sun is sinking fast. I know I shall be killed here." And on August 1, the day before he was killed, he wrote to his wife:

> Agnes darling,
>
>   If such should be we never meet again, while firing my last shot I will gently breathe the name of my wife, Agnes—and with wishes even for my enemies I will make the plunge and try to swim to the other shore.

For much of the three weeks, he played cards, usually poker. How good a player was he? The balance of opinion suggests that, if not exactly a "fish," he was not an outstanding player. He was even known to cut the odd corner. His leading biographer Joseph Rosa recounts stories of Hickok

> trimming the cards of low numbers so that the deck could be more easily thumbed. Then with the face cards untrimmed the dealer could detect the cards he wanted to deal himself more easily. The accuser did, however, add the rider: Nowadays such procedure would be regarded as cheating, but it was the way the game was played in those days.

One Black Hills chronicler wrote of Hickok that

while no one would say that he was a man to violate the peculiar code of ethics governing the gambling fraternity, it is not improbable that his reputation as a gunfighter won for him many a stake over the poker table which his cards could not win.

A famous Hickok poker story concerns a confrontation with a man called McDonald, who Hickok suspected of cheating. Hickok was all but wiped out when McDonald called a hand.

"I've got jacks full," he said, tossing the cards onto the table.

Hickok replied, "I have aces full of sixes."

McDonald reached out and turned over the cards. "But there's only one six," he said.

Hickok produced his pistol. "Here is the other six," he said.

McDonald went white. "Take the pot," he said. "The hand is good."

On the evening of August 1, 1876, Hickok was playing poker in Saloon No. 10. One of the other players was a miner in his twenties who called himself Bill Sutherland. As the game developed, Hickok was gaining the upper hand and at one point he made a substantial bet. Conceivably he went—in today's parlance—"all-in." Sutherland had no cash left but he pulled from his pocket a purse of gold dust and placed it on the table. Wild Bill won the hand. The purse of gold dust was then weighed and appeared to be a few dollars short. Hickok was in an uncompromising mood, so Sutherland went to his camp and came back with just enough to pay the debt. Hickok realized that the youngster was broke and, taking some change from his pocket—about a dollar's worth—offered it to him to buy a meal. Most versions of the story say that Sutherland was too proud to take it. But the bartender, Harry "Sam" Young, later claimed that he did take it.

The following day Hickok returned to Saloon No. 10 about noon to find three men playing draw poker. They were Captain

William Massie, a former riverboat navigator, Carl Mann, the saloon's co-owner, and a twenty-year-old called Charlie Rich who was already making a living as a full-time card player.

Hickok had always made a point of taking a particular seat, one that enabled him to have his back to the wall and a clear view of the whole room, but Rich was already sitting there and, albeit good-humoredly, declined to move. By all accounts Hickok was not concerned; he still had a reasonable, if not complete, view of the whole place and there was only a small space behind him.

After they had been playing for a while, the young loser from the previous evening, Bill Sutherland, as he was known to Hickok (it only later emerged that his real name was Jack McCall), entered the bar. Hickok observed him but didn't consider this significant; instead he concentrated on a big hand with Massie. At its end he was heard to exclaim, "The old duffer! He broke me on that hand." As he did so, McCall, who had quietly moved behind Hickok, pulled a gun from under his jacket and shot him, crying out, "Damn you, take that." The bullet drilled a hole in Hickok's head and went on to hit Massie in the wrist. Hickok died instantly and fell soundlessly to the floor. As he had predicted to Charlie Utter, Deadwood had done him in.

Charlie organized a funeral and wrote on the wooden "gravestone":

Wild Bill, J.B. Hickok killed by the assassin Jack McCall in Deadwood, Black Hills, August 2nd, 1876. Pard, we will meet again in the happy hunting ground to part no more.
Goodbye, Colorado Charlie, C.H. Utter

All this is undisputed fact.

But now, in Deadwood, some 130 years later, I want to settle the remaining disputes.

First, why did McCall do it? McCall argued at his first, hastily organized trial that he did it to avenge a brother whom Hickok had killed. According to a newspaper reporter who was there, McCall said, "Well, men, I have but few words to say. Wild Bill killed my brother, and I killed him . . . I am not sorry for what I have done." Somehow he got himself acquitted, but it later emerged there was a fundamental flaw in this defense: *there was no evidence that McCall had a brother.*

Could he have been acting as a "hit man" for others who either had a grudge or feared Hickok's presence in the town and wanted him eliminated? This is what McCall argued prior to his second trial. He alleged that a gambler called John Varnes had paid him to murder Hickok because of an earlier dispute they had had at the poker table. But a local newspaper, which published the Varnes story prior to the court case, was forced to almost immediately print an apologetic retraction. And as far as the records show, McCall did not repeat it at the trial. Instead he appears to have told the court that he was drunk when he shot Wild Bill and didn't even remember it happening.

To me the answer seems obvious. Hickok died during a poker game *as a result of another poker game.*

When he was beaten the previous evening, McCall was deprived of the gold he had either worked for—and it was hard, back-breaking work—or stolen. And he was publicly humiliated by his defeat, by being sent back to the camp for more gold and, perhaps above all, by Hickok's well-intentioned but possibly insensitively made offer of a few coins for supper. I believe the most likely scenario is that this uneducated and unstable youngster came back the following day resentful, seething with hatred for the man who had embarrassed him; to McCall there was only one way he could re-establish himself in the eyes of Deadwood and that was to destroy the living legend. He had to kill Wild Bill Hickok.

I am reinforced in this view by an item that later appeared in the *Cheyenne Daily Leader*. It quoted McCall as claiming that Hickok "as good as robbed" him of the gold dust. Another in *The Traveller* quoted McCall as saying he did it because of the way Hickok had "snatched a card from him."

If my theory is the right one, then Wild Bill Hickok lost his life because he won—at poker.

Now to question number two: what cards did Wild Bill have in his hand? Were they aces and eights? How much credence can we put on the legend of the dead man's hand? As I explore the various sources of information in Deadwood and review a number of books on Wild Bill, it becomes clear that, despite the fame of the dead man's hand, the reliability of this story has been minimally addressed compared with the wider questions about whether McCall was guilty and why he committed the crime. The fact is no one at the time much cared what the cards were and, I suppose you could say, why should they?

However, I do. This is the most famous poker hand in history, known all over the world as the dead man's hand for more than 130 years. Either it was aces and eights, or it was not. In addition to old-West historians and poker enthusiasts, this matters most to Deadwood itself, because the hand is part of the dramatic story it has polished and publicized and still promotes to the outside world over 130 years later. Deadwood earns money from the dead man's hand.

The indefatigable Joseph Rosa tells me that, despite some intensive research, no contemporary reference has been found to the cards Hickok was holding when he was shot. Mr Rosa says it was only in later years that the hand became immortalized as the dead man's hand and was reputed to consist of the ace of spades, the ace of clubs, two black eights, and the jack of diamonds, with the last card disputed.

Thadd Turner, who has investigated Wild Bill Hickok's murder more exhaustively than anyone else, supports Rosa:

Ironically, at the time Wild Bill was killed, there appears to be no written account available of Wild Bill's final cards. The aces and eights story seems to have gained acceptability in later accounts of the event.[3]

Turner concludes: "The actual cards in Wild Bill's final hand may never be identified."

Another book on sale in Deadwood, by Western writer John Ames, states:

Many myths surround the death of Wild Bill, including the famous dead man's hand. (It's not known what cards Hickok was holding at his death.)[4]

So by the time I arrive at the offices of the Deadwood Historical Preservation Society, linked to the Adams Museum, I am beginning to believe that the whole story about the aces and eights is a myth . . . that there was no dead man's hand.

However a surprise awaits me at the society's offices. The cheerful woman manning the front desk listens to my questions and says, "But we have the cards in the museum."

What!!! The actual pack???

"Well, that's what they tell me," she says. "A few years ago a family called Stephens claimed that one Richard Stephens had been making a delivery to Saloon No. 10 on August 2 and was actually there when Wild Bill was shot. In the midst of the uproar he scooped up the cards and took them home, and they were on the family mantelpiece for years. Then they were donated to the museum."

Well, what are the cards? I hurry around the corner to the museum. There they are, displayed in a glass case.

They are aces (of diamonds and clubs, not spades and clubs as usually suggested), and eights (of hearts and spades), and a queen of hearts.

Is this, then, the proof that the hand *was* aces and eights?

But who is this family and what evidence do they have that this is the actual pack? Could this man have been fantasizing, or even fooling everyone for some reason best known to himself?

I harass the museum for more information and its helpful curator offers to contact the current custodian of the Stephens family's claim to fame. This turns out to be Linda Urbaniak, the sixty-six-year-old great-granddaughter of Richard Stephens. She lives near Seattle. I send her a list of questions by email and she replies immediately. This is the gist of the correspondence:

Q: *What was your great-grandfather's occupation and what took him to the Saloon No. 10 that day?*

A: He was Richard Stephens and he was a dairy farmer delivering buttermilk to the No. 10 on his regular route after earlier deliveries in the day in Rapid City and Sturgis. He lived there on a farm outside Sturgis until 1930 when he moved to Washington (state).

Q: *Has anyone ever claimed to have witnessed him picking up Wild Bill's hand?*

A: No . . . remember there was [a] shooting going on and people were hitting the floor.

Q: *Then WHY did he pick up the cards—what led him to do it?*

A: I don't think it was a conscious act. According to my grandfather and dad, he just said that he stuck them in his pocket and forgot about them as everyone dashed out after McCall. Apparently he didn't even realize he had them until he got home the following day.

Q: *Did he just pick up Bill's hand—or the whole pack?*

A: He just picked up Hickok's hand as the cards slipped from Wild Bill's fingers.

Q: *Did he leave a letter or any notes in writing about this?*

A: If any notes were written, they no longer exist as far as I know.

Q: *Have the cards ever been forensically examined re: date etc.?*

A: No.

Q: *Did he ever mention showing them to anyone else at the time?*

A: No, but he showed the cards throughout his life to many people, as did my grandfather, James Griffith Stephens, and as did my father, also Richard H. Stephens.

She then sends me an additional note:

The cards are the ace of diamonds, the ace of clubs, the eight of hearts, the eight of spades, and the queen of hearts. They are larger than modern cards, and the placement of the patterns indicating the individual suits and values cover nearly the whole card. There are no numbers on the cards as in modern cards, and they are worn through usage and age . . .

For many years the men of my family enjoyed showing the cards to friends and acquaintances, first my great-grandfather, then his son and only child, James Griffith Stephens. When my grandfather died in 1946, my grandmother gave them to my father, Richard (Dick) Herman Stephens. My dad, Dick Stephens, donated the cards to the Adams Museum in the 1970s.

She adds that no attempt was made to authenticate the cards because "they were never intended to be displayed, were kept as an interesting phenomenon within the family, and so lack any real notarization that they are real."

Clearly Ms. Urbaniak believes—indeed believes passionately—that the cards are genuine, but the fact remains that the Stephens's story has to be taken on her great-grandfather's word alone. Is this what the museum has done . . . taken it on trust? Did it take any steps to authenticate the cards before displaying them? I put the museum's curator to the test and she emails me as follows:

The whole question of the actual cards in the dead man's hand has always been a matter of debate and it still is. We get asked about it all the time. We have a research file full of newspaper articles, magazine articles, etc. with various theories about the cards in the hand . . . were they black eights and black aces; what was the fifth card, etc. There is even a letter written by the Adams Museum's curator in 1945 in which he gives three different sources with three different combinations of cards! But when the Stephens family brought the cards in to the museum in the 1950s, I don't think anyone formally associated with our organization attempted to do any kind of authenticating. At that time, either the process of dating paper was unknown or the museum did not have the resources to pursue such testing. At this time, our official policy is to display the cards, report the details we received from the family, refer to the displayed cards as the "purported dead man's hand," and leave the rest to our visitors. After all, in Deadwood, Wild Bill Hickok has attained an almost mystical status. We've more or less decided to let the cards be as mysterious as the man. There are no plans in place to do testing on the cards to establish a timeframe for the age of the paper because that really would neither prove nor disprove the validity of the Stephens family's provenance, and we would not want to insult the family who have so generously donated an heirloom greatly valued by all of them. So, in the end, the Adams Museum's position is that we believe we have the cards held by Wild Bill, but nobody can say for sure whether we do or we don't.

Joseph Rosa now emails me to say that in addition to great-grandfather Stephens, there was one other witness in support of aces and eights:

> In the 1920s Ellis T. "Doc" Pierce, who was a part-time barber-cum-doctor, in correspondence with Frank J. Wilstach, stated that when he got to where Hickok's body lay he found the pocket hand to be aces and eights—two pair.

I lie on my bed at the Bullock, keeping a wary eye out for the ghost, and think about the doctor's story. I feel there's a flaw in this . . . but I can't identify it.

What would Sherlock Holmes spot that I was missing? Could I, in this spooky room, summon up *his* ghost?

Of course I could, and now the flaw became clear . . .

"There you are, Holmes," cried Watson. "The doctor corroborates the Stephens story. It MUST have been aces and eights."

Holmes, violin under one arm, heroin needle in the other, puffed on his pipe. "I'm afraid not, Watson," he replied. "The opposite is the case. Either the doctor discredits Stephens's account, or Stephens discredits the doctor's."

"But how, Holmes?"

"Elementary, my dear Watson. If Stephens, as the family claims, rushed over to Hickok at the time of the shooting, snatched up the cards and put them in his pocket, and then joined the chase for McCall, the cards could not have been there for the doctor to discover."

"So one of them was not telling the truth."

The counter case to aces and eights is further represented by Harry "Sam" Young, who was at the time the twenty-five-year-old bartender in Saloon No. 10. Young matters because *he was there.* Young left home in New York State at fourteen to chase his dreams in the West; he worked as a cattle herder and buffalo skinner and drove supply wagons. He first published his memoirs in 1915. I found a copy of his *Hard Knocks* in Deadwood. He writes:

> They had been playing not to exceed 20 minutes when Massie beat a king-full for Bill with four sevens breaking Bill on the hand. They were playing table stakes. Bill then asked me to bring him $50 worth of checks [chips], which I did. Charlie Utter, who had been sitting by Bill's side but a little back of him, remarked "Bill, I will go and get something to eat." I placed the checks on the table in front of Bill, standing as I did so between him and Carl Mann. Bill looked up at me and remarked "The old duffer [meaning Massie] broke me on the hand." They were the last words he uttered. There was a loud report followed by the words "Take that." McCall had shot him in the back.[5]

So while Young does not explain how he knew what the cards were, he is clear that Massie, with four sevens, beat Wild Bill who had a king-high full house.

How can the Stephens and the Young stories be reconcilable? There is one possibility—that while Young was getting Hickok the additional chips, a fresh hand was dealt and that this, not the full house, was the hand Wild Bill was holding when he was shot.

The problem with this is that Young claims Wild Bill had just exclaimed, "The old duffer broke me on the hand" when he was shot; this would suggest he was still concentrating on the full house and not yet looking down at a hand containing aces and eights. In fact Young does not mention aces and eights at all, and you would think someone writing a memoir, having witnessed this historic scene, would mention them if they were, in fact, dealt.

What conclusion do we reach? It all comes down to whether we believe the Stephens story and whether the cards in the Adams Museum are genuine.

If we do not, and there is considerable skepticism even in Deadwood, then there is no conclusive evidence that Wild Bill ever held aces and eights. Apart from the Stephens story, all we have are the conflicting reports from (1) a "doctor" who arrived after Hickok's death and says he saw aces and eights, and (2) a bartender who was watching the game and says Wild Bill had a full house, kings-up. There is no witness now alive and, of course, no photographic record.

It is also worth considering that the whole aces and eights story did not emerge at the time of the murder but much later. Why? Rosa hints that it could be vested interest—i.e., that it was Deadwood "perpetuating an air of destiny or fate concerning Hickok's poker hand." Now that I'm actually in Deadwood I can easily be persuaded this is the case. Deadwood is not just a town, it's a business, a brand, and it not only needs Wild Bill but it also needs the dead man's hand.

So, to sum up, there is no satisfactory evidence that Wild Bill ever held aces or eights . . . but no one in town is going to admit it. Sorry, Deadwood—but that's the reality.

All this said, if Wild Bill Hickok *was* holding aces and eights, what was the fifth card? Here the plot thickens, because the town's two major tourist attractions, Saloon No. 10 (nine of diamonds) and the Adams Museum (queen of hearts) are selling conflicting stories.

Saloon No. 10, as resurrected, has an obvious vested interest in this. The family that owns the current version of the saloon has pinned its reputation on the nine of diamonds and has no desire to look silly by changing its position. I call the senior member of the family and ask him what evidence he has that it was the nine of diamonds.

"Well, I wasn't there, if that's what you mean," he replies, a little more truculently than I feel the question deserves.

Well, how did he know it was the nine of diamonds? Was it just a case of this being passed down from father to son?

"That's exactly what it is."

In other words, he hasn't a clue whether it's true or not.

(The No. 10 is, by the way, a terrific saloon—good poker room with six tables; walls full of historic pictures; long, wooden bars; and a great restaurant upstairs called the Deadwood Social Club.)

Shouldn't the town's two leading tourist destinations get their act together? But, then, how can they? Saloon No. 10 has publicized its five cards for years; they're on the T-shirts. And the museum has what it claims to be the real cards on its wall. For either to change their position would add up to a considerable loss of face.

Inevitably this "rivalry" has caused some confusion in town. You would expect the Chamber of Commerce to support the town's museum. But, no . . . it has a nine of diamonds on its logo. When asked why, it replies, "because that's what's on the wall of Saloon No. 10."

The hand has been portrayed in films many times. In *Stagecoach*, a dying character has the queen of hearts as the fifth card. In *The Plainsman*, Gary Cooper held the king of spades. And a History Channel documentary showed the hand with a nine of clubs.

After careful study, the *Gaming Times* in 1998 produced five possibilities for the fifth card based on seventeen sources. They were:

nine of diamonds, listed six times
jack of diamonds, listed four times
queen of diamonds, listed twice
queen of hearts, listed three times

The fifth possibility, argued by two sources, is that the fifth card was never dealt.

Poor old Wild Bill. Dead at thirty-nine, never to see his beloved wife again, and his exceptional life and legend has been reduced to confusion and claim and counter-claim about which cards he held when he was shot. And unless someone in authority orders that he be dug up and DNA tests carried out on him and the cards (if that is possible after all these years) the mystery will remain a mystery.

At the end of my time in Deadwood I climb to its Boot Hill, an impressively atmospheric cemetery that is actually called Mt Moriah and is dramatically positioned on a hill overlooking the town.

At its heart is a proud statue of Wild Bill Hickok. Beside it is the grave of Calamity Jane, and close by that of Potato Creek Johnny, who came to Deadwood well after Wild Bill was killed and who mined one of the biggest nuggets of gold ever seen in the Black Hills. He became such a local celebrity that when he died in 1943 they buried him in the company of Deadwood's other two iconic figures.

It is snowing once more and cold and, not surprisingly, there is no one else here.

I wonder . . . if Seth Bullock still has a ghostly presence in the town, is it possible that Wild Bill does too?

I look around to confirm I can't be seen . . . then I whisper to the statue: "What was it, Bill? Was it aces and eights?"

There is no reply.

Well, *of course* there isn't.

But I'll swear that as I walk away I hear mocking laughter from where Bill, Calamity Jane, and Potato Creek Johnny are resting. Or is Seth following me from the Roosevelt Room at the Bullock? Or is it just the wind in the pine trees, causing them to creak as they gently sway and cover the gravestones with more snow?

I don't wait to find out. There's a strange atmosphere in Deadwood in winter.

Ghostly.

It's time to move on.

two

Poker in the Old West

- **Tombstone . . . another ghost, another poker mystery**
- **The Kansas cattle towns . . . cowboys and cards**
- **The poker-playing lawmen . . . guns at the table**

I'm in Tombstone for less than an hour and already I've discovered that ghosts and controversial poker games are not exclusive to Deadwood.

The Bird Cage Theater—one-time bordello-gaming club-vaudeville theater-saloon—was described in the *New York Times* in 1882 as "the wildest, toughest, wickedest honky-tonk between Basin Street and the Barbary Coast." It claims no less than twenty-six ghosts, the spirits of the men murdered there in the eight years it was open. Today some locals say they hear laughter and 1880s music as they pass the empty building late at night; employees talk of opening the doors in the morning and inhaling cigar and whisky fumes that cannot be explained. There have been many "sightings" of a ghostly man in a visor. Ghost hunters come from far and wide to investigate. While in Tombstone I see a report by the South West Ghost Hunters: though they didn't actually see a ghost, they say:

> As we moved towards the stage the battery in one of the cameras suddenly drained completely. The battery was fully charged when we entered the building. We also measured a

variation in temperature of roughly ten degrees as the area got noticeably colder; no air conditioning vents are near this area.

The Bird Cage is the oldest building on Tombstone's famous Allen Street, the others having been burned to the ground and rebuilt over the years. It was boarded up in 1889 and stayed that way for nearly fifty years until it was re-opened as a museum. In its heyday it must have been a stunning experience. Its fourteen cribs—tiny rooms with only a bed and a small table—hung from the ceiling so that the "ladies of the night" looked like birds in a cage, hence the building's name. Its bars and vaudeville theater were always packed with a riotous crowd. Wrote one historian:

You could hear the raucous music and the shouts and laughter a long way down Allen Street . . . inside the sound ratcheted higher—the piano and the violins, the clanging of beer mugs and glasses, the clattering of poker chips and dice, cards fanning, laughter, loud conversations . . . there were clouds of cigar smoke mixed with the odors of beer and whisky, overpowering perfume, cheap cologne . . . The customers were almost entirely men; indeed, the population of Tombstone, as with any new boomtown, was almost entirely male . . . The Bird Cage Theater knew its clientele and had its own mission—to cater to the purposes of those who, night after night, burrowed themselves in its dark confines . . . Here, amidst the din and depravity, they looked for whatever sparks that life in this isolated desert town could offer.[1]

Downstairs at the back, shrouded in cigar smoke, there was an oasis of calm; this was the high-stakes poker room. It's still there, and it's this that I have come to see.

The Bird Cage's owner says that all the main fixtures in the poker room, even the cards and chips, are originals from the 1880s. There are two ancient green felt tables, the smaller being a "feeder" to the larger high rollers' table, its dealers' money box still in place. Between the tables there is a Heritage wood-stove; on the floor there is an old whisky keg; on the wall two beautiful mirrors of the period. In the corner there's a small bar. On the other side of the rail is a row of small bordello rooms with only curtains between the beds and the poker players. This is where the higher-class whores plied their trade, just three feet from the game. The cards were shuffled and dealt to a background of creaking bedsprings.

According to the Bird Cage owners, this was the scene of the longest continuous poker game in history. It involved seven players plus a dealer. It cost $1,000 to buy in (when money was money!). If you wanted to stop playing but still had chips, you had to give thirty or forty minutes' notice so that, if the next player on the list wasn't on the smaller table, a runner could go down the street to find him. *And it ran for eight years, five months, and three days, twenty-four hours a day, seven days a week.* Over that time more than $10 million exchanged hands, with the house pocketing $1 million of that.

The Bird Cage promotes this story as enthusiastically as Saloon No. 10 in Deadwood promotes its version of Wild Bill's last hand. There's no question that the poker room is genuine and also that it attracted high rollers from all over the West. It's also true that Doc Holliday and Johnny Ringo had a famous fight in the place. But did the game really run for eight years, five months, and three days without a break?

As in the case of the Wild Bill hand, there is no definitive evidence and no one seems to have looked for it. Few of the vast number of books, pamphlets and articles written about Tombstone refer to this game. At a Western writers' book fair taking place in town I find all the local historians in one place and pursue them relentlessly in search of the truth. My first target is the widely published Ben T. Traywick. He says he has no information on the game. This strikes me as significant. *The* leading Tombstone historian can't verify the story. I speak to two other historians, Steve Gatto and Sherry Monahan. "A lot of people think it never happened," they say. There are about fifty researchers and writers at this event and I can't find one who can help me. Later I discover a small book on the Bird Cage; its author devotes less than a page to the game and even he is skeptical.[2] All this strikes me as surprising.

I track down the current owner of the Bird Cage by phone. His name is Bill Hunley and he's surprised that I'm surprised.

"Whoever kept records of poker games?" he exclaims. "Of course there's no evidence. But it happened."

But how did he know?

"Because the Bird Cage has been passed down from my grandfather to my father and to me, and the history has been passed down with it. My grandfather was there. He lived till he was one hundred . . . he died in 1964."

This I find interesting. We have a witness. Dead . . . but a witness.

But how did he know it was exactly eight years, five months, and three days?

"Because it began the night the Bird Cage opened and it continued until the last hand was played at three in the morning the day it closed."

Bill says that rich men came from everywhere to play there. They included multimillionaire miner and rancher George Randolph Hearst and brewer Adolph Busch.

"Of course you won't find the game referred to in newspapers and the like because bordellos and gambling were never talked about officially. And it was kept secure. That's why it was in the downstairs room at the back. But it was there. Everyone in the gambling business knew about it. It was talked about all over the West."

Bill is convincing and seems a likeable guy. On the other hand, he is also the source of some of the more bizarre Bird Cage ghost stories. (For example, the dice table which mysteriously moved itself one night when the theater was closed, positioning itself across a door labelled "Don't disturb our 26 resident ghosts." Bill says this can only be explained as paranormal, because it weighed hundreds of pounds and it later took eight men to move it back to its proper place.)

The ghost stories do not, of course, disprove the poker story but they make one wonder. To put it another way, if someone imagines (*my word*) he has a ghost (not to mention twenty-six of them), could he also "imagine" that he's inherited the world's longest poker game? And, of course, just like Deadwood's Saloon No. 10, the Bird Cage is a business with good reason to perpetuate its myths.

Still, until proven otherwise (and it probably never can be), Bill demands the place be credited with the longest poker game of all time. But here we have another problem: even if the game did last over eight years, does this make it the longest-ever game? Not according to Herbert Asbury, who described a game once played in Austin, Texas, between a Major Danielson and an Old Man Morgan, wealthy planters and old friends, who for years had a little session every night:

> At eight o'clock on the evening of June 15, 1853, they began to play as usual and the luck shifted from one to the other. Then each drew a wonderful hand and the betting became heavier. At dawn on June 16 they decided to abolish the limit. Stopping only for meals, and to change their property into cash, they continued to bet. The game went on and on, day after day, week after week, month after month. From all over Texas people came in crowds to see the two old men hunched over their cards . . . In 1870, when they had been playing for seventeen years, the cards, faded and torn, were sealed and placed in a safe deposit box in the National Bank of Austin.[3]

This story is told in even more graphic detail in another book, by Eugene Edwards, who claims the game ran for nineteen years.[4] This makes it clearer that over the whole time Morgan and Danielson were in fact each sitting on just one hand, and raising and re-raising their bets. By the end of it both had invested their entire fortune—cash, bonds, stocks, livestock, land, houses—in their respective hands, and it became clear that neither was going to call the other, so the hands were sealed up separately in tin boxes and the rest of the cards were put in another box, all subsequently deposited in the bank, each bearing the seals of the players and of a dozen witnesses. Edwards claims the two players died in the same year.

Now, I have to admit to some skepticism about this game but, even so, I can't bring myself to go back to Bill Hunley and mention this story. It could damage his publicity and his profits. I hate to see a grown man cry.

While having a drink in Big Nose Kate's saloon, I'm told of another game to investigate. Just as Wild Bill died in Deadwood the night after playing poker with his murderer Jack McCall, so it emerges that four of the protagonists in Tombstone's Gunfight at the OK Corral had also played poker together the previous night.

I find this amazing and decide to spend more time in Tombstone to investigate. But if all this is going to make sense, I have to travel back a bit in time, and to do it properly I first have to go to Kansas.

Not illogically, especially as I was raised on the other side of the world, I assume a city called Kansas City will be in Kansas and, without checking a map, I take a plane there. It isn't. It's in Missouri. Never mind, the airport isn't far from the Missouri River, border of the two states, and I'm soon driving in awe across the plains towards a spectacular blood-red sunset. From there on, it's cattle all the way.

The old rip-roaring days of the nineteenth-century cattle drives may be over, but the cattle live on—the hills and plains are dotted with giant black steers. Many, each weighing over 1,000 lbs, are crowded into corrals in the shade of huge meat-processing plants, unaware as they stoically munch on bales of hay that plans are already well advanced for nearly half their weight to hit the dinner plates of America in just a few days' time.

It's the old cattle towns I've come to see, because with the arrival of the railroad in Kansas in the 1860s came huge numbers of Texas longhorns, driven up from the lone star state to catch the trains that would take them east. With the millions of steers came cattlemen and cowboys, who after many weeks on the dusty trail would join railroad workers, buffalo hunters and a variety of desperadoes and scavengers in boomtowns that, one by one, sprung up and then faded as the railway advanced farther and farther across the West.

To cater to these drifters' appetites for women, whisky, and gambling, previously small, sleepy places like Abilene, Ellsworth, and Newton became raging infernos of decadence, with a totally disproportionate number of bordellos and dance halls, saloons and gaming houses. (In 1873, the previously tiny Ellsworth had one bank, one newspaper, and six retail stores but more than thirty gambling saloons.)

This seasonal clientele came with money. The cowboys were paid at the end of their journeys, the railway workers too. The cattlemen sold their herds; the buffalo hunters and skinners sold their hides. Most of them were single; they had worked hard. Now they wanted some fun. As a local newspaper put it, rather uncharitably: "The Texas cattle herder is a character with few wants and meager ambition. His diet is principally whisky and the occupation dearest to his heart is gambling." After weeks on the trail, with no home but their horse, their saddlebag, and the open sky, the cowboys hit the saloons like nomads finding an oasis in the desert and there, waiting for them, were the professional faro and poker players, the dice and the roulette tables.

Years later a drover called Frank Murphy recalled in the *Los Angeles Times*:

The saloons, gambling-joints and honky-tonks had one main purpose—the taking of the cattlemen's money as quickly as possible. The games were crooked . . . it needed but a day or two in town and the cowboys would be picked clean by these human vultures, fed the most horrible whisky ever distilled, cheated at every turn . . .

It's said that there were 150 professional gamblers in Dodge City alone, 80 in Newton, and 75 in Ellsworth. Some were small-time cheats and crooks, others card players of such fame that we can all recall their names today, including Doc Holliday, Luke Short, Ben Thompson, and Dick Clark, along with the gambler lawmen Wild Bill Hickok (of course), Wyatt Earp, and Bat Masterson.

It all began in Abilene, because that's where the first railway station was built. I approach this appealing and now-peaceful town by driving from interstate Highway 70 down a graceful avenue of old but well-maintained houses to the main street. There I stroll around a park celebrating the life of a famous former citizen, Dwight D. Eisenhower; his grave, his Presidential Library, and his boyhood home are all on this site. Then on to "old Abilene town," a rather tumbledown replica of the cattle town of the 1880s with some original log cabins. Actually it's a rather unconvincing reconstruction, but when it was "real" it went within four years from being an unknown backwater to the notorious boozing, gambling, and whoring capital of the West. For a year Wild Bill Hickok was Abilene's marshal. While he became famous for his ruthless administration of the law, he actually spent most of his time playing poker, deploying his deputies to do the legwork.

The big poker games were played either in the Bulls Head Saloon or the Alamo, the games mainly five-card stud and draw poker.

The Bulls Head was run by gambler Phil Coe (the man Wild Bill Hickok eventually shot dead) and a tough, gun-toting, gambling Texan called Ben Thompson, who would allow losing players to trade in their six-shooters for chips. If the player lost, the guns were sold to pay the debt. Thompson left a trail of dead bodies and defeated card players all over the West, but he always managed to escape with "self-defense" verdicts and remain surprisingly popular with gamblers, even those he beat. Perhaps this popularity was due to accounts of him entering his own gambling joint in Texas and watching his own house faro dealer, whose name was Lorraine, wiping out all comers. To the shock of the players, Ben pulled out a gun and shot each of the stacks of chips off the table, shot up the dealer's box, and then fired the remaining bullets into the hanging lamps. He turned to the players and said, "I don't think that set of tools is strictly honest, and I want to help Mr. Lorraine to buy another."

Thompson's gaming room was particularly popular with Texans, but Wild Bill Hickok's spiritual home was the Alamo. It was one huge room. You entered it by three impressive double-glass doors that were never closed and, apart from the bar of polished mahogany with gleaming brass rails, there were only gambling tables where faro, monte, and poker were played. It was conveniently positioned so that on a rainy night you could walk to the town's leading cat house without getting wet.

After Abilene, the railroad, the cattle, and the whole whisky-drinking, fornicating, gambling circus moved to Ellsworth. In fact this gutsy little place survived more than the cattle boom; in its early days there were floods, catastrophic fires, a typhoid epidemic, attacks by Native Americans, and a takeover of the town by desperadoes (ultimately hanged from the limb of a cottonwood tree). But, according to Kansas historian William G. Cutler, none of this was worse than the effects of the cattle boom. This, he wrote, "was somewhat detrimental to morality":

The thugs, blacklegs and cut-throats, with the attendant train of prostitutes that usually accompany them . . . made it, for a time, far from being the place in which a piously inclined person would wish to reside . . . When, in the following year, the cattlemen took their trade further west, the citizens of Ellsworth were much relieved and felt greatly rejoiced . . . The dangerous characters having been removed, the town settled down to peace and quietness and . . . breathed a purified moral atmosphere.[5]

As befits a town whose local radio stations are today dominated by hell-and-damnation preachers and right-wing political demagogues, it still breathes a "purified moral atmosphere." You could say it's inordinately proud of being restored to a quiet backwater, and given the trials and tribulations of its earlier days maybe this is understandable.

Next to experience the "boom-and-bust" impact of the cattle trade was Newton. To get to it we have to travel east, across country; it's a few miles north of Wichita, the state capital. Now a haven of peace and tranquillity, in 1872 it too was as wild as they come. Newton was the venue for many high-stakes poker games. Nearly 10 percent of its citizens were professional gamblers, most of them operating out of the inappropriately named Gold Rooms—unlike many of the big saloons of the day, this was not a place of elegance and good taste; it was basic, to put it mildly.

One of the more chaotic gunfights ever—what became known as the Newton General Massacre—is said to have occurred as a result of a poker game in Newton in 1871. However, there are conflicting stories about its cause and who was involved. One has Bill Bailey, a Texan gambler, playing at a place called the Red Front Saloon; at one point the town marshal, Mike McCluskie, who was watching, accused Bailey of cheating. Bailey reached for his gun but was outdrawn and watched sullenly as McCluskie turned over the cards. Bailey had dealt an opponent four kings but he himself had four aces. The game ended there but, the story has it, Bailey later confronted McCluskie at a local dance hall. Over fifty shots were fired, five men were killed, and another five wounded. Another account claims the fight was over a faro game at Perry Tuttle's saloon, with McCluskie being killed by a man called Anderson. Whoever, or whatever, as one writer rightly points out, "most of those who were shot had no part in the quarrel that triggered the cannonade, proving once more what a dangerous place a gambling table could be in a frontier town loaded with short-fused, gun-toting characters."[6]

Ultimately these cattle towns made way for what became the most famous of them all, Dodge City. Legend has it that when a ticket collector on the Santa Fe train asked a disconsolate (or drunken) ticketless passenger for his destination, the passenger said, "I want to go to hell." "Well then," said the collector, "you want to get off at Dodge City."

I arrive from Highway 40 as it is getting dark and, as I pull into a motel car park, I notice three or four groups of men, all of them armed with rifles and shotguns. This is a bit disconcerting: I know this once was a dangerous place, but has it not changed? Then I recall the posters at the state line: *Kansas welcomes hunters*. Of course—it's the first day of the hunting season, and the "killers" have come from all over the country . . . just as the buffalo killers and the gunfighters did when the trade in buffalo and cattle was at its peak in Dodge in the latter part of the 1870s.

Unlike the other cattle boomtowns, Dodge City was well established before the longhorns came to town. A gateway to the old West after the opening of the Santa Fe Trail in the 1820s, it had become over the following years a launching place for wagon trains headed west into Colorado, a stopover point for mail riders, and a supply base for troops engaged in the Indian Wars. The arrival of the railroad in the 1870s reinforced its growth. As buffalo were slaughtered in the millions, and almost wiped out as a species, Dodge City became the place from where they were shipped. Foul-smelling buffalo hunters and skinners thronged the streets. Dodge City was already becoming notorious as a lawless town, but it was when the Texas cattle business came, just in time to replace the dying buffalo trade, that its legendary phase as "Queen of the cow towns" and den of iniquity began.

Frank Barnard, a Texan newspaper proprietor who had come to Kansas with a herd of cattle, told his readers that "some things occur in Dodge that the world never knows of. Probably it is best so."

In 1878 a New York newspaper reported that "there is more concentrated hell in Dodge City than any other place of equal size."

Undoubtedly there was a greater concentration of professional card players in Dodge City than ever assembled elsewhere, at least until the World Series events began in Las Vegas, Nevada, over a century later.

One of the difficulties in determining how much poker Wyatt Earp, Doc Holliday, and the others played is that most sources refer to them as "gambling" without specifying what form of gambling it was. We know Wild Bill Hickok loved draw poker, but Earp, Holliday, Masterson, and most of the other well-known names also engaged in faro dealing, and probably this was the main source of their income because it produced rich pickings for clever card manipulators. There is evidence, however, that poker was their personal game of choice.

Asbury writes:

> Faro was king . . . [but] at short cards, poker was supreme; it was the game most favored by the few professional gamblers who played square, and by Wild Bill Hickok and the other great gunfighters in their hours of relaxation. Most of the superstitions still religiously observed by dyed-in-the-wool poker players originated in the games of the frontier saloons.[7]

These included the belief that it was bad luck to count your chips, and, more colorfully, that defeat and destitution faced anyone who played poker with a one-eyed gambler.

This last superstition owes itself to another of Eugene Edwards's stories. It concerns a one-eyed man playing Omaha and having an extraordinary run of luck. Eventually one of the other players became convinced he was cheating, so he placed his revolver on the table and said, "I am not making any insinuations or bringing any charges, and I will only say this, that if I catch any son-of-a-gun cheating, I will shoot his other eye out."[8]

(A similar story has a man losing several thousand dollars in a poker game in Kansas City. He, too, was convinced he was being cheated but couldn't prove it. So he eventually rose to his feet and said, "Gentlemen . . . I was assured that I would find this a gentleman's game . . . you *are* all gentlemen and I know it . . . but I've got only a few dollars left, and if one of you gentlemen would be kind enough to tell me where I can sit in a horse thief's game, I believe I'll go round there.")

Faro, a rather complicated game requiring special equipment, including a special table, a dealing box, and a device called a case-keeper, was in theory fairly balanced between the house and the player, assuming the dealer was "square." For this reason, and because it led to less violence than poker, it was wildly popular in the 1800s, not just in the cattle towns and mining camps, but all over the West.

Faro meant playing the house, or alternatively playing a professional faro dealer who was allowed to set up his or her stall in a gaming house or saloon, whereas poker often involved players dealing to each other. Both provided plenty of opportunity for cheating, but poker more so. As a result more gunfights took place over disputes at the poker table than for any other reason, but, even so, poker was especially popular with the cowboys because it could be played around campfires and didn't call for the elaborate equipment needed for faro. In saloons the cowboys who didn't throw their money away on dubious games of faro played poker at the lower-end-of-the-scale tables while local business figures and professionals played for higher stakes in the back rooms.

These days it may seem surprising that lawmen, such as Hickok, Earp, and Masterson, spent so much time at the faro and poker tables, but the reason for these combination lawmen-card players was well explained by Robert DeArment in an article in *Wild West* magazine in 2005:

> It was no accident that many of the top-flight gunfighters of the Western frontier were members of the sporting fraternity. Tough, steel-nerved young men who had acquired gunfighting reputations . . . found themselves in demand as dealers in gambling resorts. There were two reasons for this: First, gunfighters of renown attracted patronage, as miners and cowboys were quick to seize the opportunity to match wits and gambling skills with frontier celebrities across a green felt table. Second, since the open display of large piles of cash was a constant attraction for criminals of all sorts, ranging from sneak thieves to hold-up men, the mere presence at the table of famous personalities known to be adept at the art of the draw-and-shoot discouraged any attempt to steal.

DeArment developed this argument further in his book:

> Most of the gunmen who gave Dodge City its first notoriety . . . were professional gamblers. Many served as law officers in Dodge and elsewhere, but their first allegiance was to the gaming table. The progression usually went as follows: A young gambler, in order to protect himself from hard-bitten, gun-toting frontiersmen, practiced daily the art of the draw-and-shoot; inevitably he was challenged at his game and downed his man; a reputation as a fast man with a gun was attached to him;

a job riding herd on troublemakers in a border town was offered, and he accepted because a marshal's position offered him a steady income while still providing time to pursue his first calling of gambling . . . it was in the role of quick-shooting frontier lawmen that many Western gamblers gained renown . . . Bat Masterson, Wyatt Earp, and Doc Holliday gained a kind of immortality as frontier lawmen, [but] all were gamblers by profession.[9]

We have been passed an image of Wyatt Earp as an uncompromisingly tough lawman, an image firmly established by his time in Dodge City and the other Kansas cattle towns, yet he held relatively junior posts—a constable in a Missouri township, a deputy in Wichita, an assistant city marshal in Dodge City. As with Wild Bill Hickok, there are far more stories about Earp's activities than one lifetime could possibly allow for, and his reputation as a gunfighter appears exaggerated. The best of Earp's biographers, Casey Tefertiller, clears Earp of being a reckless killer:

He killed only when he saw no other choice, and his victims [were] criminals . . . he was not a man-killer who delighted in death, and he was never a gunfighter, at least not in the sense that later movies generations would understand the word.[10]

Of the gambling and the poker playing, Tefertiller writes:

Wyatt Earp . . . may have spent much of his time at the gambling tables, but that was expected as his job was to protect the business . . . he was no plaster saint but he was the kind of man the citizenry wanted walking in front of the procession during dangerous times. Men like Earp were also the men who the "good" citizens wanted out of town during peaceful times. Earp seemed most at home with the gambling crowd, surrounded by prostitutes, with men whose morals would not meet high standards. Wyatt Earp had been an honorable and effective lawman, one of the best of a generally unsavory lot.

Because of his powerful personality, Earp was the central figure of a group whose names were to be closely associated with him forever more. One of these men signalled his arrival in the advertising columns of the *Dodge City Times* in June 1878:

Dentistry

J. H. Holliday, dentist, very respectfully offers his professional services to the citizens of Dodge City and surrounding country during the summer. Office at room No 24, Dodge House. Where satisfaction is not given, money will be refunded.

Doc Holliday, a legendary dealer and player of faro, but also a cunning and probably profitable poker player, had befriended Wyatt Earp in Texas and, it is believed, was drawn to Dodge City as much by the latter's presence as by the gambling opportunities. The son of an affluent Southerner who was a veteran of the Civil War, Doc was raised in Georgia. Tragically he contracted tuberculosis from his mother, and shortly after he qualified as a dentist this "alternately melancholy and volatile" twenty-one-year-old left for Texas, hoping for a better climate for his health. For the rest of his thirty-seven years he lived under the shadow of inevitably premature death and, by his actions, often appeared to be deliberately confronting it. While he practiced for a while as a dentist in Dallas, he increasingly coped with pain by drinking whisky and dealt with depression by gambling. It was in Texas that he met his lifelong on-off companion and lover, "Big Nose" Kate Elder (apparently thus nicknamed not because of the size of her nose but for her capacity to stick it into other people's business).

One story, later told by Wyatt Earp in an interview for a California newspaper, sums up the volatility of Holliday and this relationship with Kate:

Doc Holliday was spending the evening in a poker game. On his right sat Ed Bailey . . . The trouble began with Bailey monkeying with the deadwood [*the discarded cards*]. Doc Holliday admonished him once or twice to "play poker"—the seasoned gambler's way of cautioning a friend to stop cheating—but the misguided Bailey persisted. Finally, Holliday pulled down a pot without showing his hand, as he had a perfect right to do. Thereupon Bailey began to throw his gun around . . . but before he could pull the trigger Doc had jerked a knife out of his pocket and with one sideways sweep caught Bailey just below the brisket.

Well, that broke the game up and soon Holliday was being guarded with gamblers clamouring for his blood. You see, he had not lived in Fort Griffin very long, while Ed Bailey was well liked. Big Nose Kate, who had a room downtown, heard about the trouble and went up to take a look . . . What she saw and heard led her to think that his life wasn't worth ten minutes purchase, and I don't believe it was . . . She set fire to a shed at the back. It all happened exactly as she had planned it. The shed blazed up and she hammered at the door yelling "fire." Everybody rushed out, except the marshal and the constables and their prisoner. Kate walked in, bold as a lion, [pointed] one of her six-shooters at the marshal and handed the other to Doc Holliday. "Come on, Doc," she said . . . and the two of them backed out of the hotel, keeping the officers covered. All that night they hid in the willows down by the creek, and early next morning . . . the two of them got away safely and rode the 400 miles to Dodge City.

Wyatt Earp also wrote about Doc Holliday:

Doc was a dentist whom necessity had made a gambler; a gentleman whom disease had made a frontier vagabond; a philosopher whom life had made a caustic wit; a long, lean, ash-blond fellow nearly dead with consumption, and at the same time the most skilful gambler and the nerviest, speediest, deadliest man with a six-gun I ever knew.

He was later to be described as arriving in Tombstone a "living dead man," constantly "choking, coughing, and spitting up blood," turning to whisky for pain relief, allowing ill-health to ignite a flaming temper, and, thus, often getting into trouble.

Other friends of Wyatt Earp included Bat and Ed Masterson, also both lawmen and card players. Bat Masterson is another whose legend exceeds the reality; he and Ed met Wyatt Earp while buffalo hunting and followed him to Dodge, where, in 1877, while Bat was briefly sheriff, Ed was shot and killed after an encounter with cowboys who had been playing in an all-night poker game. Once while playing poker in Deadwood, Bat won a gold mine, only to lose it the next day to a full house of kings and queens.

Luke Short, an immaculately dressed and clever card player who could also handle a gun, was another who made a mark on the cattle towns before going on to Leadville and ending up in Fort Worth, Texas. He played faro or poker with a Colt revolver with a sawn-off barrel in his pocket and was always ready to use it.

Life in Dodge City today thrives around an inordinately long main street, now called Wyatt Earp Boulevard (like Deadwood and Tombstone, Dodge City knows how to market its legends). We can see plays in a theater built into the historic Santa Fe depot and follow the tracks left by wagons on the original Santa Fe Trail. On the site of the town's old Boot Hill there is perhaps the best reconstruction of a Wild West main street to be found anywhere. There are over 20,000 authentic artifacts: the Fort Dodge jail of 1863, still intact . . . a saloon and cigar shop that in 1877 sold over 5,000 fresh cigars a week . . . a "tonsorial parlor," where, after a long ride, the cowboys could have a bath, their hair cut and a tooth pulled or tonsils removed . . . over 2000 firearms . . . and so on.

In a Dodge City treasure house called the Kansas Heritage Center I find an account of the memorable day a former governor of Kansas came to town looking for some easy poker pickings.

The *Dodge City Times* in 1877 reports:

The once famous boss of the state, ex-Gov. Thos. Carney of Leavenworth, arrived on the 6 o'clock train . . . to buy hides and bones for a St. Louis firm. It seems that . . . the Governor's real business in Dodge City was to entice our unsophisticated denizens into the national game of draw poker and fleece them of their loose cash . . . the talk he made about the hide and bone business being merely a blind to cover up his real design.

The Governor's reputation and dignified bearing soon enabled him to decoy three of our businessmen into a social game of poker, "just to kill time, you know." Gov. Carney's intended victims were Col. Charles Norton, wholesale dealer and general financial operator, Hon. Robert Gilmore, and Chas. Ronan, Esquire (three of Dodge City's well-known gamblers). The game proceeded merrily and festively for a time, until . . . at last the Governor held what he supposed to be an invincible hand. It consisted of four Kings and the . . . joker . . . which the Governor very reasonably assumed to be the Ace of spades.

As four of a kind at that time was the highest possible hand you could hold, having as a fifth card the ace of spades would indeed have made him unbeatable. Unfortunately he had misread his hand, the joker in this particular pack and the ace of spades being similar in appearance. But back to the local newspaper:

The old man tried to suppress his delight at his hand and to appear unconcerned when Col. Norton tossed a $100 bill into the pot; but he saw the bet and went $100 better. Norton didn't weaken, as the Governor feared he would, but nonchalantly raised the old gent with what he supposed was a fabulous bluff. Governor Carney's eyes glistened with joy . . . and he hastened to see the Colonel and add the remainder of his funds, his elegant gold watch and chain. Norton was still with the game, and the Governor finally stripped himself of all remaining valuables . . .

A breathless silence pervaded the room as Gov. Carney spread his four Kings on the table with his left hand, and affectionately encircled the glittering heap of gold, silver, greenbacks and precious stones, with his right arm, preparatory to taking the spoils. But at that moment a sight met the old Governor's gaze which caused his eyes to dilute [*sic*] in terror, a fearful tremor to seize his frame, and his vitals to almost freeze with horror. Right in front of Col. Norton were spread four genuine and perfectly formed Aces . . . Slowly and reluctantly he uncoiled his arm from around the sparkling treasure . . . With a weary, almost painful effort he rose from the table and, dragging his feet across the floor like balls of lead, he left the room . . . The next eastward bound freight train carried an old man, without shirt studs or other ornament, apparently bowed down by overwhelming grief, and the conductor hadn't the heart to throw him overboard. Gov. Carney is not buying bones and hides in this city any more.

Incidentally Col. Norton, whom Carney had greatly underestimated, for he was a highly skilled poker player, came to a sticky end: some years later he accused a man of cheating and was shot dead at the table.

I also find in the Heritage Center a cutting from the *Ford County Globe* on a fascinating dilemma faced by a local pastor who would find poker chips in the collection on Sundays:

The cowboys always drop a poker-check in the hat and place the parson to the inconvenience of going down to the poker rooms to have them redeemed . . . Latterly some of the Christian tenderfeet have objected to the parson's visits to the houses of the ungodly—not from the scandal thereof, but because they fear the softly seductive influences of these abodes of sin may draw the worthy man from the paths of rectitude . . . so the matter was soberly considered and the decision was promulgated just before the sermon last Sunday . . . The deacon would be requested to redeem the reds and blues, while the whites were to go to the sexton for services.

Speaking of clergymen, one is reputed to have turned up in the Lady Gay Saloon in Dodge City. When asked how he could justify playing poker in this place of low repute, he replied that gambling was God's way of rewarding the virtuous with winnings and punishing the wicked with losses. After a few hands he was found to have an ace up his sleeve. He defended himself by telling all and sundry they had witnessed a miracle . . . that the ace must have been placed there by the Lord himself. Nevertheless he was asked to leave the game, albeit escaping from the saloon without the bullet holes that would have accompanied a less saintly figure.

By the end of the 1880s the cattle trade was moving north to Chicago and the cow towns were returning to the obscure backwaters they had once been. The gamblers began to transfer from the cattle towns to the mining towns. One, farther north, was so taken over by card playing that it changed its name to Pokerville. Another famous mining town and gaming center was Leadville in Colorado. Ben Thompson turned up there at one point and later wrote: "of its gambling houses . . . there are so many and all are so crowded that you cannot pass through them from morning to morning; they never close."

Leadville grew from a hamlet of one hundred inhabitants to a disorderly city of fifteen thousand in a year and a half. No less an authority than the *Encyclopaedia Britannica* described Leadville as "one of the most turbulent, picturesque, and in all ways extraordinary of the mining camps of the west." It is said that at its peak it had 120 saloons and 118 gaming houses where you could play faro or poker or gamble in other ways. Of them all, the place for high-stakes poker was the Board of Trade Saloon.

While some headed north or west, to Leadville and other mining towns, Wyatt Earp liked what he was hearing about a town in Arizona called Tombstone. By all accounts, a gold strike there had launched a gambling craze that offered rich pickings. So, in October of 1879, he set off for Tombstone.

His friend Doc Holliday followed him. Shortly after, so did Bat Masterson and Luke Short.

And so, 127 years later, do I.

The poker gods are on my side because by coincidence the town is celebrating the 125th anniversary of the Gunfight at the OK Corral. Tombstone aficionados have come from all over the United States, all immaculately and impressively dressed in 1880s costume. The streets are full of Wyatt Earps and Doc Hollidays, of Big Nose Kates and Ike Clantons, of cowboys and miners, madams and ladies of the night. The effect is astonishing. I walk into the Crystal Palace Saloon and I'm the only one in the place dressed for the twenty-first century. It's like being transported back by time machine. Groups of cowboys, guns in holsters, spurs on boots, hang around street corners and saloon doorways, or ride their horses slowly down the dusty street. Formally dressed business figures in black suits with long jackets and shiny waistcoats, ivory-handled pistols in their big leather belts, stroll down Allen Street, arm in arm with their ladies in long dresses. And everywhere men are being shot. At 10:05 a.m. Curly Bill shoots Marshal White in the alley by the Bird Cage Theater; at 10:30 a.m. Luke Short shoots Charley Storms on Allen Street between 5th and 6th streets; at 11 a.m.

the Earps pistol-whip Ike Clanton between Fremont and Allen Streets . . . and on and on the bullets fly.

From a high vantage point I witness the Gunfight at the OK Corral—except that it isn't at the OK Corral. Another myth bites the dust . . . the fight actually took place on vacant ground between Fly's boarding house and photo gallery and the Harwood family home at the corner of Fremont and 6th. The OK Corral is a few feet away. From my position above the vacant lot I see the Earp brothers and Doc Holliday walking down Fremont Street, all in long black coats . . . Sheriff Johnny Behan tries to intervene and is brushed aside . . . the four men enter the lot and come face to face with Ike and Billy Clanton, Frank and Tom McLaury . . . words are exchanged, and then the shooting begins. When the smoke has cleared, the McLaury brothers and Billy Clanton lie dead and, apart from Wyatt Earp and Ike Clanton (who runs away), everyone else is injured.

The following morning I witness an atmospheric and moving funeral procession for the dead men. Based on records of the time, and with everyone in 1880s costume, it slowly proceeds down Allen Street, the three hundred mourners led by the Clanton and McLaury cowboys carrying a sign charging the Earps and Holliday with murder, followed by the Black Maria hearse—the actual one that took Frank McLaury to Boot Hill—and the women of the family in black. All this is accompanied by the drumbeat and mournful trumpets of the town band. The sidewalk is packed with spectators, impressively silent because the scene is so beautifully re-created that it's possible to believe the deaths have just occurred, and the anger and tears are real.

That night they project old Tombstone films onto a screen on the side of a truck blocking one end of Allen Street. The sound of cinematic gunshots echoes down the lonely side streets, competing with the sizzling of steaks on the local barbecues and the country and western music from the Crystal Palace and Big Nose Kate Saloons. It is unforgettable. But even this cannot compare with the spectacle at the Oriental Saloon.

The Oriental Saloon and Gambling Hall, at the corner of Allen and 5th, was (and is) one of the most famous places of its kind in the West. When it opened in 1882, the *Tombstone Epitaph* described it as

> the most elegantly furnished saloon this side of the favored city of the Golden Gate. Twenty-eight burners suspended in chandeliers afford an illumination of ample brilliancy . . . To the right of the main entrance is the bar, beautifully carved . . . In the rear of this stand a brace of sideboards which are simply elegant and have to be seen to be appreciated . . . The back area is suitably furnished after the style of the grand club room with conveniences for the wily dealers in polished ivory . . . The selection of the furniture and fixtures displays an exquisite taste.

Owned by a man called Milt Joyce, it was to be the home of some of the West's most famous poker players. Wyatt Earp dealt faro and played poker there and at one time had a small holding in the saloon. Doc Holliday dealt and played there. So did Bat Masterson and Luke Short. Twice badly damaged by fire and restored, it was the scene of some memorable confrontations. Holliday shot and injured another player there. "Billy the Kid" Claiborne was killed in a gunfight with the Oriental's bartender, "Buckskin Frank" Leslie, after the latter had thrown him out of the saloon. In 1881 Luke Short was dealing in the Oriental when he got into a dispute with a veteran gambler called Charley Storms, pistols were drawn, and Storms bit the dust. Both Leslie and Short were judged to have acted in self-defense.

For a while the Oriental was leased by Dick Clark, perhaps the most renowned gambler and poker player ever seen in Tombstone, and even beyond. Clark was born in New York and raised in Michigan. When he was twenty, he turned up in Denver, where he became a miner, before fighting in the Civil War. He emerged from that experience a skillful and committed card player, a familiar figure in all the cattle towns of Kansas in their heyday, often playing high-stakes poker with wealthy ranchers coming in from Texas to sell their herds. A newspaperman in the area at the time wrote of Clark: "He has the reputation of being one of the best-hearted and cleverest poker players in the country. His face, while engaged in play, is one of the most impassive I have ever seen."

Clark came to Tombstone in 1880 and spent most of the rest of his life there, becoming the "boss gambler" of the town. He took over the Alhambra and ran that. According to historian Sherry Monahan, the Alhambra

> was one of the finest of the time. The bar fixtures were made of walnut, mahogany, and rosewood. They were adorned with wrought and filigree work, neatly gilded and finished. There were extravagant sets of Bohemian, Italian, and French glassware with splendid designs and patterns. The bar stock was expansive and included the finest drinks, the best liqueurs, and cigars.[11]

Clark would undoubtedly have played in the high-stakes poker game at the Bird Cage. He also travelled all over the West to take on other high-stakes players. He lent class to Tombstone. He had a huge reputation for his skill as a poker player, for his gentlemanly conduct, for accepting defeat in good humor, and for generosity to his fellow players. He was the doyen of the profession, his standing similar to that of Doyle Brunson today.

But back to the Oriental, and I now witness another spectacle: on this 125th anniversary of the gunfight, they have for the evening re-created the main gaming room. Faro and poker and blackjack tables are lined up in rows from the front of the saloon to the back. At them sit the men and their ladies in their

1880s evening finery, playing by lamplight. It is another unforgettable scene.

They call Tombstone the "town too tough to die." Well, like Deadwood, it's undoubtedly a survivor, building a business out of its history and a community around one street, the rebuilt and atmospheric Allen Street. But it still has a beating heart. The locals are still living their history. The buildings on the main street may have been re-created and/or restored but, unlike Deadwood's main street, Tombstone's Allen Street is as rough and ready as it was in the beginning, unpaved and closed to traffic, a horse rail blocking each end.

Its history is faithfully recorded in old copies of the local paper, the *Tombstone Epitaph*, and I go to look at the old printing press and read up on the place.

From its columns I learn that Tombstone's "founder" was a prospector called Ed Schieffelin. He had panned for gold all over the West and now, thirty years old and described as tall and wild looking, he and a few others braved the real possibility of murder by Apaches or being killed by scorpions or tarantulas and took on the harsh southern Arizona landscape. There, Ed stumbled across silver. He filled a bag with samples, erected markers to stake his claim, and went to Tucson. An assayer confirmed the quality of the silver and with Ed and his brother formed a partnership to build a mine. Others quickly followed as word spread of a "mountain of silver." Ed had already named his claim "Tombstone" and this was to become the name of the first of the partnership's three mines and subsequently of the town that quickly grew from one hundred people living in small cabins on Allen Street to a population of over ten thousand. Ed, now rich, travelled the United States but eventually died of a heart attack in a lonely cabin in Oregon, where he had been happily living out his last years. He was forty-nine. He was returned to Arizona and buried in the hills near Tombstone where he had prospected, dressed for

eternity in his old red flannel shirt and ragged prospecting outfit, with his pick, shovel, and canteen beside him.

Like all mining towns, Tombstone was a rough place, with a
majority living in tents, packed with rough-and-ready bordellos, saloons, and gaming joints, its now-famous Boot Hill cemetery kept busy by frequent knife killings and gunfights. (A
poster outside the undertaker's still says: "Why walk around
half dead when we can bury you for 22 dollars?")

As a gambling town it for a while took pride of place in all
the Southwest; a poker player could find a game in every single building on one side of Allen Street, as well as in some
buildings on the other, and on surrounding streets too.

But Tombstone's place in history owes itself to the presence
there of some of the West's most famous gambler-gunfighters.

One was Johnny Ringo, notorious cowboy, outlaw, cattle
rustler, enemy of the Earp family. While I'm in Tombstone, his
biographer, Steve Gatto, tells me of a game of poker that took
place in Galeyville in Arizona one night in 1881. Johnny Ringo
lost all his money there, only to return later with a companion.
One was armed with a Henry rifle, the other with a six-shooter.
They held up the poker players and took about $500 and a
horse. Ringo was later to face trial three times in Tombstone,
but each time the poker players refused to turn up and testify,
clearly deciding that this was one hand it was safer to lose.

But of all Tombstone's personalities the two who were to
leave an indelible mark on its history were Wyatt Earp and Doc
Holliday, because of the Gunfight at the OK Corral. It was to
become legendary and Wyatt could never escape it. Biographer
Casey Tefertiller wrote of him:

> It baffled him that history would not just leave him alone. Other
> people had killed and left their pasts behind . . . He could run
> fast and far, but he could never escape from Tombstone and the
> five months when his actions stirred the conscience of a nation.

Tombstone, with its web of ambiguities and uncertainties, would haunt Earp for the rest of his life.[12]

Raised by their father to believe in family loyalty, the Earp brothers had remained close and, in 1879, Wyatt had persuaded other members of the family to join him on the wagon train with their partners and wives. In Tombstone they set about building a compound of houses. Wyatt was thirty-one at the time, James thirty-eight, and Virgil thirty-six. They were later joined by Morgan, who was twenty-nine. Virgil already had a commission as a deputy US marshal, James became a barman, and Wyatt began his life in riding shotgun on stagecoaches. He later became a deputy sheriff for a time. But much of his time was spent in the Oriental and other saloons, dealing faro or playing poker.

Doc Holliday arrived after a winning gambling break in the Arizona town of Prescott and, despite from the start becoming involved in a number of ill-tempered fights, was one of the first to be signed up as a deputy when the Earps needed a posse. He would turn up with a sawn-off shotgun. He became an even more controversial figure when he was fingered as being part of a raid on the stagecoach between Benson and Tombstone (he vigorously denied this and threatened to kill anyone who repeated the story; he was eventually charged but found not guilty).

Whether operating within or outside the law, this was now a dangerous man, as anyone can become when he has so little to lose. One biographer, Bob Boze Bell, writes tellingly of Holliday at this time: "We can't even accurately list the number of men he killed . . . what we do know is that *he was willing*. Any man who went up against Doc Holliday knew one thing: he didn't care. He *wanted* to die."[13]

So by 1878 the Earps and Holliday were well-known personalities in Tombstone. Virgil Earp had won respect as a lawman, and Wyatt was a mover and shaker in gambling circles.

From time to time the Earps were the main members of a posse sent out to catch a bank robber here, a rustler there, and a few stagecoach ambushers in between. Holliday was equally prominent, both as an associate of the Earps and as a player in most of the town's saloons, ever present at either the faro or poker tables. But as Tombstone developed from the usual rough-and-ready mining town into a busy and lively "city," with quality saloons, banks, newspapers, and business houses of all kinds, there emerged on its fringes a new breed of "cowboy," many of whom made their living by rustling cattle and robbing stagecoaches. The town had a love-hate relationship with them: many of the more "respectable" citizens despised them for what they were, as well as for their uncouth debauchery in Tombstone; others, especially the bordello and saloon owners (and the butchers, who purchased their stolen beef at knock-down prices), welcomed them for the money they contributed to the town, most notably on drink, gambling, and women.

If there was one factor that united the cowboys it was a dislike of the Earps and Holliday, with whom there was a series of incidents, culminating in two on October 25, 1881. First, Virgil Earp found an armed and drunk Ike Clanton on the street threatening to kill any Earp he could find. Virgil struck him on the head with his revolver and took him to the judge to be fined. Then, Tom McLaury threatened Wyatt Earp outside the courthouse and Earp knocked him down and left him lying in the dust.

Even so, many argue that the gunfight was never really intended to happen by either party. That the whole thing wasn't totally out of control is evidenced by a game of stud poker played the previous night in the Alhambra saloon. Virgil Earp was playing (and possibly Doc Holliday). Also in the game was Sheriff Johnny Behan (not a friend of the Earps), Frank McLaury, and, for a time, Ike Clanton. When asked later how these men, who were to confront each other with guns the following day, could play a peaceful game of poker the night before, Behan is said to have replied: "Well, poker is poker."

One story has Ike Clanton losing $300 in the game and leaving in a bitter mood. Another story has Ike angry because throughout the game Virgil Earp kept a six-shooter on his lap; this definitely did rile Ike because he complained about it in his testimony at the Earp trial.

As I search the records in Tombstone, I wonder . . . was a poker game the cause of the gunfight, just as poker was the cause of Wild Bill's murder? I look for more detailed information on the game, but there doesn't appear to be any and I—reluctantly—conclude that there's no evidence that the poker game pushed Ike over the edge and led to the Gunfight at the OK Corral; more likely the money he lost and the "insult" of the openly displayed gun were just two more things about which to be mad at the Earps.

In any event, the following morning the McLaurys and the Clantons turned up on the vacant lot near the OK Corral. The word was out they were looking for a fight and the Earps decided that, as far as these cowboys were concerned, enough was enough.

To this day controversy rages about who began the shooting, and whether the Earps took the law into their own hands to tame the likes of the Clantons and the McLaurys or whether they were acting properly to preserve the peace on behalf of their fellow citizens (Virgil, after all, was still town marshal). The town is still deeply divided. At the time the *Tombstone Epitaph* was a supporter. Commenting on the gunfight, it said: "The feeling among the *best class of our citizens* [my italics] is that the Marshal was entirely justified in his efforts to disarm these men, and, being fired upon, they had to defend themselves, which they did most bravely."

The Earp brothers and Holliday were, however, arrested and stood trial. Fortunately for them, the judge took a similar line to the *Epitaph*: "I cannot resist the conclusion that the defendants were fully justified in committing these homicides; that it was a necessary act, done in the discharge of official duty."

The funeral reflected the feeling on the anti-Earp side and, to be fair to the *Epitaph*, it reports the event accurately:

> The funeral of the McLaury brothers and Clanton yesterday was numerically one of the largest ever witnessed in Tombstone . . . Headed by the Tombstone brass band it moved down Allen Street. The sidewalks were densely packed for three or four blocks . . . it was a most impressive and saddening sight and such a one as it is to be hoped may never occur again in this community.

As local historian Ben Traywick says:

> It was a gunfight in which everyone lost. The McLaury brothers and Billy Clanton died in flame and gun smoke. Until he died, Ike had to live with the fact that he ran away . . . for the Earps it was the end of their hopes of wealth and prestige as respectable businessmen in Tombstone. Two months later, Virgil was shot from an ambush and crippled for life, Morgan was shot from a dark alley and killed. Wyatt, one brother crippled, another dead, rode out of Tombstone never to return.

After a period when he acted beyond the law in seeking to avenge his brothers' killings, Wyatt Earp went on to live relatively peacefully as a professional gambler until he was seventy-nine, far outliving his friend Doc Holliday, who travelled the West, still playing cards, increasingly ill, until in 1887 he died at the age of thirty-seven at a health resort called Glenwood Springs. Amused that he was dying of ill health rather than riddled with bullets, he is said to have uttered as last words: "I'll be damned—this is funny."

Tombstone is today a peaceful town off the Arizona beaten track, but somehow it keeps the controversies and memories alive. It is still split between supporters of the Earps and Holliday, and supporters of the Clantons and McLaurys.

As I walk down Allen Street, especially on this weekend when the town has dressed itself in 1880s garb, it begins to take a grip on me. I find myself beginning to assume a John Wayne-like gait and my right hand begins to hang loose, near where a gun holster would be. (In Tombstone this particular day, you only looked crazy if you did *not* walk like this.)

I wander down the road to Boot Hill. One of the best poker players of all time, Dick Clark, is buried here.

So are the Clantons, and Tom and Frank McLaury—their marker starkly declares they were "murdered on the streets of Tombstone 1881."

Another marker takes my eye, one for a man called Moore. It says:

Here lies Leslie Moore
Four slugs from a 44
No Les, no more.

That night I take a last walk down Allen Street. The 125th celebrations have ended; the colorfully dressed "cowboys" and "gamblers" have gone home. The Bird Cage is shut and silent. The debate over the Gunfight at the OK Corral is over for another day. But the country and western band is still playing at the Crystal Palace. As I pause to listen I note a poster on the wall:

"No-limit Texas hold'em at the Crystal Palace . . . a chance to win a seat to the World Series of Poker . . . Monday and Tuesday 6 and 9 p.m."

So they're still playing poker in Tombstone.

three

Drama on the river
. . . cheats and card sharps on the Mississippi steamers

June is not the best time to be in the Mississippi town of Natchez. It's hot and humid and can be uncomfortably sticky. If you're wandering around Natchez-under-the-Hill, a fashionable wining-and-dining area that divides the Mississippi River from the impressive old plantation mansions on the hill above it, even the descent of dusk and a breeze from the water do little to help. Of all the advertising outside the bars and restaurants, two words have overriding appeal: *air conditioning!* What it was like in the old days when this was a den of iniquity equal to any hellhole in America, heaven only knows.

In those days Natchez-under-the-Hill, like The Swamp in New Orleans or The Landing in Vicksburg, was a squalid and unruly haven for criminals, prostitutes, and crooked gamblers, all catering to the lustier of the men who worked on the river (and the plantation owners or their sons who would descend from the Hill to sow their wild oats). Anyone with money was in danger of being robbed or swindled. If you lost at poker in one of the gambling dens, as you surely would, it was unwise to complain you were cheated, for, according to one historian, if you did you would be "knifed, shot, or gun-butted to pulpy oblivion and then tossed into the river."

Asbury describes it as

literally and figuratively [a] stink-hole of creation—mazes of narrow streets and alleys teeming with gamblers, murderers, footpads, burglars, arsonists, pickpockets, prostitutes and pimps, and ruffians who would gouge out a man's eye or chew off his nose for the price of a drink. Every flimsy cabin, clapboard shanty, and abandoned flatboat with its bottom stuck in the mud was . . . a brothel, a dancehall or a low tavern . . . all of them ran wide open 24 hours a day. Brawling and debauchery of every description were virtually continuous, and murder was so common as to attract only passing attention.[1]

Of course it's all been gentrified as a tourist attraction these days. If you're looking for poker today, you head for a riverboat called the *Isle of Capri*. The state of Mississippi for years inexplicably insisted that gambling was acceptable only if it took place on water; thus, even today, most legal gambling, including poker playing, takes place on boats that don't sail: they stay firmly attached to the shore so that the players who get bored or go broke can easily be replaced. (In Tunica they've been particularly imaginative, building conventional casino resorts over canals and swampland; thus you'll find Bally's and Sam's Town, the Gold Strike and the Horseshoe, and other names associated with Atlantic City and Las Vegas all claiming to be built over water.) The *Isle of Capri* is a typical riverboat-casino, friendly, with a restaurant, 143 cabins, and a swimming pool. Everyone is wearing shorts or other casual clothing; nowhere can be seen the beautifully dressed, glamorous Mississippi gambler of legend. This is a shame because it's this world I wish to explore.

Unfortunately there's no one alive to tell the tale, but as I delve back into the old newspaper records and memoirs written at the time stories emerge that make even poker playing in the old West seem a tame affair.

At the beginning of the 1800s card playing on the river was the pastime of men who sailed flat boats loaded with freight. They would play cards by lantern light on the deck at night and then head for the lawless gambling dens of places like Natchez-under-the-Hill when they docked. Then came the river steamers. These majestic boats carried freight such as cotton, but also passengers. The poor travelled in cramped and uncomfortable quarters, sometimes with the freight. On some boats they had to supply their own food and blankets to lie on.

But for the affluent—rich farmers or plantation owners, slave traders, business or professional men of standing—no expense was spared. They travelled in luxury, consuming food and wines and spirits of the highest quality and relaxing in chandelier-lit lounges of real grandeur. By 1860 there were well over 700 of these riverboats on the Mississippi, their elegance only slightly spoiled by the two high chimneys at the front, belching out black smoke. Steamers like the *Natchez* and the *Robert E. Lee* were described as floating palaces.

With these palaces came the professional gambler: black knee-length coat, white ruffled shirt, expensive leather boots, gold watch and chain, gentlemanly, persuasive . . . and crooked. There were hundreds of them and they were cheats and swindlers—almost without exception. You did not lose at poker on the riverboats; you were robbed. Many of them worked in pairs, even teams. They always pretended they didn't know each other, often coming aboard at separate ports. They had a variety of tricks for attracting the unwary into a game. Once it was under way, they would work together to ensure one or the other of the team would win. One practice was called "iteming"; one of the team would appear to be occasionally watching the game but would, in fact, be observing others' cards and signalling to his partner by puffs of cigar smoke or other methods what cards his opponent held. One such cheat even came aboard "disguised" as a fiddle player and would signal hands to his partners by a change of tune. They used marked cards and cold decks. Many would be in collusion with the barman. They would supply him with a number of cold decks prior to the game and when the time was ripe would call for a fresh deck, ostentatiously open it in front of the others in the game, and then deal predetermined hands. The aim would be to give the "sucker" a top hand—say four kings—and thus induce him to bet heavily, then throw down a better hand—in this case, four aces—and take the pot. Sometimes for the cheat it was as simple as dealing a winning hand to himself—or to a partner; these men were magicians with cards. A popular trick was to deliberately lose for an hour or so and allow a naive opponent to build up a stack, and then increase the pace of the game, with the betting becoming heavier as the opponent's confidence built, until at a well-chosen moment the opponent would be dealt the sucker hand; every dollar would end up in the middle and he would have at that precise moment a change of "fortune" and lose the lot.

For the professional gamblers the set-up was ideal. There were men with plenty of money on board but without the experience of playing disciplined poker with good players, let alone card mechanics. After a day or two on the boat they would become bored and, after a lavish dinner washed down with wine, port, and brandy, their decision-making faculties were not finely tuned. They may have been men of substance in their own world, but at the poker table they were out of their depth—they were there to be taken. And taken they were.

One river gambler at the time, Tom Ellison, described it thus:

> It was dead easy money . . . all the time. Everyone who travelled had lots of stuff, and everyone was willing to bet, and bet high . . . It wasn't gambling, it was robbing; but that's what went as gambling in those times. The fellows had to be pretty slick, I can tell you . . . I've seen fellows pick every card in the pack, and call it without missing once. I've seen them shuffle them one for one from top to bottom, so that they were in the

same position after a dozen shuffles as they were in at the first. They'd just flutter them up like a flock of quail and get the aces, kings, queens, jacks all together easy as pie. A sucker had no more chance than a snowball has in a red-hot oven.

Even amidst this colorful crowd there were some outstanding personalities. There was Jimmy Fitzgerald, who needed three slaves to carry his cases of expensive clothing and who was probably the most expensively dressed of all the card sharps. There was John Powell, who some believed was that rarity, an honest riverboat gambler. He once took a young man for all his money, only to see the loser shoot himself; Powell was so upset that he lost his killer instinct and went on to lose his $500,000 lifetime winnings and died broke. There was Canada Bill, famous for a line that summed up poker players everywhere; told that the game he was playing in was crooked, he groaned, "I know, but it's the only one in town."

And then there was George Devol, the most famous of them all, because of his exploits as a poker cheat and a fighter but above all because he is the only one of the riverboat gamblers to have written a book of memoirs, still being sold today under the title *Forty Years a Gambler on the Mississippi.*

Devol was born in Ohio in 1829 and when he was ten years old ran away from home to be cabin boy on a riverboat. Within a year he had learnt to manipulate cards so that "I could cheat the boys. I felt as if I was fixed for life." His brother persuaded him to work in the boat-building business for a while, but he finally concluded that there was a better life to be had as a riverboat gambler. "I told him I intended to live off fools and suckers. I also said, 'I will make money rain' and I did come near doing as I said."[2]

Devol was a scoundrel, a consummate cheat and a renowned fighter with fist or head. While he usually carried a pistol, his main weapon was his head—he claimed that his skull was an inch thick over his forehead and he would simply butt any assailants with the power of a charging buffalo. He travelled the Mississippi for years, cheating and conning the affluent passengers with almost every trick in the book. Sometimes he worked alone; often he had a partner.

In his autobiography, Devol shamelessly describes his cheating:

> I was on board the *Sultana*, bound for Louisville, and got into a five-handed game of poker. When we landed at the mouth of the Cumberland, two of our party got off to take the boat for Nashville; that left our game three-handed. For fear that another would get away, I thought that I must get in my work without further delay; so I excused myself for a few moments and went to the bar. I got a deck just like the one we were using, and ran up three hands, giving one three Aces, one three Kings, and myself four treys. We played a short time after my return, and on my deal I called their attention to something, and at the same time came up with the cold deck. The betting was lively. I let them do the raising, and I did the calling until it came to the draw. They each took two cards, and I took one, saying, "If I fill this flush, I will make you squeal." I knew they both had full hands, and they just slashed their money on the table until there was over $4,000 up. Then I made a raise of $1,200, and they both called. "Gentlemen," I said, "I suppose you have me beat; I only have two pair." "Oh!" says one, "I have a King full," and the other one said, "I have an Ace full." "Well boys, I can down both hands, for I have two pairs of treys." The game came to a close, for there was no more money on the other side.[3]

But he had a kind of conscience. From time to time he would return his "winnings" when he felt he could be causing real distress. And he preferred to cheat other cheats, rather than honest men.

I have often given a sucker back his money, and I have seen them lose it with my partner, or at some other game on the same boat. I have won hundreds of thousands from thieves who were making tracks for some other country to keep out of jail and to spend their ill-gotten gains. I enjoyed beating a man that was loaded down with stolen money more than anyone else. I always felt as if it was my duty to try and keep the money in our own country.[4]

He was scornful of the behavior of many of those he robbed, the so-called "gentlemen" he met on the riverboats:

They are not brave enough to take the name, but they are always ready for part of the game. A gambler's word is as good as his bond, and that is more than I can say of many businessmen who stand very high in a community. I would rather take a true gambler's word than the bond of many businessmen who are today counted worth thousands. The gambler will pay when he has money, which many good church members will not.[5]

As for his acts of charity, he is quite open about his dishonesty, so why should he be disbelieved when he writes:

I was playing poker with a gentleman aboard the steamer *John Simonds*, bound for Louisville, late one night, and had won a few hundred dollars from him, when he got up without saying a word, and went to the ladies cabin. In a short time he came back with a small velvet-covered box in his hand, and said to me, "Come, let us finish our game." He opened the box, and I saw it was full of a lady's diamond jewelery. I said, "What are you going to do with those?" Said he, "I will put them up as money." "Oh no; I have no use for ladies jewelery." "Well," says he, "if I lose I will redeem them when we get to Louisville." I told him I was not going above Vicksburg. "Well," says he, "if you win, leave them with the clerk and I will pay him." I then loaned him $1,500 on the jewelery, and we sat down to play. It was about 3 a.m. when we commenced, and before they wanted the tables for breakfast I had won the $1,500 back. We drank a champagne cocktail, and he went to his room. The barber was at work on me, so that I was a little late for breakfast, and the steward had to take me into the ladies cabin to get me a seat. There was a gentleman, a very beautiful lady, and a sweet little child at the same table; the lady's eyes were red, as if she had been crying. I looked at the gentleman, and saw it was the same person who had lost the diamonds. Somehow, my breakfast did not suit me; and the more I looked at that young wife and mother, the less I felt like eating. So at last I got up and left the table. I went to my room, got the little velvet box, wrapped it up, and carried it back. They were just leaving the table when I returned. I called the chambermaid, and told her the lady had left a package, and for her to take it to her room. After it was gone I felt better, and I ate a square meal. The gentleman came and thanked me, and wanted my address; but as I never had anyone send me money lost at gambling, I told him not to mind the address; for I knew if I did not give it, I would not expect anything, and therefore would not be disappointed.[6]

Devol lived into his seventies and it is said that he won $2 million, mainly by cheating at draw poker, but lost most of it because of the classic poker player's problem: a leak. In his case it was faro. A writer in the *Cincinnati Enquirer* sums it up: "Had he never seen a faro bank he would have been an immensely wealthy man . . . one night before the war I saw him lose $32,000 at one sitting. He left the table without enough money for a cup of coffee."

There are many dramatic stories of encounters on the riverboats but three have become legendary.

The first occurred in the early 1830s. Four men were playing poker. One of them, a relatively young man returning to Natchez from New York, where he had been on honeymoon, was down a fortune . . . about $50,000. What made it worse was that it was money he had been trusted to carry from New York to some business leaders back home. As his position became desperate and he was on the verge of throwing himself into the river rather than face shame in Natchez, a man joined the crowd of spectators. He saw immediately that the game was fixed. He joined the high-stakes game and soon afterwards saw that one of the players was drawing a card from his sleeve. He took the player by the wrist and with the other hand put a knife to his throat and demanded to see the hand. As he expected, it contained not five cards, but six. Four of them were aces. The newcomer announced he would take the pot as he had the only legitimate poker hand.

"Who the devil are you?" cried the cheat.

"I am James Bowie," the man replied.

The cheat went silent, and the inventor of the Bowie knife, and later hero of the Alamo, scooped up $70,000, handed $50,000 to the young man, and walked away.

(Other versions of the story have Bowie shooting the cheat; alas there is no one around to verify this—least of all the cheat!)

The second involves a father who discovered his son playing poker and being swindled out of $8,000. When he saw his son lose his last $500 to a crooked gambler producing four eights to beat four sevens, the father took the vacant chair. An observer said, "One thing soon became evident—that the newcomer was playing at one adversary only. He betrayed no anxiety to win money from any of the others but lost no chance to bet with the gambler. The others saw it, and, one by one, dropped out, leaving the two to their duel. They all felt that some kind of a story was being enacted and were all unwilling to interfere with it." As one high-stakes hand led to a pot of

$10,000, the father drew a pistol and demanded that the gambler show his hand. It contained three aces. The father then spread out the other cards, revealing three more aces. He then took the money. The gambler tried to knife him, but the father took him by the throat, lifted him from his chair, took him out on deck, and tossed him overboard.

The third comes from that remarkable poker storyteller Eugene Edwards in his book *Jack Pot*, published in 1900. It concerns an Army paymaster who found himself playing with three card sharps. He dropped $500 before he guessed he was probably being swindled, but instead of giving up he settled down to concentrate on every detail of the others' behavior. Under his close scrutiny they played straight for a while, then began to crowd him out of every pot by continually raising and re-raising each other. He bided his time until he was dealing and—quite fairly—dealt himself three queens. He raised and was re-raised and then the betting really began, the other three raising the paymaster and also each other until it became clear that they were not going to allow him to call. When the pot reached $2,600, one of them raised it to $6,500. The paymaster, realizing that the three could now walk away with the money and split it between the three of them, protested he couldn't afford to call and asked the raiser to cut the pot so that he could. He was told that he knew the game was no limit when he came in and that he had fifteen minutes to raise the money. So the paymaster sent to his stateroom for his valise. He opened it and took out wad after wad of crisp banknotes and laid them on the table. "Now, gentlemen," he said, "since you insist upon playing without limit I will see your $6,500 and raise it $50,000. I'll give you fifteen minutes to see the raise or I will take the pot." The three slunk away. The paymaster carefully put the money back in the valise and, greatly relieved, returned it to his cabin. He had been playing with the money he was taking to pay the troops, and if he had lost he had planned to kill himself.[7]

By the 1880s most of the riverboat gamblers had gone. There were few men left to cheat because the Civil War had devastated the plantation owners and ended the slave trade. Trains were replacing boats as a mode of travel. And there were more attractive opportunities elsewhere—at the gold and silver mines and in the booming cattle towns farther west. While many of the gamblers would end up in these places, this golden era of the Mississippi steamboats would be the last one in which so many outright card cheats were operating in one area at one time.

As the era of excess, whether it be on the Mississippi or in western boomtowns, was replaced in the emerging twentieth century by a more stable social order, poker became more of a social activity and a popular home game. It would not be until after the Second World War that it began to re-emerge as a professional game—especially in southern states such as Texas. Only then did the second age of poker really begin.

The second age of poker

Fadin' the white line

. . . the life and times of the Texan Road Gamblers

four

Poker in the Lone Star State
... or "how to get out of town with the money"

It's a sunny autumn and I'm driving the highways and by-
ways of Texas. Nearly all the best-known ghosts at the table are
from this state. The World Series of Poker (WSOP) was
founded by Texans, and Texans won eight of the first nine
World Series main events. Yet, despite producing some of the
best players the world has ever seen, and—in hold'em—the
most popular form of the game, Texas has resolutely kept
the professional game illegal. Thus nearly all the big names in
poker history, the legendary fraternity who from the 1950s to
the 1980s achieved worldwide fame as "the Texan road gamblers" and went on to dominate both the World Series and the
game's Hall of Fame, were outlaws, their nomadic and often
dangerous lifestyles not that dissimilar to their nineteenth-
century Wild West predecessors, except that the Texans travelled by car rather than horse.

For them poker was not just about playing cards; it was
about endless hours driving country roads, fadin' the white
line from gas station to gas station, town to town, motel to motel, and game to game . . . it was about identifying and beating
cheats, coping with police raids and arrests, and surviving hijackings and shootings. Winning at poker was the easy part;
getting out of town with the money was the real challenge.

Carl McKelvey, perhaps the last of the old-style road gamblers still driving these roads (the others are either dead or playing somewhere else), says, "You lived daily with cheats, the law, hijackers, and game operators who didn't want to pay out at the end of the game—so it was a tough business. These players today—the heroes, the stars—if they had to go through what we had to go through to be a poker player, they wouldn't be a poker player. They couldn't do the things that we did. We were a different breed. They're card-room players and we were road gamblers. Not only did we have to protect ourselves but we also had to conduct ourselves right because we had to be asked back. The standard of behavior in Texas was especially high because otherwise you'd get your nose broken, or worse . . . a lot worse."

Unlike those who today play in front of attentive crowds and television cameras, the Texan road gamblers played in dark corners and dangerous places, protected only by the way they handled themselves (and, if necessary, their guns). Fadin' the white line demanded courage, an acceptable personality, and stamina. While there were some big games and sometimes some big wins, often the pickings were relatively small, and from them expenses had to be covered and, by some, families kept. As well as the long, tiring journeys and countless days spent waiting in soulless motel rooms for the game to begin, there were sometimes crushing defeats. To survive they had to be hard men, capable of doing whatever they had to do to survive in hard times.

Amarillo Slim says that to be a road gambler you had to do four things:

1. Find the game
2. Beat the game
3. Not get arrested
4. Not get robbed

In the '50s and '60s most towns had a game if you knew where to find it, and a man known as "the boss gambler" to control it. He was a tough character in a world of tough characters—it was he who decided who could play in town, it was he who kept order, and it was he who paid off the police and the judges. If he didn't like you, at best you would be frozen out of the game; at worst you could get arrested by his friends in the force. If you were approved, you played poker untroubled by the law. Often he had a respectable front: the only way that poker could be played legally while allowing a house charge, or "rake," for the promoter was if it were licensed to be played in a club with a charitable purpose, thus AmVets, Elks, and Redmen clubs were all used as fronts for poker. Byron "Cowboy" Wolford, who ran more than one Elks Club, wrote:

> The reason that people got Redmen and AmVets charters was because you could only take a drop [i.e., take a share of the money that was bet] legally if you had a fraternal charter. Your reason for taking your drop, you explained to the officials, was to support the fraternal organization, make charitable donations, pay the rent, and so on. You didn't need to be a veteran to get an AmVets charter, but we always got it in some veteran's name because it looked better that way.[1]

"Explaining to the officials" sometimes involved passing over bulky envelopes!

Sometimes the games would be in a shady den, out the back of a bar or liquor store, or in a barn; usually they would be in the boss gambler's or houseman's home, with good home cooking and plenty of liquor for the few who liked a drink while they played.

Normally there were three kinds of players in the game. There were the locals, some of them small-time recreational players, some semi-professionals; there were the road gamblers, the real professionals, who drove the length and breadth of the state seeking out the bigger games; and there were the "producers"— wealthy amateurs who were the prime target of the pros, often men who had made fortunes in oil or gas, or were big ranchers, men who worked hard to make their money and were ready to play hard with it, and who loved a game of poker and were ready to pay for it. Cowboy Wolford wrote:

> Folks have asked me whether the road gamblers just played against each other, wondering how any of us could make any money always playing against the other top hands. Naturally, that's not how it was. Let's say that Mac knew someone from Waco who had money, what we called a "producer." Mac would make a call or two and we'd drive to Waco to get in the game with him, not with the other professional players. There were always three or four men from the area who had money and who were not top players, men who just liked to play poker, and they're the ones we want to play with—they were the producers of the road show.[2]

There were about thirty or forty road gamblers in Texas, nearly all of whom were world-class players. Some stuck to their own territory—east or west or south of the state; others travelled the length and breadth of Texas, occasionally beyond it, some with partners, some alone. All were looking for a "good game" and that meant one with serious money. That in turn called for at least one significant "producer" at the table, and hopefully more. But the smaller games had their "producers" too. Nolan Dalla, a later-generation Texan poker player who has become a highly respected writer on the game, tells an amusing story about a relatively modest "producer":

> I was playing in a $10–$20 stud eight-or-better game. It was played almost every day and we all knew each other. Every

now and then a player everybody called Cowboy used to come in. He wore a big Stetson and always had a pocketful of money. When Cowboy was in the game it was like fish-fry. I mean, the guy just loved to play—and he played *every hand*. For anyone who knew what he was doing it was bonanza. One day Cowboy finally got sick of losing. He announced he was fed up with eight-or-better and was going to another game across town where they were playing $10–$20 hold'em. The other game was due to start in half an hour and Cowboy reckoned he just had time to get there. Well, wouldn't you know it—as soon as Cowboy left, the game immediately broke up. I mean, it was more like an evacuation. You could have shouted "fire" and the room would not have cleared any faster. Players jumped in their cars and made a mad dash across town to get seats locked up before Cowboy arrived. Three of us made it in twenty minutes. A couple of other players walked in a few minutes later. Finally Cowboy arrived and looked at a table comprising exactly the same players he had just left. Without blinking, he said, "I guess y'all got tired of playing stud eight-or-better too."

Hijackings were an accepted hazard of the business. Poker players were an ideal target because they were outlaws; they couldn't call the police for help. If they were halfway clever, the hijackers couldn't lose. Where else could they find piles of cash sitting on the table and no protection from the law?

The stories are many and colorful. The door would just burst open, the hijackers would be masked and carrying guns, and usually they would force the players to undress and leave them in their underwear so they couldn't easily follow them to the getaway cars. The players would just try to stay calm and hope the thieves were professionals who would just take the money and go. What they didn't want was to be robbed by a half-crazed drug addict, a guy capable of blowing their heads off for no reason at all. As veteran Texan star T. J. Cloutier says,

"When they came in with the guns, you gave them what you had and that was it. You could always make the money back, but you couldn't get your life back."

Of course there was more to fadin' the white line than avoiding being cheated or robbed; the games were tough, and the top Texan road gamblers became highly experienced, uncompromisingly ruthless players. They studied the game; they may not have had the books and simulators and DVDs we have today, but they never stopped learning. Doyle Brunson, Amarillo Slim, and Sailor Roberts spent hours in the car or in their motel rooms talking about hands, sharing experiences, working on their games. It is no coincidence that when they moved to Las Vegas, the Texan road gamblers were for a time unbeatable.

This, then, is the territory and the tradition I'm about to explore as I launch myself on the poker trail in west Texas. I take Highway 27 to the twin towns at the hub of west Texas, Midland and Odessa. This is where the "black gold" began to flow in abundance at the end of the 1920s, transferring sleepy cow towns into pulsating business centers at the heart of massive oil fields. (As well as oil—and some may say less to their credit—the twin towns produced two US presidents, George H. W. Bush and his son, George W.)

Had I been a Texan road gambler, I would have undoubtedly played at the Golden Rooster in Odessa. This was in a hotel called the Inn of the Golden West run by a gambler known as "Pinkie" Roden. Doyle Brunson would probably have been there, and Amarillo Slim, and often the third member of their bookmaking and poker partnership, Sailor Roberts. Lawrence Herring (known as "Broomcorn") would probably have been in the game, and sometimes Jack Straus and Bill Smith. And Johnny Moss, too. He ran an illegal craps and poker joint in nearby Graham in the 1930s before ending his travels in Odessa, no doubt attracted by the benefit to old bones of 300 days of sunshine a year.

Moss is long gone (he died in 1995 when he was eighty-eight), but his ghost haunts every place in Texas where poker was played. He was the first of the Texan road gamblers. By all accounts he was in his prime for thirty years from the late '30s to the '60s; a great poker player, some say the best ever, he was—also by *nearly* all accounts—not a likeable man. As one contemporary put it: "His personality worked at the poker table but nowhere else." He could be mean and miserable, some say, and not above a trick or two. He was in later years a nasty abuser and bully of dealers. Those who knew him invariably talked about his eyes. One contemporary described them as "hooded like an alligator's, they regarded the world with a cold intensity that was simultaneously inspiring and chilling." Another wrote: "His eyes were piercing, all-knowing, fearless, scary, cold, predatory, and conceited. It was as if he could see right through you and the backs of your cards. His eyes seemed to be permanently half-opened, scanning the room, studying every detail."

However—and it's a big however—you have to set Moss within the context of exceptionally hard beginnings and also the uncompromising poker world he first encountered.

He was born on May 14, 1907, in the tiny town of Marshall in northeast Texas. He was still an infant when his mother died and was only four when his father was seriously injured and became a cripple for life. The family was so poor that Johnny abandoned school at only eight to sell newspapers on the streets of Dallas. From then until he died, he was a professional hustler, his only education being what he could pick up in pool halls and poker rooms.

It was as a kid on the streets that he met Benny Binion, the Dallas crime boss, later owner of Binion's Horseshoe in Las Vegas, who became a friend for life and who was to fund him when he became a frequent loser in his last and failing years. At fifteen, another friend from the streets showed Johnny how to cheat at poker—how to mark cards, how to find the cards in the deck and know who he was dealing them to, how to manipulate the shuffles and cuts, how to slip cards into and out of his pockets. But young Johnny noticed that his friend never seemed to have much money, so he decided to put what he had learned to better use by offering to be a "lookout man" at the Otter's Club in Dallas. In effect, he became a cheat catcher, earning three dollars a day. Not only did he spot the cheats but he also learned how to play poker—draw poker, five-card stud, and a lowball game called "deuce to the seven." He also learned what makes poker special: you don't have to have the best hand to win. By the time he was twenty, he was on the road, seeking out and playing in games all over the state.

In those days there were not as many opportunities to play as there would be later, in the '50s and '60s, so he also gambled on his skills at pool, bowling, dominoes, and especially golf, and even tried motorcycle racing, applying to them all the same determination to win. He was an astonishing all-rounder. Then there were the dice and, of course, the horses. As the '30s Depression came to an end and was succeeded by the oil boom, he found himself in much bigger games. He won some big money, and he lost some big money . . . sometimes in the same week. Once he won $250,000 in a game in Dallas and told his wife to buy the best home for them she could find; it took her four weeks and by then he had lost the lot betting on horses.

He began travelling beyond Texas; in later years he often talked about someone he called "Little Man," a racketeer in Alabama who may have been short in stature but not in ambition—according to Moss, Little Man organized poker games with $100,000 buy-ins in which it was possible to see more than a million dollars on the table at one time. Moss claimed to have won a lot of money in those games. (Moss was known to exaggerate, but if these games were anywhere near as big as this, then they were the precursors of the big game in Las Vegas in later years.)

For over fifty years Johnny Moss lived by and from gambling, and above all from poker. When the leading Texan road gamblers moved to Las Vegas and the World Series began in 1970, he was elected world champion by his peers. The following year it was decided the title should not be awarded but properly contested in what was to be the first major freeze-out tournament. He still won it, and he won it again in 1974, beating Crandell Addington in the heads-up finale. By now he had begun to run his own card rooms in Las Vegas. He did this at the Horseshoe, then the Aladdin, and finally at the Flamingo. He still played but he was finding it harder to last the distance in the longer games. He also allowed himself to be drawn into forms of poker he was less skilled at. As he became a grumpy old man, and increasingly a loser, he became harder and harder on the dealers, many of whom came to hate him. Despite being a Moss fan, the young Mike Sexton was one who was discomforted by his behavior: "He'd scream and holler at the dealers and fire them on the spot sometimes. He was terrible in terms of berating dealers—it was awful." And all this time, whenever he was in financial trouble, his friend Benny Binion was there to underwrite him and keep him in the game.

There are pictures of Moss taken in Las Vegas at the end of his career. He is dressed like Burt Lancaster in the film *Atlantic City*. By then he was a rather sad figure. But don't waste your pity; it was those who played him, or took his bets, that we should feel sorry for. And the Texan road gamblers owe him because it was Johnny Moss who helped lay down the track they were to follow in later years.

Thomas "Amarillo Slim" Preston could never be a ghost; he's always been too much of a grandstander. Ghosts tend to be the silent type; Slim, even approaching his 80s and not in the best of health, is vocal.

On my way into Amarillo I pass a dozen or so Cadillacs buried end-up in a field. It's surreal, and so is the Big Texan

Steakhouse on the former Route 66. While I wait for Slim, I contemplate a seventy-two-ounce steak. This is at least six times the size of steak I would usually have, and I'm a big eater, but I'm told that if I can eat all of it in an hour, together with potatoes, beans, and salad, followed by fruit pie, I can dine for free. The Big Texan says more than 30,000 have tried and nearly 15 percent have succeeded, including an eleven-year-old boy and a sixty-nine-year-old grandmother. I'm tempted to bet Slim he can't tackle the steak. Slim has never been backward about taking a bet; he once rode a camel into a hotel in Morocco because someone bet him he wouldn't dare. But I decide not to tempt him; you don't hustle a hustler. So when he arrives in a battered-looking old pick-up truck, we settle for bacon and eggs. He piles his plate high. How, I wonder, does he remain so slim when he eats so much? The answer is he doesn't: he picks at his food while we size each other up.

We're both a bit edgy. I'm anxious that he feels relaxed and talks freely; he's clearly deciding whether he can trust me. He's right to be wary. I have a hard question to ask . . . but I'm keeping that for later. In the meantime he finds it reassuring that I actually want to help him feed the horses on his ranch, and soon we're on our way.

As we climb into the pick-up, he points out some bullet holes in the door. Just a couple of days earlier someone had tried to rob him. Slim flat refused to give him the money. The bullet holes are eloquent testimony to the way he lives life on the edge. (A few weeks after I spend this day with him he is robbed in his home and some money and his prize Amarillo Slim belt buckle are stolen. All this he takes in his stride, filling local newspaper columns with caustic comment on his attackers.) Now he settles himself behind the wheel and we're bumping up and down across his ranch—approximately 3,500 acres. Clad in a yellow golf shirt, jeans, and a baseball cap, he's soon feeding me his well-worn one-liners, each followed by a loud cackle and vigorous tooting of the horn.

"The cattle were costing me a fortune—don't ever have a hobby that eats." (Cackle, cackle. Toot, toot.)

"Hell, I was so slim I looked like an advance man for a famine." (Cackle, cackle. Toot, toot.)

"You can shear a sheep many times, but you can skin it only once." (Cackle, cackle. Toot, toot.)

I'm trying to stay objective about Slim, because I've heard bad things about him, but I like this. It's a performance, a well-rehearsed performance, but not *just* a performance—I doubt if it matters whether I'm there or not. This man in this beat-up truck on this dusty road is doing the two things he loves most—talking, and looking at land that he owns as far as his aging eyes can see. Slim is much more than a poker player; he has a life.

What do I know about him? That he's seventy-nine years old and has lived all but a few childhood years in Texas, that he's always been tall and thin, that he became a pool hustler when he was sixteen, that he's now been outwitting lawmen and tax-men to survive as an illegal bookmaker, gambler, and poker player for more than sixty years, and that unlike his peers he has invested his winnings and, truth be told, is these days probably happier with his horses than with human beings.

In the 1950s he formed a bookmaking and poker-playing partnership with Doyle Brunson and Sailor Roberts and all three went on to become world champions by winning the main event at the World Series of Poker—they were that good.

Slim won the world title in 1973 (in controversial circumstances, as we will discover later) and altogether won four World Series gold bracelets and around $1 million in tournament prize money, though most of his winnings were from guys who had more money than sense and were willing to pay up just to say they had played him; two such were the drug-dealing brothers Lee and Jimmy Chagra from El Paso.

Then one night he appeared on the famous *Tonight Show* with Johnny Carson and became the first celebrity poker player. He appeared on the show eleven times and did more than anyone else to make the game respectable.

What have I heard about him that's bad? That Slim only cares about Slim, that his hustling doesn't stop short of those who believed they were his friends. There are even those who say he hasn't been "that good" a poker player—more of a con man at the table. There are three kinds of Slim-watchers: those who like him; those who good-naturedly say, "Well, Slim is Slim," and can take him or leave him; and those who really don't like him.

Two of the "dislikers" are Bobby Hoff and Carl McKelvey. They were close friends of Brian "Sailor" Roberts (who became their partner after he split with Doyle and Slim); in fact, they loved Sailor Roberts. And they claim that Slim let Sailor down badly.

McKelvey says, "Sailor was having some problems with the law and he was on probation, so Slim set him up in El Paso in a bookmaking operation with two of the local people there. The FBI uncovered it and it was a big case and they linked Slim to it, but Slim got himself out of it and Sailor ended up getting three years in a federal prison. Bobby Hoff had a little money and I had no money at the time and I think it cost us $5,000 to help him out, so we scraped it together, but Slim didn't lift a finger to help him. Slim dumped Sailor in El Paso."

Bobby Hoff supports this story: "Sailor had no money, so I went to El Paso and I paid Sailor's lawyer fees myself and Slim called every day to see how the trial was going . . . this was supposed to be his dear friend and he never offered one time to send any money to help him. Not only that, he actually held a twenty-four-carat gold chain of Sailor's as a security on $2,000 that he said Sailor owed him; the chain was worth at least $6,000. I saw him once and he had that chain and I sent someone to give [Slim] the $2,000 and told him, 'If he doesn't give you that chain, just tear it off his neck.' The way he abandoned Sailor was a terrible thing."

I hear a number of "Slim the hustler" and "Slim the hard man" stories. Naturally he rejects them all. He knows he has critics—even enemies—but puts it all down to jealousy. Anyway, it's time I let him talk for himself, because we're way out on the ranch now. There are no buildings. It's just rough scrubland and cactus and mesquite, the occasional windmill. He has recently sold most of his cattle and all he has left are his horses. He has a name for each of them, carries them pails of water, unloads bags of feed from the truck, talking all the time—whether it is to me or the horses, I'm not clear.

So, he does not live on the ranch? "No, I live in Amarillo in a 6,800 square foot home with a mountain out the back. There's a king-size electric swimming pool, four holes of golf in the backyard, and a professional tennis court in the corner. It has an illegal fence around it, ten feet and solid. I'm inside the city limits, but I got my own well and water. I'm not supposed to but a lot of public officials can take a bribe." (It does not appear to cross his mind that this sounds bad. Nor does it occur to him when he's telling stories about dodging the taxman that, if everybody did, there would be no roads for the road gamblers to drive.)

And the ranch? "It would be in the top twenty in this part of Texas, I guess. I have some others, two in Texas and three in New Mexico. Some are bigger and some are smaller. And I have a stable of racehorses in California." He also owns four eighteen-hole par-three golf courses in Amarillo and Dallas, Alabama and New Mexico, and from time to time he's owned pizza places and ice-cream parlors. On the way to the ranch we had passed what he described as "a little tract of land I'm buying"; this "little tract" is 790 acres.

The Slim "empire" has to be worth a lot of money. Where did it come from? "Well, it came from poker and bookmaking, of course."

He begins to talk about his skill at sports handicapping (he claims to be the best) then diverts himself onto the tax people.

"They had me in and said, 'Mr Slim, we want to see you in Waco, Texas, at ten o'clock, Friday morning, at the First National Bank and I said, 'Gentlemen, you got a better chance of getting a blow job out of the Statue of Liberty than you got getting me to come down there. I haven't got no business in Waco.' And they said, 'We'll get a subpoena and come and get you.' Of course I knew what it was about. I had a safe deposit box down there. So I said, 'Well, I guess I'll be down there.'"

"So I'm there and as we go downstairs, you have to sign in with this old lady, and she looked up and said, 'Oh, Mr. Roberts, how are you?' and I said, 'Fine, young lady, how are you?'

"By that time they had three special agents down there and somebody like a court reporter who recorded all the proceedings and two officers from the bank, but none of them noticed she called me Mr. Roberts. So they read this court order to open the box. It was one of these big boxes, and one of the agents dipped down in it and brought out a handful of $100 bills. They have four clerks trying to count it and they were shaking like leaves. So this one agent, he said, 'Damn, there's a lot of money in that box,' and I said, 'It looks like more money than I've ever seen.' So he said, 'Isn't that your money?' and I said, 'No,' and I said, 'We've already agreed that it's not your money, so if it's not mine and it's not yours, let's split it.'

"Anyway, when it came to court, they couldn't prove it was mine, so after hearing me, the judge says to the other side: 'Get out of my court and don't ever come back in here with a case like this. I don't want to hear it, this is thrown out.'"

Was that reported in the newspapers at the time?

"Not exactly as it was. It said, 'Slim wins again.'"

"Thing is, they knew it was mine but they didn't grasp that it was my signature on there as Mr. Roberts, even when that little ol' girl said, 'How are you, Mr. Roberts?'"

We begin to talk about the hijackings in Texas. Was he actually playing in a game when they came in with guns?

"Goddamn, yes. A lot of times. Last time we got robbed in Austin they made everybody drop their trousers and told us to scratch the ceiling. Doyle Brunson was there. Doyle's kind of crippled and he couldn't raise his arm and they said, 'Say, Fatso, we said scratch the ceiling,' and Doyle tried to explain he couldn't and they slapped him on the side of the head with a shotgun, and then Doyle got his arm up, no problem; in fact, he damn near climbed that wall.

"I remember we were playing at Killeen. That was a big hold-up. They came in jumpsuits and Halloween masks and with sawn-off shotguns and they got a big score down there. There was probably $150,000 on the table. Their introduction was a string of bullets across the ceiling with a machine gun. I was in the kitchen having a bowl of soup. I had a big stack of money and I just put it in my soup and covered it up with crackers and they never found it.

"Then there was a bad experience in Atlanta, Georgia. They stripped me naked and wired me up. They tore my handkerchief in two and put half of it in my mouth and then put duct tape over my mouth. Of course I thought they were going to give me the water treatment . . . At that time a lot of the hijackers, if a guy didn't come up with the money, they'd hold him under the water and, believe me, you will give it up. And that's what I thought they were going to do and the guy said, 'We're going to take a thirty-minute head start and we'll call back to the hotel and tell them you're here and they'll come up and let you loose.' But I still thought they were going to put me under the water and as soon as they left I naturally struggled to get loose and that wire cut me. Blood on white enamel looks scary and I was bleeding like a stuck hog in the bathtub, naked. And I hear a key or somebody opening my door and I thought, 'Goddamn, there's a maid.' So I start banging my head on the side of the tub and finally she comes to the door and opens it and screams, and you could have heard her for twenty miles."

He tells me about the partnership with Doyle Brunson and Sailor Roberts: how they had met at a game in Midland, and how Sailor and Doyle a few weeks later came to Slim's house for a three-hander. Slim claims he won all the money and had to lend them some to go home. What impressed him was that they actually mailed him what they owed. He decided these were men he could trust.

So they got together and combined poker with bookmaking and it all lasted for years. They roamed Texas together. They would fix the game they were going to by phone or on their way home from the previous night's game. They would either take Doyle's car or Slim's station wagon, with Slim usually driving. ("I drove fast and I knew the roads.") They would drive hour after hour, Sailor usually sleeping, Doyle and Slim talking poker. They would check in to the best-looking hotel or motel in town, Slim and Doyle sharing a room and Sailor sharing one with the girl of the moment (and there always was one, even if the moment was just an hour). Some of the games lasted all night, some three days. Security in Slim's case was a Smith .38, carried in his pocket to the game, mainly in case of attack when he was leaving with money. Doyle carried a gun too. After a time they knew where every game was, who would be playing and what kind of stakes they could expect. The bankroll, expenses, buy-ins, winnings, and losses were shared.

In the meantime the bookmaking became big business. Doyle and Sailor ran an office in Midland and Slim ran a branch in Fort Worth as well as looking after San Antonio. Slim also did most of the handicapping. They had eight people manning the phones and taking the bets. This went on for over a decade.

"We were efficient at it, and all three of us were knowledgeable about sports. We had a good, clean reputation. If you won something from us, you got it. This was all illegal, but I had judges and district attorneys and sheriffs in the can. Everywhere I went, I went under a fix."

Is he still doing it?

"No, but I let a guy lay off to me. There's some books which are pretty good sized books and anytime he gets over $20,000 for a game he calls me and gives me $15,000 of it because he doesn't want to take a chance on losing that money on one game, so he lays it off to me."

The partnership with Doyle Brunson and Sailor Roberts finally broke up when the three of them went to Las Vegas full of confidence only to have their bankroll wiped out in a humiliating debacle of a game involving Puggy Pearson at the Dunes. Whether each blamed the other, or the team just had the stuffing knocked out of them, who knows, but they went their separate ways: Sailor to link up with Hoff and McKelvey, Slim to become a "personality," and Doyle to build a career in Las Vegas that would eventually make him a giant—*the* giant—of the game.

While Slim has been chatting away, it has got real hot under the Texas sun, and he's sweating and suddenly he appears to gasp for breath. I give him my bottle of water and he gratefully gulps some down. Then he points to the skeleton of a heifer— just white bones lying in the dust. "It must've been sick and the coyotes got it. It wasn't there a day or so back, so they must have stripped it of meat overnight. That could have been me. I fell off my horse one day and I couldn't get back on my feet; I was just lying there in the heat of the day and I thought, 'I'm going to die out here,' but luckily one of the men who were working the ranch for me was driving by in a truck and saw the horse standing there and guessed what had happened. If he hadn't picked me up, the coyotes would have got me too."

This reminds me he is an old man and not a particularly well one. As we begin to drive back to Amarillo, I ask him about it.

"I went into critical care three times and intensive care twice in the last year and a half. I had five so-called specialists and one of them said, 'It's obvious he isn't going to make it so let's get him out of intensive care and put him in critical care.' I came to for a minute and I cursed his ass. I ran him out of the emergency room and then I said to the other four: 'I bet all four of you exorbitant goddamn thieves that I walk out of here.' Not one of them could look me in the eye."

Then he adds: "Of course they probably could have won, as they make you get in a wheelchair when you leave." We both laugh. (Cackle, cackle. Toot, toot.)

It's time to ask the difficult question. I know that Slim has always been proud of his family and that three years back it was shattered by a big row that caused his wife of fifty years to divorce him and one of his children to go to the police. Slim ended up before a grand jury and was indicted on three felony charges of indecent assault (the charge being that he inappropriately touched his twelve-year-old granddaughter). He later pleaded guilty to three misdemeanor charges and was given a two-year suspended sentence and fined $4,000.

The word spread throughout the poker community and Slim's world fell apart. "It almost killed me because it intensified all these health problems. It got me a divorce and it cost me business deals and a couple of million dollars. But I could stand that . . . I'm not complaining about that. What was bad was that it damaged my family.

"I never said one word to anyone at the time. And I never said a word after. Don't you find that curious, that I didn't try to defend my name? I was charged with a felony when it was not a felony; that's what they eventually decided—they decided it was at worst a misdemeanor; that's like getting a parking ticket. There wasn't nothing to it. And I only got that verdict because I preferred to plead guilty than hire smart-assed lawyers who would have beat up on my family. It was heartbreaking, but I took it on the chin and for a while I stayed away. Spent time with my horses."

As far as poker was concerned, he became a relative recluse. He was shunned at the World Series in 2004 and stayed away the following year. Then in 2006 he returned, slipping quietly into Las Vegas, a shadow of the showman he had been. At the World Series, Nolan Dalla sometimes identifies famous players and introduces them to the crowd. I was there in 2006 when he spotted Slim taking his place unnoticed in the far corner of the huge room at the Rio. There were more than 3,000 players and spectators packed in. He took his microphone over. Then he paused. Should he introduce Slim? What was the mood out there? Finally he leaned over and said to Slim, "I'm going to introduce you in a moment; just stand and raise your hat." He took a deep breath and said, "Folks, in this corner we have one of the game's legends. He did more than anyone else to publicize and popularize our game. Let's have a big welcome for Amarillo Slim."

For a fleeting moment there was silence.

Then the whole room broke into warm applause. Slim just sat there, nodding at Nolan in gratitude, a glimmer of a tear in his eyes.

In poker there's always another game . . . another hand . . . another chance. So it was for Slim. Some three years after his fall from grace, at least the world of poker was ready to forgive him his sins.

Time to move on.

Time to play poker.

And they wanted the old showman there.

As I drive Highway 20 en route to Dallas, I think about Slim. He's a hard man. But, like Johnny Moss, he came from a hard place. Do I like him? I don't know. But I can't find it in my heart to disparage him either. He is a man of his time and place and, for all the bravado, he conveys a sense of vulnerability now. He tells the same old stories he's always told but without the same old energy. It's my guess that the man who all his life has so loved and needed an audience is now lonely. And probably doesn't have long to go. The game is nearly over.

One thing I know: he loves his horses. And there's a place, out at the far end of his ranch, on a brow overlooking a valley and the Canadian River, where he is accountable only to himself and history, and there he appears to be at peace. Sometimes he goes out and spends the night there, in a little tent, his horse grazing nearby. When his time comes, and even he expects it to be sooner rather than later, I hope they think to bury him there.

Now I'm in Dallas, and, of course, I pay my respects to the Redmen Club, a poker institution run, until recently, by Cowboy Wolford's brother, Ray, and a partner. It's been around on one site or another for at least sixty years, always operating outside the law. Nearly all the Texan road gamblers played there at one time or another—three generations of them, beginning with Moss way back in the 1930s, and including such legendary names in Texan poker circles as Corky McCorquodale, the rodeo star Cowboy Wolford, Bob Hooks, Cotton Bullard, Blondie Forbes, Bobby Chapman, Johnny Wheeler, Fred Sarge Ferris (who came from Shreveport, Louisiana), Everett Goulsby, a man who bet such huge sums on sports that he could literally change the odds across the whole country with one bet, and Robert A. Brooks, who made his money in Alaska, at one time partnered Cowboy Wolford in a poker club in Dallas, and was so respected that he was always called Mr. Brooks.

The Redmen Club, with its seven poker tables, its television monitors always set on the sports channels, and its popular kitchen, is still there (but shortly after my visit is raided and finally closed down).

Had I been around in the old days I could have also played in a game run in Dallas by Charlie Bissell, a man who was about as wide as he was tall, seriously fat, and who appears to have been universally despised, but ran one of the higher-stakes poker games and was, therefore, humored. T. J. calls Bissell "the Big Texan" and says of him: "He was the most hated man you could meet in poker, but he ran a clean game and provided the best food you've ever had at a poker game, so we played there anyway. You had steaks like you wouldn't believe and big salads and desserts. And some of them were really big games . . . At least once a week we had $100,000 on the table. I remember Betty Carey once won $51,000 one night in a $5–$10–$25 no-limit hold'em game. She had all the hands in the right spots and the guys weren't giving her credit for the player she was. She ate them alive."

Another semi-legal place was the AmVets Club. Cowboy Wolford once sat down to play the owner of this seedy joint and ended up winning the whole club. (Cowboy may not be a legendary name in poker, but he was all over the place in Texas in those days and good enough to become runner-up in the 1984 World Series. Another of the Texan road gamblers to be born into extreme poverty, he became one of the state's best-known rodeo riders and developed his poker skills in late-night games after the show was over. He died at seventy-three in 2003.)

Benny Binion, about whom much more later, was of course the big man in Dallas in the early days, more of a top crime figure than boss gambler, and one of his hit men, George McGann, was a regular in the poker clubs. He was a contract killer who was himself killed as a result of a row in a poker game in West Texas; the man he was playing with left the game, went to his car, took out a gun, and came back and shot him in the head. Another occasional player was Troy Inman, who was known to leave a game and, gun in hand, wait outside to rob the winner.

One man you definitely didn't want to meddle with was Henry Bowen, who ended up as one of Binion's bodyguards and fixers; not only did he know where the bodies were buried, he usually buried them! (Bowen, a big man who often wore bib overalls, had robbed the occasional bank in his day and was stitched up by the police for a murder in Oklahoma and spent years on death row. In fact he had been at Johnny Wheeler's rodeo in Texas, hundreds of miles away, when the murder took place, and owed his life to the poker community, which kept pressing for a reprieve until he was eventually cleared.)

None of these were top players; McGann, in particular, was a real loser. T. J. Cloutier says that McGann once ran out of money playing at the AmVets Club and, in a temper, pulled a gun and robbed everyone at the table. He came back to the game the next day and nobody said a word.

T. J. tells a great story about McGann: "There was a guy called Tippy-toe Joe who used to play heads-up with him and won a lot of money off him over the years. One day McGann lost his cool after losing to Joe for the umpteenth time and took out his gun and demanded, 'Give me all you've got.' So Tippy-toe Joe had to sign over $10,000 in $100 travellers' cheques. As they're leaving the place Joe, who had beaten this guy out of a fortune over the years and didn't want to lose him, said, 'We're not going to let this little incident ruin our game, are we, George?'"

Carl McKelvey describes McGann as "a homicidal maniac." McKelvey says, "His other partner was Stanley 'the Creeper'; they called him that because he'd hide in the bushes and creep up behind someone and shoot him in the head when he was coming home. Ironically, to meet them you would never believe it . . . you would think George was a schoolteacher, and Stanley was well mannered, a bit feminine. But these were bad guys. I was once given a ride to Midland by these two killers. We were there after legal drinking hours, it was about two in the morning, and the only place you could play poker and get a drink was in a really rough place called the Flats, the black area, and this guy RJ is *the man* and his joint is *the place*. When I walked in with George McGann and the Creeper, I could see everyone looking edgy because they were all scared to death of George. He'd already killed two of them over there. So he said, 'Sit down there, Carl. Here's $1,000, we're going to stake you.' But what I didn't know was RJ was a thief and he was cheating . . . he had a hole-out table that enabled him to slip a card into the game when he wanted to. And they played hold'em with the joker as ace or to complete a straight or a flush. So I'm playing along and a big pot comes up when I'm playing this guy. I think I had ace-queen and there was a queen after. So I moved all my money into the pot and he reached for his chips, intending to slip a joker into his hand, and then he froze like a deer in headlights, because he saw George McGann was standing behind me and watching him. He looked like he was paralysed. The card that could beat me was within his reach but he saw George there and he knew George was staking me and he was terrified of George so he folded and I won the pot."

Linked to Dallas, there is the old cow town of Fort Worth. There I go to see the famous Stockyards, right off Exchange Street, where, for the benefit of outsiders like me, they still stage a round-up each day . . . actually it's pathetic, half a dozen bored cowboys herding a few tame and tired longhorns down the street at what seems a yard and yawn a minute. This is where the poker was played in Doyle Brunson's day, in the pool halls, beer joints, or top-floor hotel rooms of Exchange Street. "This was the toughest place I've ever played in," Sailor says. "There were forty of us that hung around together there and, apart from Sailor and me, they were all either dead or in the penitentiary by the time they were thirty-five. It was a common thing to open the newspaper and read that one or two of them had got killed. I was playing there one day and some guy burst into the room and shot one player in the head; it was splattered all over the wall. Well, everyone got up and ran. There's a river out the back and we all ran into it. There were some hard guys in Fort Worth—really hard guys."

From Dallas-Fort Worth, I pay a brief call on Denton. It's just up the road. There, in the days of the Texan road gamblers, I could have played in Hugh Briscoe's game on Sundays. Briscoe was a wealthy man who owned over five hundred acres of land and loved to play poker. When he lost, he would sell off an acre or two to cover his costs, until he ended up losing all five hundred acres and retaining only the land occupied by his house. His game attracted some of the big names—T. J.

Cloutier, Bobby Baldwin, Robert A. Brooks, Cowboy Wolford, Catfish Bullard, and Ken Whatta Player Smith, who became famous for wearing what he claimed was Abraham Lincoln's top hat and crying out when he won a hand, "Whatta player," a point he proved at the highest level.

From Denton, I drive back to Richardson, an affluent suburb of Dallas at the heart of the Telecom Corridor. The street I enter is clearly the preserve of its better-paid professionals. You could imagine a doctor, dentist, banker, or business executive living at Number 1106. What you would not expect to find there is a professional poker player.

He doesn't even look like a poker player; you expect a poker player to look like he's been up all night, to be a drinker and smoker, to look . . . well, a bit dissipated; you don't expect him to be six foot five, with the frame of a football player, and with the healthy appearance of a non-smoker, non-drinker who destroys four eggs (plus bacon, etc.) for breakfast every morning and probably would have devoured that seventy-two-ounce steak at the Big Texan and asked for more.

This is T. J. Cloutier, one of the best players never to have won the World Series main event. He's been on the final table four times, second twice. He has six WSOP gold bracelets and has won over fifty professional tournaments, including taking the Jim Brady Diamond Classic in LA three years in a row. And it all began on the road in Texas.

We settle in his little study, surrounded by pictures and trophies accumulated over fifty years of playing poker. He tells me he is not a genuine Texan, having been born in California. At school there, he excelled at baseball, basketball, and football, and won a sports scholarship to the University of California and played in the 1959 Rose Bowl. After time in the army he played professional football in Canada for five years. He then joined members of his family in a food business in San Francisco, but, when his marriage broke up, he decided on a change and travelled down to Texas with one hundred dollars in his pocket and the chance to work on the oil rigs. He had already played poker in California, and now began to play more regularly and make money, so he decided to do it full time. Thus began a career that has made him one of the best known and loved players in the game.

He began playing poker at the Brass Rail in Longview. Then he heard about Harlan Dean's game in Shreveport, just across the border in Louisiana, so he went there in the late '70s and played pot-limit hold'em.

"After I was there a couple of years I heard about Charlie Bissell's game in Dallas and the first twelve times I played in it I won. I was driving two hundred miles from Shreveport and then driving back. That was every Monday, Wednesday, and Friday. Bill Smith and I played together and a lot of the time I staked him and I would stay at his house. After I had won twelve times in a row Charlie Bissell said, 'I'm going to drop the latch on you unless you give me half your play,' so I said, 'OK, why not?' because I liked playing in this game. This is not unusual—Slim Lambert, the boss gambler in San Antonio, often insisted on a piece of the action if a player was winning regularly. Anyway, everybody liked to play in Charlie's game because it was the best no-limit hold'em game going and it was three times a week, and at least one out of the three times there would be $100,000 on the table in chips. You paid 5 percent when you bought your chips and if you bought $5,000 or more, you got them for 3 percent."

Why was Bissell so hated?

"He'd do things like call me up and tell me what an asshole someone was, and then he'd call them up and tell them what an asshole I was, and everybody knew he was bad-mouthing everyone else. Then his game got busted by the police and he became a snitch and anytime a game started up in Dallas you'd see him going through the parking lot taking down licence plate numbers. But to be fair to Charlie, for most of the time his was the most honest game.

"Bobby Chapman was boss gambler here in Dallas for a time. He was a big-time bookmaker who also ran a car lot and he loved to play poker. He didn't play it well because he'd get drunk, and every card game in Dallas used to keep a six pack of Schlitz beer in the refrigerator just on the chance he might show up. He used to play on the theory that he would buy a lot more chips than anybody else and if he could win one out of five hands he'd bust you, and it worked lots of times, but everybody wanted to play against him.

"I played at Bissell's one day and we were getting towards the end of the month and I had to get all the bills paid. I'd won $2,700 so I decided this was a good time to go home. Then I got a call to say Chapman was on his way to the game, so I picked up the money I had won there and went back to the game. Chapman brought in $200,000 and he put down $20,000 buy-in. Of course I put down my $2,700, and I looked down and I had ace-king of hearts. His money was already in on the blinds, so he called the $2,700 and he had two tens and they held up, and I had to go back home. It was exactly twenty-two minutes from when I got the phone call to the game until I got back home . . . and it cost me $2,700."

We're looking at a map of Texas, identifying the poker games T. J. played in.

Longview? "An older guy, Sam MacFarland, was the main gambler in Longview and all the games were built around him. He would carry a big chunk of money in a little paper bag, but if he ever needed credit out of a game he could always get it. He always said if he ever got to the point where he couldn't drive himself to a game, he was going to end it all. One day he called me up and said, 'I want you to do a favor for me,' and he gave me four different bags to take to the places where there were four poker games and to pay off what he owed, and when he got back home he blew his brains out. That was just because he couldn't get around anymore. He did just what he said he was going to do. But he wanted to make sure he didn't owe a dime before he died."

Odessa? 'They were all games that Slim and Doyle worked. That was Doyle's area. In Midland-Odessa they had a famous game with some bookmakers and drug dealers where everybody got all shot up. One guy accused another of cheating and they stood up and started firing guns at each other. A couple of them died on the spot, and one of them was wounded badly and he ran out the door and pounded on a neighbor's door to try and get help, but they'd heard all the shooting and they thought someone was trying to break in, so they opened the door with a shotgun and let him have it and they killed him. Talk about a bad beat!"

And so the stories roll on. But T. J. soon began to make an impact beyond Texas. He really hit the big time when he began to focus on tournaments. "The main thing cash-game players can't handle in tournaments is where the antes and blinds jump every hour or so and they have to adjust their game to that. So I worked on that. And when I first started out on the tournament circuit, I started learning how everybody played. I have an almost photographic memory for how people play poker. If you and I played poker twenty years ago, I'd forget your name but I wouldn't forget how you played and it's beautiful to know that. I don't have to write that down and that's always worked for me. It's a huge strength. And you've got to have what we call iron balls, too. If you've started a bluff, you've got to go all the way through with it. It's been my objective for years to have more chips at the end of each level than I had at the last one, so I'll make a play here or there. It's the timing of the plays that counts and that's something you can't teach somebody. I categorize everyone on the table and I'm watching everything that goes on. I know who's playing a lot of excessive pots and who I can go over the top on without a hand, and you have to use that in your favor."

The first time he came second in the World Series main event he found himself heads-up with one of his closest friends, Bill Smith. But the real heartbreaker was his defeat by Chris Jesus Ferguson in 2000. He went into the final table as short stack but with a plan to sit tight and let the others take each other on and, hopefully, knock each other out. And that's exactly what happened. When it came to the heads-up, he was still there, albeit with only 400,000 chips to Ferguson's 4,700,000. Even so, T. J. came all the way back and took the lead. "I kept chipping away at him and once we were more or less on equal terms I was looking for him to miscalculate the value of a hand, and eventually he did. I had ace-queen and opened for 130,000. He had ace-nine and raised me, and I then went all-in. Well, he sat there for about five minutes. He told me later that he didn't think he could beat me heads-up and that he had been waiting to gamble on a hand. Anyway, he called and the flop came two-king-four. There was a king on the turn. So all I had to do was to avoid a nine and I had won . . . yet I could feel the nine coming. I even knew it would be the nine of hearts. And it was."

T. J. had suffered one of the most crushing moments in the history of the game. The ultimate tournament player had been denied winning the ultimate tournament by the ultimate in bad luck. Phil Doc Earle, one-time Houston player and World Series gold bracelet winner, was there: "With 95 percent of the money in the pot, it only needed for Chris to receive any one of thirty-nine of the remaining forty-two cards in the dealer's hand and T. J. would become world champion and achieve the dream of all poker players, the Holy Grail of poker fame, immortality, you name it, it all applies.

"T. J. was denied the dream by a thirteen-to-one shot. Oh, the cruelty, devastation, sense of failure, and loss he must have felt in his gut and heart . . . yet he stood up, stared for a moment in silence, then put out his hand to Chris and said, 'You played well enough that you deserved to win.' Then he had a mike stuck in his face and was asked what he felt about the draw out: 'That's poker,' he said. There was a remarkable unpretentious dignity about him at the moment that was unforgettable."

For over fifteen years T. J. had a partnership with multimillionaire Lyle Berman. Berman would buy him into events and take a share of whatever T. J. won. "As far as he was concerned he was investing and he ended up ahead of the deal, and from my point of view I never had to worry about buy-ins because the money was always there. It was a good partnership." He now has other partners. Buy-ins are still not a problem. He enjoys teaching, writes books—useful books—with his friends Tom McEvoy and Dana Smith, and takes part in poker boot camps. During the 2006 World Series he left Las Vegas for two days to teach a whole family how to play tournaments. They paid him $15,000 plus his expenses.

What was the most memorable hand he played?

"That's easy—it was one when I had no cards. It was in Shreveport and I had the nuts in a hand of pot-limit hold'em. I was playing a guy called Wayne Edmunds. I had $7,000 in the pot. Then, for some reason, the dealer picked up my cards and tossed them into the muck. I couldn't believe it; one second I had the winning hand, the next it was gone. But Wayne had his head down, looking at his cards, and he didn't see what had happened. So when he looked up, I kept my hands high, as if I was holding the cards close to my chest, and bet $3,000. He folded and I won the hand with no cards."

With every one of the old-timers there is a question I wish I didn't have to ask. With T. J., it's about his dice habit. T. J. is famous for losing his poker winnings at the craps table.

Would he be a lot better off if he hadn't been addicted to craps?

"There's no telling, but I'm not going to go back and relive my life. I've had a hell of a life. And I only play at the craps table occasionally. I could play craps every day, but I don't do it. I don't think about it when I'm home. I just care about it when I'm out there [actually in the casinos] . . . But a lot of times I play for a lot smaller money than a lot of people think I'm playing. I haven't lost nearly the amount of money people think I have. And I haven't lost any more than other poker players lose on sports betting and crazy bets on the golf course. I probably lost as much helping my brother."

(T. J. spent about $500,000 trying to keep his brother out of jail. "He was older than me, but he always wanted to be me and he'd go out and write bad checks in poker rooms and stuff and get himself in trouble over gambling. He died last year, but I spent a lot of money trying to keep him out of jail. He actually went to jail a couple of times when I couldn't do anything about it.")

"But," he continues, "there's no denying I play craps. The only time I ever win on craps is when I start with small money. If I start from $400–$2,000, I might win, but if I start with $20,000 I have no chance."

Then why does he do it?

"I don't know, I guess it's the action . . . I spend a lot of time in casinos waiting to play poker in tournaments and things. You get bored. I'm going out to Las Vegas this week and I bet you I play craps at some point. I won't play it for much money because I'll make sure I won't take much with me.

"To tell you the truth, I hate to talk about it because I know it's my addiction or affliction and I don't have any qualms about admitting it, but I hate for some wise guy who doesn't know me to come into a poker room and say, 'Did they get you again at the craps table?' or something like that. It's none of their damn business."

We adjourn to the local hamburger joint. It's lunchtime and full, but they quickly make room for him. There's a lot of nudging and pointing. Everyone knows T. J. Everyone likes him. He always has time for anyone who wants a word. His wife, Joy, joins us. She's tiny compared with him, but you can tell she holds her own in the relationship. They're fun to be with and I have no desire to leave. But I have places to go . . .

It's possible from Dallas to rejoin Highway 20 and travel across the part of East Texas that once pulsated with oil fields, taking in Tyler (a major beneficiary of the oil boom of the 1930s, where Cowboy Wolford was born and eventually ran his own game, and where Johnny Wheeler owned a ranch and played high-stakes poker), Gladewater, Longview, Kilgore, and Marshall (where Johnny Moss was born). When the oil was discovered, these small, unremarkable towns became a modern version of the cattle or mining boomtowns of the frontier days out West and drew the same mix of workers (the oil men) and opportunists (not least the Texan road gamblers).

Just over the Louisiana border is Shreveport, a kind of "honorary Texas poker town" from where Sarge Ferris came, and where T. J. played a lot in his earlier poker days. The guy who ran the game in Shreveport was Harlan Dean. It took place in his house and is still remembered by many for the cook's unbeatable hamburgers. It's been said that Harlan was so mean that once, when the cook wasn't around, he sent out for one roasted chicken to meet the needs of seven players for two days, but T. J. remembers him more kindly: "Harlan was a character; in fact, if I got broke I'd call up Harlan or he'd call me up on Sunday morning and I would say, 'I'm broke, can't come,' and he'd say, 'Come on down, you can have some chips,' and, if he got into difficulty in the game and didn't want it to stop, you could borrow the whole chip case if you wanted."

Now it's time to turn south. I tick off the poker places on the map as I drive by: towns and cities such as Killeen, Belton, Lockhart, Austin, Alice, and Robstown. Then there's Waco, where a guy called Bud Brown ran a game in the Elks Club. Cowboy Wolford wrote of it:

That joint was something else—it was upstairs and had a big bar at the front and a poker room in the back with windows that had been all shuttered over with plywood for years. The Elks finally decided to knock off the plywood and put in windows to get some ventilation. Two of the old gamblers who had been playing there for nearly twenty years keeled over dead within a month—I figure they couldn't stand the fresh air.[3]

As I'm heading south my thoughts turned to rumors I had heard about cheating, even by the best players. I wonder about the partnerships and whether they involved complicity at the table.

The line between playing straight poker and playing beyond the rules—or, to call a spade a spade, cheating—was not as clear in those days as today's players would imagine. There was a considerable element of what you could call "gamesmanship." Most professional players probably did what they had to do to win, knowing that if they didn't create an edge, their opponents would.

They were not there for the fun. They didn't endure the hours on the road, the lonely days and nights, and the dangers and setbacks for the love of poker; they were there to earn their living and, in the case of men like Doyle Brunson, Amarillo Slim, and Johnny Moss, to keep their families. So, many of them—I'm not saying all—entered those rooms intending to do whatever it took. That did not necessarily mean they were professional cheats in the sense that cheating was their business; but it would not be surprising if occasionally they strayed beyond the straight and narrow.

Herbert Asbury writes interestingly about the highly respected nineteenth-century poker player Dick Clark in his book *Sucker's Progress*:

> To the Dick Clarks of the frontier, gambling is an honorable calling, on a par with, if not a cut above, banking and the law. [But] the high roller had to learn every crooked trick in order to be on

his guard against them . . . If, like Dick Clark, he called himself a "square gambler," he set for himself certain standards and scruples. He would not think of holding out an Ace or hiding a cold deck under a bandanna in his lap . . . but if he had the ability to stack a deck while shuffling or to reverse a cut so smoothly that the other players could not detect the move, he saw nothing unethical in employing his hard earned talent. When professionals sat down to play "hard cards" for heavy stakes, the use of such skills was considered very proper and even necessary. A man making his living with cards could not long survive if he relied only on the whims of that fickle lady called luck. Dick Clark was as straight a gambler as the West ever knew, and yet he wore a large diamond ring that he would turn into his palm when dealing in a big game and use as a mirror. The layman might find it difficult to comprehend the ethical difference between the use of Clark's ring and [other ways to manipulate the game] but to Dick Clark and his peers the distinction was marked and fundamental. Anyone could stack a deck in private and hide it under a bandanna; it took a master and countless hours of practice to be able to read the faces of cards as they flashed across the tiny diamond mirror in the palm of a hand.[4]

Paula Mitchell Marks echoes the theme in her book *And Die in the West*:

Cheating—if done with finesse—was considered part of the game . . . obviously, when a gambler cheated, he wanted to do it in such a way that he could not be challenged. Professional gamblers had to be men who knew how to avoid trouble.[5]

She quotes a Tombstone saloonkeeper as saying: "Wherever skill of the mind or the fingers could be employed to bring in the money, Dick Clark and his brethren used what they had."

Now, as I drive across Texas, I ask myself: if Amarillo Slim, Doyle Brunson, and Sailor Roberts, two of them carrying guns, were driving the white line in the same car, staying at night in the same motel rooms, meeting all their expenses and playing in the same games off the same bankroll, were they really always straight? If at the end of the game they had to pay into a bankroll they all shared, why *would* they try to beat each other? Are we really to believe that on those long drives they didn't devise signals? Were they never tempted to push up the betting between them in order to force opponents to abandon their hand?

Poker player and writer Nolan Dalla says, "I think that back in those days things went on . . . probably even some of the big names we respect today didn't always win on the up-and-up. But I'm sure they would tell you it was defensive in nature. It was just part of the game.

"All the gamblers from that era were opportunists. Gambling then was not how it is now. You have to look at it in the context of the era. You could not survive in poker unless you knew about cheating and maybe practiced it to a certain extent. I think the distinction that they would draw, if they ever told you the truth, is that they never took money off people who truly couldn't afford to lose it. Or they would say they were putting one over on people they knew were themselves scam artists or dubious people. I'm sure they had a kind of moral justification for their actions. But if we're to judge them, we have to judge them in terms of the era they lived and played in."

There has always been a question mark over Johnny Moss. He admitted learning how to cheat as a kid. Yet he was adamant that for nearly all his career he was strongly opposed to cheating. In his interview with Jon Bradshaw for the book *Fast Company*, Moss claims, "I ain't never cheated, ain't never connived." In his self-published biography by Don Jenkins he took the same line:

> When cheating enters a game, Johnny signals his displeasure in
> no uncertain terms. He feels the cheaters are stealing from him

. . . because Johnny can play better than the other players, the money will eventually belong to him. The cheaters are taking the money from the game before he can win it legitimately.[6]

Some of his contemporaries back him up. Crandell Addington, who played with Moss many times, says, "Moss cheated? I don't think so. I played with him a lot of times and I can't imagine it."

T. J. Cloutier differs. "When he was a younger man, he was not only the best player but he could cheat with the best of them. He bragged about it in his older age, not only to me but also to others, so I'm not saying anything out of school. Johnny Moss was for Johnny Moss, and that was him. If he got the opportunity to cheat, he would."

In a magazine interview, Doyle Brunson was unequivocal. "Moss was a cheat," he said.

Still, one has to say in his defense that poker in those days was not like it is today. Nolan Dalla's point about acting in self-defense is a valid one; often it was a case of fighting fire with fire. Amarillo Slim loves to tell a story about spotting a hole in the ceiling from where someone could see his hand and signal to one of the players whether he should bet or fold, i.e., someone was cheating big time. So he waited for a particularly big pot and then deliberately let a card be seen, but when the hands were turned over the card was not there; he had switched it. His opponent leapt to his feet, white-faced . . . but then froze. He couldn't say a word, because if he did, if he charged Slim with cheating, he would have admitted he was cheating too. Slim left the game a happy man. He, too, would call this self-defense.

Moss survived on the road in Texas for well over thirty years. He played in every kind of place with every kind of player. He was arrested and cheated and robbed, won big sums of money and frequently went broke. He was undoubtedly a great player, but did he not have a few little tricks to help him in the hard times? We can't go back and re-create those times, so we don't know, but what we do know is that in later years, when he ran card rooms in the casinos of Las Vegas, he encouraged the dealers to cheat the recreational players who came on holiday or for fun. He did it by taking an outrageous rake out of the game. He ran what was called "a snatch game." The dealers would snatch as many chips as possible. Not from the professionals who would have quickly spotted it but from those who had little experience and simply didn't know what was happening to them. They were being robbed. (These were the days when casinos didn't think it worth their while to have a poker room and rented the space out to someone like Moss, who then controlled what happened.) So, despite his protestations, he was no paragon of virtue.

As for the Brunson-Preston-Roberts partnership, I put the question to both survivors, Doyle Brunson and Amarillo Slim.

Slim says, "You know, what tells you a lot is that in all those years and all those games we were never once accused of signalling one another our hand. I tell you, that's really something, because everyone knew we were partners, and yet never once did anyone suggest we were colluding."

But if there were just two of them in the hand, what was the point of going on?

"There wasn't. One of us would bet and the other would throw his hand away. That didn't hurt anyone."

It seems to me that this makes the game easier for the partners than their opponents, but I ask whether he came across much cheating.

"Yes, but we knew the cheaters and if we hit town and there were guys working in that game, out of courtesy we'd either leave or they would leave. We were not going to stand to get fucked with our money, and by the same token we weren't going to tell anyone what to do. That's why I always got along with both the thieves and the players."

I don't know whether Slim ever cheated, but it's clear from his answer that, if he didn't, it was a pragmatic decision, not a moral one.

Doyle Brunson says, "Everybody knew we played together; we never made a secret of it. We could never do anything out of line because it would have been too obvious. Often when we contested a hand by raising and re-raising we showed our hands afterwards. All those years we never at one time had a problem with it because we just never did anything out of line and we would show our hands and say, 'Well, like, that's what I had.'"

Cowboy Wolford addressed this question:

Everybody was aware who was playing with the same money but that didn't bother anybody. Road partners didn't usually play in the same game, but even if they did, the other players didn't fear any collusion . . . I've seen bankroll partners playing in the same game, each man for himself, not getting anything from the other guy—they played their hands. Of course they stayed out of each other's way.[7]

Well, I can't do more than put it to them, and that I've done.

It's a weekend and what better place in all Texas—indeed all America—to be on a sunny autumn day than in San Antonio. I spend a leisurely Saturday afternoon paying my respects to past heroes at the Alamo. The city has been built around the old mission, so it's a short walk from where I'm staying to what has become a shrine to the 189 brave Texans who defended it from 3,000 Mexicans for thirteen days before all were killed. Here I see the burial places of Davy Crockett and Jim Bowie. There's a canal winding its way through the middle of San Antonio. The banks on either side are known as the River Walk (or Paseo del Rio) and they're lined with colorful cafes, restaurants, and wine bars, and on Saturday night it is a great place to be. I'm not surprised to find it attracts more than twenty million tourists every year.

I find my way to the Castle Hill area where Tom Moore, Slim Lambert, and Red Berry ran a nightly game. This was by invitation and high stakes, and is where Crandell Addington first made his mark. Now *there's* a name to conjure with. Between 1974 and 1979 Crandell Addington made FOUR World Series final tables, coming second to players of the caliber of Moss and Bobby Baldwin, and ultimately made the main event final ten on seven occasions.

Given the size of today's fields, this record will probably never be broken. I decide to seek him out.

He's in his office on Sunday morning. He's wearing a casual shirt, jeans, and boots. This makes me one of the few in the world of poker to have seen him without a tie, because if ever there was a contest for the best-dressed player in the whole history of the game, Crandell would win it by a distance. I've seen scores of pictures of Crandell playing poker, usually at the World Series, spanning thirty years, because he was there at the beginning, and he is *always* immaculately and imaginatively dressed, always wearing a jacket and tie and usually an expensive Stetson. "Well, it gives me a bit of table presence that others don't have," he says. "And it helps, because wearing a coat and tie reminds me to remain disciplined."

Of course there's more to Crandell Addington than being a flashy dresser. This is one of the great poker players. Not only does his final table record in the World Series main event have few equals but he was also a big cash-game winner, both on the road in Texas and later in Las Vegas and elsewhere.

Like fellow Texan Amarillo Slim, Crandell these days has a life outside poker. He's chief executive and chairman of the board of a biotechnology company that is developing a drug it believes could make a major impact on some forms of cancer. Even so, the glass case in the office is full of poker trophies and it's clear that recognition as one of the game's big names matters to him.

He points out the window towards Castle Hills. "They had a full-scale casino that ran on the weekends at 6701 West Avenue; that was the big home owned by Tom Moore, eight acres, and he had a huge area out the back where they had craps, 21, roulette, and people came from far and wide. Of course all this was illegal, but that didn't bother anyone. For six days a week the highest stakes poker game in the United States took place there. One of those days it was a limit game, but the other five days it was no-limit hold'em. It wouldn't be unusual—and, remember now, this was in the early 1960s—for there to be $100,000 on the table in any one hand—now you can multiply it by eight to calculate it in terms of today's stakes. Most of the players were just wealthy men who liked playing poker, but Tom would invite friends like Doyle Brunson and Sailor Roberts and Johnny Moss. It was the type of game that good players were looking for because there were these producers who had made their money in oil, or cattle, or real estate, but who couldn't put a hand together. Tom Moore and Slim Lambert and Red Berry were the boss gamblers in San Antonio at the time."

Crandell played poker at university, and the father of one of his friends played in the game. "I left college in 1961 and was recruited by one of the big five accountancy firms in the USA; in the Southwest region I was the number one recruit. I went to work downtown on the starting salary of $375 a month. I was playing poker around San Antonio and I heard about this big game out on West Avenue. I asked what the buy-in was and they said $500. Remember, I'm working for $375 a month. But I was winning money playing poker, so I could afford it. So I was allowed into that game and thought I'd died and gone to heaven.

"In 1963 I was twenty-five, and they thought I was just a kid and I was going to lose my money and that will be the end of it, but it didn't work out that way. After about six months Tom Moore called me and said, 'Come out a little early today before the game starts.' So I went out there and he and Slim Lambert were sitting there and they said, 'You need a partner,' and I said, 'Nope, I've got plenty of money, I don't need a partner,' and they said, 'You *need* a partner,' and I said, 'Oh, I get it.' . . . So from that point they took half my play."

That was the deal to allow him to stay in the game?

"Yes. And I left work and for ten years or so I just played poker."

Crandell had become a Texan road gambler. He started playing in games all over the state and beyond. He was one of the few to travel down to Mexico to play. But unlike many of his contemporaries he could see a world beyond poker.

"I became an operator in some oil and gas ventures . . . an operator is the party who develops the prospect. You go and lease the ground, and you do the drilling and the production and so on. So I did that for a few years and also helped develop a couple of properties."

As a result he is now a rich San Antonio businessman who sometimes plays poker, but he's still so respected in the game that he was summoned to Las Vegas in 2006 to be inducted into the game's Hall of Fame. I was there and was impressed, both by his aristocratic appearance and carefully chosen Southern gentleman's outfit, and when in his acceptance speech he quoted Thoreau ("Most men lead lives of quiet desperation, and go to their graves with a song still in them"), this, I concluded, was no ordinary poker player.

I now ask him about the Moss encounter in the World Series in 1974 when he placed second.

"Well, I could have won. We played back and forth for a long time and finally a hand came up where, if I had won this hand, I would have broke Johnny. I had a big lead on him in chips anyway. I flopped three sevens and he slow-played two aces. He checked on the flop and the turn and, even though there was an ace on the river, I was convinced I had him. I decided to check on the river and let him try and take it from me. When he did, I called, and of course he had three aces and he got hold of a lot of chips. That was a hand I'll never forget. Then we played and played and finally I tried to win a hand with a pair, but he turned a set of threes on me and that was the end of the game."

We talk about his time on the road. Did he carry a gun?

"I did. I carried an automatic pistol. Mainly to get to the car after the game.

"I played along the river and that's how I first learnt how much a million dollars in $100 bills was. I saw it weighed. There was a grocery store like an old meat market and they had these scales they used to weigh these things on. They had a few tables in the back where they drank a beer or two, and they had a huge game back there. I was the only guy in the game whose first language was English. One night I'm playing down there and they got into an argument about how much a million dollars weighed and I'm listening to this argument going on in Spanish and one of them says, 'Wait a minute,' and about five minutes later he comes back in with a big duffel bag and he goes up to the front where they've got this scale up on the counter and he starts emptying this duffel bag of all these $100 bills wrapped up in rubber bands. Someone said, 'You aren't going to get all that up on there,' and that was true, it was too much bulk for the scale, so the guy finally puts $250,000 on there, because that was all he could get on there, and then he just multiplied by four. About a year later they arrested a load of people who had no visible means of support and yet had these huge houses down there. You can guess where the money came from. Anyway, that's how I learnt how much a million in $100 bills weighed.

"I played once in Monterey. There was a big horse race there. So afterwards they said, 'OK, it's poker time,' so we went over to this bar. It was against the law to play poker in Mexico too, or at least it was then, so they said, 'We can't play out here, but we can play in the bathroom,' so we took some tables in the bathroom. It was just a big room and there were no toilet stalls, no urinals, nothing, so it all ran down these small tile walls and into a tiled trough at the bottom—if you get my drift. So they set the tables up in there and we started playing. We had a hell of a poker game there."

Crandell Addington may look like, and have the manners of, a Southern aristocrat, but he has played poker in some strange places.

I'm now back on the road south and as I drive mile after mile I begin to wonder whether some of the game's mysteries will ever be solved. As I discovered in Deadwood, Tombstone, and other gambling towns of the 1800s, exploring poker's past is made difficult because there are virtually no records. If you want to know about baseball, football, golf, the Olympics . . . there's no end to the facts and statistics; school kids can reel them off. But not poker.

Take the origin of Texas hold'em. This is by far the most popular form of poker, the one adopted for the main event at the World Series of Poker, but no one appears to know when and where it began. I assume my best hope lies with the old-time Texans—Amarillo Slim (seventy-nine years old), Doyle Brunson (seventy-four), Crandell Addington (sixty-eight)—but, for all their years in the game, even they don't know.

Doyle thinks it came from Waco, probably in the 1950s.

Crandell says, "The first time I ever saw hold'em was around 1959. My friend's father was playing in the big San Antonio game (one that I played in later on—from about 1963). They didn't call it Texas hold'em at the time, they just called it hold'em. And my friend introduced it to me and some of the other guys at college who were playing mainly draw poker. I thought then that if it were to catch on, it would become *the* game. Draw poker, you only bet twice; hold'em, you bet four times. That meant you could play strategically. This was more of a thinking man's game."

At least Slim recalls exactly when he first saw it.

"It was in 1959 in Brenham, Texas, a little old town between Houston and Austin. At that time one of the best poker games in Texas was played above a feed store in downtown Brenham. I remember I liked the game right off because every time a card lands on the board it changes the possible best hand. We all know that two aces are the best hand to start with, but come queen-ten-three—now there's a lot of hands that can beat two aces. Now, that makes a game!"

All three of these veterans were playing poker in the '50s *before* they came across Texas hold'em. Could this mean the game was invented in the mid-'50s? This would explain why they all came across it at roughly the same time. I was coming round to this view until I re-read the Don Jenkins book on Johnny Moss. It is hopelessly vague about dates, but, as best I can work out, Jenkins is writing about the late '20s or '30s when he states:

The Elks Club [in Dallas] offered a ten-handed hold'em game, which was different than any game [Moss] had played before. Each player was dealt two down cards for the first round of betting. Because there were mandatory "blind" bets, the play was either to call or raise the bet or to fold on the first round.

After the first round of betting was equalized, there were three cards dealt, face up, in the center of the table. These were called the "community cards," which each player used in conjunction with their two down cards. These three cards were also termed "the flop" . . . There was a second round of betting.

When that round of betting was equalized, there was a fourth card placed face up in the center of the table . . . this was also a community card to be used by each of the players. A round of betting followed the placement of that card, which was called "4th Street."

The last card available was a fifth community card, face-up, in the center with the other four . . . it was the last card of each hand . . . When the last round of betting was completed, each player used their two down cards and the five up cards to make their best five-card hand.[8]

This is a surprising revelation, because, without question, the game described is what we know today as Texas hold'em.

If this part of the Jenkins-Moss book is true, they were playing it in Dallas in the '30s, well over twenty years before it was "discovered" by Doyle, Crandell, Slim, and others in the late '50s.

The next reference to hold'em in the Jenkins-Moss book comes after an account of how Moss spent two years in the Navy and the Marines during the Second World War. Jenkins writes:

He returned to Dallas (in 1945) to find one nice surprise . . . most of his cronies had added a new game to their repertoire—hold'em. The high action game had spread quickly across the south. Johnny never let on that hold'em was one of the first games he had learnt. He simply asked them how it was played and had a picnic as people all across the south tried to teach him.[9]

As I've already noted, I think the Jenkins-Moss book is unreliable. It is the Moss story as told to Jenkins and it's careless about dates. But the claim that Moss learned the game before the Second World War and came back to Texas to find it catching on has a ring of truth . . . if only because there is no reason why either should make the story up. Moss was known to embellish a story, especially if it strengthened his reputation, but this story made no difference to his reputation one way or the other.

But if it is true, why did hold'em not take off and eclipse draw and stud and become *the* number one poker game until so many years later? How do we explain that Doyle, Crandell, Slim, and others didn't see it until the late '50s? Of course, one answer is that these three only appeared on the circuit about then. Anyone playing with Moss in the '30s and '40s is now either dead or nearly one hundred years old (Moss was thirty-seven in 1945), and none of them left records.

It could be that hold'em was around in the '30s, but mainly in the South, and according to some initially in the Corpus Christi-Robstown area, and that it only really took off, albeit slowly, in the '40s and '50s, when it was picked up by a generation of players who travelled more widely and took the game with them. We know it hit Las Vegas at the end of the '60s when a number of Texans introduced it at the Golden Nugget. (Corky McCorquodale is usually given sole credit for this, but Crandell Addington and some of the other Texans all claim a part.) By the time it was adopted for the main event of the World Series of Poker, it was being described by Doyle Brunson and others as "the Cadillac of poker."

But as for the exact origins of this compelling form of poker . . . well, I have found no one who really knows. It is another of the secrets that remain with the ghosts at the table.

From Crandell Addington and San Antonio I head to the southeast, to Brenham, Victoria, and Houston. In Brenham, the big man was Martin Cramer. He was the boss gambler there and ran one of the biggest games in Texas in a rustic, old building downtown. His card room looked like you would expect in places like New Orleans in the '20s and '30s—high ceiling, old-style bar, fans whirring above the table. Players liked it; it was one of the best places to play in Texas. Cramer had himself well covered with the police and the judges but not, alas, with the gangsters. He was murdered.

I have one final objective on this journey: I want to learn a bit more about another legendary road gambler, Sailor Roberts, and I think I know how to do it. I've now passed Victoria, where his friend Bobby Hoff was born and raised. Bobby is now in California and I'm hoping to meet him later, but I drive on to Houston and, as I hoped, I find Carl McKelvey having dinner in his brother's Greek restaurant. We adjourn to the porch and gossip. Carl is sixty-four and one of the last of the Texan road gamblers, still on the road, still seeking out games, especially the one he likes and plays the best: pot-limit hold'em. Carl has never won a World Series gold bracelet, but he's been a runner-up three times and made the money on many other occasions. He was a boyhood friend of Bobby Hoff and Steve Lott, and they became gamblers together, travelled to Las Vegas together and there met Sailor Roberts.

Sailor was so-named because he spent four years in the US Navy during the Korean War. He was a hedonist who also had a talent for poker. He won the World Series in 1975 on a final table that included his old Texan road gambling mates Doyle Brunson and Amarillo Slim. He also won a WSOP gold bracelet in a 1974 deuce to seven low ball event. This was his favorite game. But if he had a greater talent it was for winning the affection of his fellow man and woman; despite his addiction to drugs and his exceptional devotion to women, he is still looked back on fondly by everyone in the game.

I tell Carl what T. J. Cloutier once said about Sailor: "Boy, did Sailor love the girls and parties. I remember one time when he was older and drove to San Angelo to play poker. Over about three months he beat the game out of $85,000—and it wasn't a big game, just pot-limit hold'em with $5 and $10 blinds. But by the time he left town he had less money than he arrived with— that's how much he liked to party with the girls. I mean, he was a party animal. He loved three things: playing golf, playing poker, and going out with the girls. And the good times took him for every dime he had . . . the girls were ripping him off, and he knew it but he didn't care—he just wanted to live life to the fullest. But he did more for down-and-out players than anyone else. If a guy was down on his luck, Sailor would give him a bankroll."

Carl laughs at the description. "It's right on. Sailor was the type of person that would never say anything bad about anyone. I never met a man like him. He would never say anything bad about anyone, no matter what they did. He wouldn't hold any grudges, always glad to see you, and if someone needed help he was there and he couldn't say no. He was such a unique man. I loved him . . . he was a man who I wanted to be like. He loved the good times and he loved women. He and Bobby and I used to party a lot and have a good time."

Sadly the partying extended to drugs and the three of them all became addicted to cocaine with disastrous results. Ultimately associated health problems killed Sailor, and also dogged Carl and Bobby. "In those days they said cocaine wasn't addictive, it was a social drug, and everybody was using it, so we used it too and we thought it was all right. Little did we know it was a cruel joke.

"There came a point when Sailor was doomed and he knew it, and he refused to stop taking drugs and drinking because he said he was going to die anyway, so he kept going. Bobby Hoff tried to take care of him in Los Angeles and he would give him some money to go and play poker and he would take the money and go and buy drugs and he was driving Bobby crazy, so Bobby asked me for some help on this. I called Bobby and Sailor answered the phone and he said, 'I got to get out of here, please send me a ticket,' and I did that and got him a place to stay and I said, 'You can't do this to yourself. You're my hero and it's killing me. I can't stand it. You gotta quit.' But he wouldn't take care of himself, and all he wanted to do was fool around with the girls and smoke crack. He gave up . . . because he knew he was dying and he thought, 'What the hell, I'm going to have a good time.' That was the way he looked at it, and there was nothing Bobby or I could say or do for him to pull him out of that.

"So what can you say? A man is going to die and he wants to live the way he wants to live . . . are you going to tell him not to?"

Sailor Roberts, world poker champion in 1975, one of the great Texan road gamblers, died in a hospital in California in 1994. He was sixty-four. The final killer was sclerosis of the liver, caused by hepatitis. He left behind him a lot of friends.

I ask Carl about the southern Texas circuit. "There were great players on this circuit . . . Victoria, Corpus Christi, San Antonio, and Houston; there was a big game in all these places. There were some great players. People like Sam Moon, who had a game in Corpus Christi, one of the biggest games in Texas at that time. I ran it for him. Sam was a gambler all his life and in his later years he seemed to run into a run of cards that was unbelievable. He was a tall, thin man, slow moving, didn't say much, but he had real presence about him. He was a very aggressive player, a good player (he made the final table in the World Series in 1979), but a real 'steamer' when he was losing. He was an honest man and he was on the square. Speedy Meyers and Buck Buchanan were coming in from Killeen. Bobby Hoff would be there, T. J. would come down from Dallas occasionally. Every weekend there would be $30,000–$40,000 winners. There was a game here in Houston that Jesse Alto and Danny Hunsacker ran. It was at the time in 1978–79 when Houston was booming with oil money, and there was a lot of cash in the game then. We played in a penthouse in the center of town. There were several high-stakes games in Houston at that time, but Jesse's was the biggest. He was a small, energetic guy, full of charm. And he had taken care of the police. You could win $20,000–$30,000 in those games; Jesse lost $160,000 one night and that was a lot of money back then."

(Alto has an astonishing record in the World Series main event: second to Brunson in 1976, fifth in 1978, third in 1984, sixth in 1985, fourth in 1986, and ninth in 1988.)

Did he carry a gun?

"I carried a pistol with me at all times. I carried it to get me to the car. I never had to use it. But we got hijacked here in Houston twice . . . once when I was a young kid, with a double-barrelled shotgun, and that was scary. I got robbed four times in all. I've also been arrested numerous times."

His last words to me beautifully sum up the lives of the Texan road gamblers: "We used to call it the three ifs . . . *IF you can beat the game, IF you get paid, IF you get out of the place with the money.* It was tough."

And now it's time to leave Texas. I have to move on because poker moved on. The great days of the Texan road gamblers eventually came to an end. The producers ran out of money or became disillusioned. The law killed some games, the hijackers finished others. Players grew older; game organizers died.

But there was another factor that ended the days of the Texan road gamblers.

Benny Binion, the Dallas crime boss, boyhood friend of Johnny Moss, had some years earlier filled the boot of his car with dollars and fled to Las Vegas. Now he was making things happen there. And, as the word spread of rich pickings, one by one the poker players followed.

The third age of poker was about to begin.

The third age of poker

Las Vegas

five

The Godfather—Part I

Dead man talking—the truth about Benny Binion

It's November 30, 1987, and there's a birthday party in Las Vegas . . . a spectacular party, over the top even for this town where excess is the norm. There are 18,000 guests. The entertainers are world-famous country and western singers Willie Nelson and Hank Williams Jr. The toast is proposed by the casino mogul Steve Wynn. When the four-tier birthday cake is carried onto the stage, all eyes turn to the eighty-three-year-old man in the white Stetson sitting in an armchair at the center of the arena, and the chant begins . . . *"Benny, Benny, Benny."*

This is the crowning moment of Benny Binion's life: Benny the family man . . . Benny the philanthropist . . . Benny the entrepreneur . . . Benny the small-time gamblers' protector and the poker players' patron saint . . . Benny the founder of both the World Series of Poker and the game's Hall of Fame . . . Benny who, Steve Wynn now tells the cheering Las Vegas crowd, is *"the greatest guy we ever met."*

Now let's slip back in time to the 1960s. Ed Reid and Ovid Demaris are researching their book, *The Green Felt Jungle*, and interview a retired police captain who was active during the gang wars of the Benny Binion era in Dallas, Texas. They quote this exchange:

Question: Can you give us some insight into Binion's MO?

Answer: His MO was always the same—kill 'em dead and they won't give you no more trouble.[1]

Could this man being feted by 18,000 in Las Vegas in 1987—the pioneer of modern professional poker—*the greatest guy we ever met*—really be the same man whose modus operandi in Dallas was *kill 'em dead and they won't give you no more trouble*? Who was the real Benny Binion? The genial, beardless Santa Claus of Las Vegas described by Al Alvarez in *The Biggest Game in Town*? Or the psychopathic killer who emerges from accounts of his Dallas days?

I decide to find out.

It isn't easy. Benny in his Las Vegas days met poker's needs: his Binion's Horseshoe became its home, his World Series its summit. Many of the game's veterans recall him only as a benevolent and generous old man, and now that he's dead they consider it indelicate, or even ungrateful, to ask where the man and his millions actually came from. Yes, they knew he had bribed police and politicians. Yes, they knew he was—or had been—a gangster, a man who hired killers, but who when questioned about it would ask why he would do that when "*I can do my own damn killin'*." But they also knew him as the man who laid the foundations of the multimillion-dollar business that poker is today, and as the poker player's friend who backed some of the game's legends when they were on a losing run and would help just about anyone with a loan or a dinner or a room at his beloved Horseshoe. In his later years they loved to be in his company and hear his stories, to be part of the "club" he created around himself.

Of course, if you believe "you can only judge a man as you find him" (and it's not an unreasonable philosophy), you could buy Benny. In his latter Las Vegas years he worked on his image as a laid-back, friendly character with a fund of stories. And as he grew older and the past receded into the distance that image prevailed. As Al Alvarez wrote: "Age, reputation and great wealth turn tough people into lovable old characters."[2] Sally Denton and Roger Morris wrote that once he left his Dallas crime base and moved to Las Vegas, "the outrageous was now merely colorful, his bloody past a quaint caricature, another civic attraction. He became known as the wily sage and grandfather of Glitter Gulch."[3]

Over the years some have written of Binion's dual image.

A. D. Hopkins, a leading Las Vegas journalist of the time, wrote:

> His reputation as a killer, which he acquired in his youth, [may have] followed him to his grave; but he [also] gained the active affection of thousands of Las Vegans, who also saw a philanthropist, a generous and fair employer, and a brilliant innovator in the city's key industry.[4]

Denton and Morris wrote:

> From the beginning, Binion was two men: the "square craps fader," the honest game boss who covered any bet, who might even give money back to hapless losers or remember loyal employees with turkeys at Christmas; and a barbaric outlaw of terrifying means, leaving the buckshot-mangled bodies of rivals or renegades beside railway tracks or half-buried under quicklime all over North Texas.

This question—who was the real Benny Binion?—is one any poker historian must address because Benny, and the whole Binion family, played an unparalleled role in the growth of the game. For forty years Benny was *the man* as far as poker in Las Vegas was concerned. The Godfather. Today he is a ghost whose shadow still falls across the game and whose friendship some of poker's greatest names still find difficult to explain.

So it is that I head back to Dallas to see for myself his old haunts, to scour fading newspaper reports of the days of the Great Depression and Prohibition—his days—and talk to some of the road gamblers who knew him, and share stories with others who have researched him.

Let's cut to the chase and confront Benny the killer first.

In the files of the *Dallas Evening Journal* there's a story published on May 26, 1933:

> A jury in Judge C. A. Pippen's Criminal District Court, Wednesday, gave Benny Binion, 29, a suspended sentence when he pleaded guilty to the murder of Frank Bolding, a bootlegger [on] October 5, 1931.
>
> The State could produce no eyewitness to the shooting, although five witnesses were put on the stand who testified that they saw Bolding as he approached the house, and that a short time later they heard several shots.
>
> Binion took the stand on his own behalf. He testified that a friend had warned him by phone earlier that day that Bolding had bragged he was on his way to Binion's home to kill him.
>
> The accused man stated that Bolding called him out to the backyard and attacked him with a long-bladed knife. Binion said he fired five times at Bolding. Eddie Carroll, ambulance driver, testified for the defense. He stated that when he reached the scene of the killing, he found a long-bladed knife by Bolding's body.

It remains a mystery as to why Benny pleaded guilty to murder if he was acting in self-defense, a claim the court at least partially accepted in giving him a suspended sentence. In fact Benny's own son, Ted, many years later suggested that the victim's knife had not actually been drawn; the implication is that Benny had made a small deal with the ambulance-driver witness while waiting for the police. Ted added that Benny was safe pleading guilty because he knew the court would take into account the bad reputation of the victim: "The guy was so bad, who cares?"

However, a more likely explanation, not suggested by Ted, is that a deal was made with the Attorney General or the court; given the number of judges and law officials in Benny's pay, this would not be surprising.

Whatever the reason for his plea, the fact remains that Benny *did* plead guilty to murder: he admitted to the world, *"I am a killer."*

(Benny was questioned about this killing many years later when the Las Vegas Gaming Commission was considering him for a gaming licence. Binion told them: "That was just a nigger I caught stealin' whisky.")

Self-defense was claimed a second time when Benny and an associate were charged with the murder of a man called Frieden, who had recently come to Dallas from California and dared to invade Binion's rackets territory. The *Dallas Times Herald* reported on December 12, 1936:

> Judge Noland G. Williams on Monday dismissed murder indictments against Benny Binion and H. E. (Buddy) Malone that charged them with the policy racket slaying of Ben W. Frieden, 56 . . . Frieden was shot and killed by his automobile Friday afternoon September 12 on Allen Street.
>
> The murder trials had been [suspended] twice because the witnesses to the shooting had disappeared. The state had been trying for six weeks to find the missing eyewitnesses.
>
> District Attorney Hurt recommended the charges be dismissed. Hurt's motion pointed out that it was a self-defense case, that witnesses testified at the habeas corpus hearing that Frieden was armed and fired the first shot in the encounter, and further that there was insufficient evidence to convict.
>
> Binion and Frieden were rival policy game operators. The evidence showed Binion went to Frieden's car and they had an argument, during which Binion slapped Frieden.

> Frieden then drew his pistol and fired at Binion. Both Bin-
> ion and Malone . . . returned Frieden's fire . . . It was deter-
> mined later that Frieden died instantly with a bullet to the
> head.

In fact there were those who believed that Benny, having
walked up to the car and committed cold-blooded murder,
then shot himself in the shoulder, self-inflicting the wound to
prove self-defense. One was John L. Smith, who wrote: "When
Binion was indicted, he claimed his shoulder wound had been
inflicted by Frieden. Never mind that Frieden was unarmed or
that the bullet came from Benny's own pistol."[5] Gary W.
Sleeper, in his book, *I'll Do My Own Damn Killin'*, also says
"some suspected that Binion's flesh wound was self-inflicted."
Sleeper explains Binion's revolver had been fired three times
but only two of his bullets were found in Frieden's body, "raising the very real possibility that Binion had in fact used his
third bullet to inflict his own wound."[6]

There are many other allegations about Benny's involvement
in killings, but these are the two occasions when he was actually charged and, as the newspaper accounts show, in the first
case there were no witnesses and in the second the witnesses
conveniently disappeared. Their absence could owe a lot to
Benny's reputation for being unforgiving of his enemies.

The police officer quoted earlier described the approach of a
contract killer called Lois Green, who carried out occasional as-
signments for Benny:

> Lois had a system, a regular procedure when he wanted to plant
> a victim. He would send a couple of his boys out ahead to dig a
> pit and leave some quicklime stashed nearby . . . Take the case
> of Otto Freyer, a real tough monkey who shook down gamblers,
> pimps, and even raided some of Benny's games . . . Freyer was
> taken to one of these pits, stripped naked, shot in the guts with a
> double-barrelled shotgun, kicked into the hole, and covered

with lime while he screamed for mercy. He was still alive when they finally buried him.[7]

Why, if he was such a notorious disposer of his enemies, did Benny only ever face two murder charges? The answer lies partially in the influence he had with those in power and partially in the difficulty in those days—pre-DNA and the other sophisticated investigative techniques and equipment now available—to win a murder case without witnesses. Gangland murders were especially hard to prove; the victim was not there to testify, and, as for witnesses, they tended to fade away like snow in the spring. It's been said that between the '20s and the '50s it was easier to beat a murder rap than a charge of breaking and entering. Chicago's Al Capone was responsible for countless killings but (like Benny Binion later) could only be convicted on tax evasion charges.

As for the killing: it was just business. The retired police officer told Reid and Demaris: "Big-shot bootleggers . . . have to kill to stay in business. Otherwise they wouldn't be in business long enough to earn the title. Show me a big-shot bootlegger . . . and I'll show you a cold-blooded murderer every time."[8]

Jim Gatewood begins his Binion biography with what he calls "Benny's Law."

Rule number one is: *Do them before they do you.*

There are others, and all of them have been repeated to me by those who knew Binion in Las Vegas:

My friends are always right and my enemies are always wrong.
I'm not gonna tell you anything but the truth, but there is a lot of the truth I'm not gonna tell you.
When you come to a tough place in the road, never look back and never holler "whoa."[9]

This last "law" was Benny's defense for who he was and what he did. If he said it once, he said it a million times:

"Tough times make tough men" . . . in other words, you had to do what you had to do.

So, back to Texas, to Pilot Grove, north of Dallas, about twenty miles from the Oklahoma border. This is where Benny Binion was born on November 20, 1904 . . . born and nearly died, because he was ill with pneumonia five times before he was two years old. Benny would later claim he never went to school for a day in his life and couldn't read or write. Thus begins the myth creation; in fact, the Gatewood biography quotes a childhood friend as saying, "Benny had a good head on his shoulders and had no trouble with schoolwork." Benny himself, in an interview in his latter years, referred to reading a book while in prison. What is true is that he didn't have much schooling and was probably semi-illiterate.

His father traded horses and mules and decided that it would be best for the kid's health if he went out on the road and got plenty of fresh air; as a result (just like Johnny Moss, who was later to become a friend on the streets of Dallas), he never really had a childhood, spending all his time with men. He left home at fifteen and by the time he was twenty he had already accumulated a lifetime's experience scraping a few dollars here and there, gambling, selling liquor, horse trading, and living by his wits in places such as El Paso on the Mexican border.

He made his way to Dallas in 1923 at the ideal time for someone of his ambitions. It was the Prohibition era and the Great Depression was just a few years away. Both created considerable opportunities for the unscrupulous to profit. Gatewood claims that Benny marked his arrival in Dallas—and declared his intentions—by buying two .45 automatic pistols, a .38 revolver with an ankle holster, and a Winchester model twelve-pump sawn-off shotgun. If so, by the time he was in his late teens he was already buying the tools of a trade: Benny had not come to the big city with conventional work in mind.

For one so young and uneducated he had a remarkable talent for making contact with, and winning the confidence of, older men. He now set about befriending three who would play a crucial role in his life. One was an influential deputy sheriff called Bill Decker, a man who by force of personality almost ran the city for three decades. Benny developed a friendship and understanding with Decker—albeit, as far as one knows, not a financial one—that worked well for both for over twenty-five years. The second was Joe Civello, a local Mafia boss, who, it is said, helped launch Benny's career as a bootlegger. The third was Warren Diamond, the Dallas gambling boss, who managed the St. George Hotel and ran a gambling joint there. He was known as "Knuckles" because of the brass knuckles he always carried with him. Benny was for a while an aide to Diamond, making deliveries, collecting protection money, working in the casino. He became like a son to him, so much so that when he announced he was going to open his own games, Diamond let it happen; anyone else could have expected to be looking down the barrels of a sawn-off shotgun. When Diamond retired, Benny "inherited" Diamond's business and contacts.

Even in his early twenties, Benny managed, with a combination of street cunning and fearless and ruthless "man management" skills, to establish himself as the rising star on the Dallas crime scene. He became a major bootlegger and then took up the numbers racket, or, as it was described by its operators, the "policy wheels" business. This involved using insurance companies as the instrument for selling an additional policy that was, in effect, a kind of lottery or raffle ticket. Once a week the numbers would be put into a wire wheel and one would emerge as the winner. This was illegal, but, as the Great Depression began to bite, it became big business in depressed times, creating work for the unemployed and bringing financial relief to the lucky winners. Not that this was a charitable venture: Benny kept 80 percent of the income and distributed only 20 percent to those who so desperately needed it. This business quickly built up to the point where he was coordinating a number of policy wheels across Dallas and making the beginnings of his fortune, even with the expense of having to pay off policemen and employ thugs, who either had to protect the policy runners (salesmen) from being robbed or deal with those who were stealing from their boss. It was not unusual to find the dead bodies of policy runners beside the railway tracks or in fields of weeds on the outskirts of town. (It was about this time that Benny allegedly placed an order for five Thompson submachine guns.)

Benny increasingly based his operations in the Southland Hotel, a place built by criminals that combined high-quality public areas with hidden hallways and passageways for easy escape. In 1926 Benny opened his craps game in Room 222. By 1929 he had a combination of legitimate and illegal businesses, all fueled by the success of bootlegging and the policy wheels.

He now entered a difficult period: first he had to handle the Bolding murder charge, escaping with a suspended sentence; then he lost his friend and benefactor, Warren Diamond, who committed suicide while suffering from cancer; then he lost his brother Jack, killed in a plane crash; and then he got some really bad financial news: Prohibition was to be repealed, bringing to an end the lucrative trade in illegal alcohol.

But, if this financial news was bad, it was hardly catastrophic: the policy wheels continued to turn and produce handsome profits, and Benny was now in the gambling business, running ten or eleven casinos in the Dallas area. He owned part of the famous Top o' the Hill high-stakes casino in Fort Worth. A deal had been made with the police whereby these illegal operations would not be closed down but would pay regular fines; the city didn't officially want gambling, but it did want money, so the fines were a form of taxation. Benny was later to claim that he paid $600,000 a year in fines. That was a lot of money in those days—but the games went undisturbed and, compared with

Benny's overall income, it was a tolerable business expense. He also had a variety of coin-operated "machines" around the city—pinball machines, slot machines, jukeboxes, and pool tables. He even had trailers with craps tables inside them travelling around the country fairs. All of this required a small army of enforcers and thugs to protect the collection and banking of the money. Then it called for enforcers to watch the enforcers. No one could be trusted.

Benny was involved in every racket in town and, over twenty-three years, rose to be the undisputed crime boss of Dallas, the Al Capone of the city, police and judges in his pocket, killers ready to deal with any "problem." His hold on Dallas increased when several members of the Civello crime family were found guilty of narcotics trading and sent to Leavenworth Prison—in the case of Joe Civello, for fifteen years. It also introduced a new factor—with Civello out of the way, there was a vacancy for someone to handle the Mafia drugs operation in the city. But if Benny had a virtue it was that he disliked the drugs business and he never did have any part in it. Indeed he would often argue that he dealt in good clean fun—drinking and gambling—and never the dirty business of drugs and prostitution.

He was now offered by the Mafia the chance to get into drugs, using his numbers runners to also sell dope, but, encouraged by Bill Decker, who offered to help Benny nail his competitors and enemies in return for help in keeping drugs out of Dallas, Benny refused to become involved in the trade. This made him a nuisance to the Mafia. He was now a target. He invested in a bulletproof, bomb-resistant Cadillac. But he had another form of defense, namely his friend Decker. When four hit men arrived from Chicago, Decker and a number of deputies were waiting for them at the train station. They were sent back from whence they came.

There is little doubt that at this time the Binion law, "do them before they do you," was being enacted more and more.

For instance, about now Benny was approached by a man called Ivy Miller, an associate of Benny in a North Dallas policy wheel and craps game, who complained his business was being undermined by a newcomer called Sam Murray. On June 14, 1940, Benny and Ivy Miller staked out alternative entrances to Murray's bank and waited for him to come to pay in his takings. It was Miller who found himself face to face with Murray; there was shooting and Murray was left dead on the pavement. Benny, who had been at the other entrance, quickly slipped away and was never charged with complicity. Miller was arrested but, despite numerous witnesses, ultimately freed because of "insufficient evidence." (He was later shot by his own son after an argument over money.)

In his book on this period, Sleeper writes:

> The shots that killed Sam Murray ignited a war for control of gambling in North Texas that raged until the mid-1950s. For 15 years gamblers killed each other with shotguns, pistols, rifles, machine guns and dynamite. They deposited bodies on country roads and city streets, in back alleys and front yards, and in parking lots and shallow graves. They killed each other for profit, revenge, and for hire. Theirs was a war of intrigue and double-cross, marked by constantly shifting alliances and shadowy motives. The police knew why the bodies were piling up and who the killers were. Yet, not a single gambler was ever tried, much less convicted, for a major crime of violence . . . The killings in Dallas were discussed with great concern in the murky backrooms frequented by the Chicago "outfit" and . . . even attracted the unwelcome attention of the United States Senate. And when they talked about the killings in Texas, they talked about Cowboy Benny Binion.[10]

Benny had become involved in a gang war with a ruthless maverick called Herbert Noble who was building up a rival numbers racket and even running a competitive craps game. It is said that Noble and his associate, Raymond Laudermilk, decided to remove Benny altogether and began by assigning a sniper to shoot him as he passed by in his Cadillac, but the bulletproofing withstood the test. Benny responded by contracting the murder of Laudermilk; he was found shot in a car abandoned in the street. (His killer was later shot himself, before coming to trial.) Subsequently, Noble had to survive no less than a dozen attempts on his life. As a result he became known as "the clay pigeon." In fact the various attempts to kill him and a series of miraculous escapes would have been comical if it had not all been so deadly serious. Without doubt everyone stopped laughing when his wife was killed by a bomb when she unexpectedly used his car. The explosion was heard miles away; the car and Mildred Noble were blown to pieces. This drove Noble crazy and he came up with an ingenious scheme to bomb Benny's home from an airplane. He was actually found by the police with the plane, the bombs, and maps of the area where Benny lived. In the end he, too, was blown to pieces in his car . . . on the thirteenth attempt on his life. While this story figures in all accounts of Benny's life, and it has always been assumed Benny was responsible, he vehemently denied it, claiming that Noble had other enemies.

By the end of the Second World War Dallas was becoming increasingly lively for Benny. He was always at risk of a Mob-inspired hit. Wars for territory were becoming more and more bitter and violent. And the political climate was changing, too. The war in Europe was over and there was a new mood abroad. In a stronger economy the rackets business was losing its momentum. Benny heard that a Senate inquiry into illegal gambling and political corruption was being planned with himself as one of its targets. And—the last straw—the men at the top of Dallas law enforcement were changing, with a new district attorney and a new county sheriff. He didn't know them and they were not accepting his money; instead, he found himself facing a grand jury indictment for operating a numbers racket. He summed it up by saying, "My sheriff got beat in the election."

So in 1946, for Benny Binion, now forty-two years old and millionaire crime boss of Dallas, life was becoming too problematic. And probably he was tired. For over twenty years he had held together his ever-growing empire, always having to be the strong man, always having to watch his back for challengers from both within his business and outside. Benny always had a streak of common sense. Like the gamblers who survive, he knew the odds against perpetual winning were prohibitive. It was time to get out of the game. He put several million dollars in the boot of his worthy Cadillac and with his family he headed west, leaving, according to Reid and Demaris, "buried in police secret files details of crimes that would stagger the imagination of even the most prolific of detective writers."[11]

His destination was the Nevada town of Las Vegas.

Las Vegas is now such a famous place, its neon-lit image so well established, that it is difficult to believe that it came late to the gambling scene, long after gaming was well established on the Mississippi riverboats, in the old West, and in states like Texas. Indeed, the city itself is relatively new. In the 1860s when Wyatt Earp, Doc Holliday, and the others were playing poker and faro in luxury saloons in Dodge City and Tombstone, Las Vegas was a dot on the map, a watering hole, the attraction to passing humans its natural springs. These created an oasis in the middle of the Mojave Desert. Spanish travellers at the time were so inspired by the springs and their grassy surrounds that they named it "The Meadows"—or, in Spanish, *Las Vegas*. At the beginning of the twentieth century there were only thirty people there. It is perhaps appropriate that it owed its growth to a corrupt politician, one William Clark, who planned to build a railroad from California to Salt Lake City and decided Las Vegas would be an ideal place on the route for his repair shops. Simultaneously he and a competing hustler called McWilliams bought up the land and began to market it vigorously. The sales were a success, but Las Vegas never really took off as a town until it had a lucky break, namely the decision in the 1920s to build the Boulder Dam (it later became the Hoover Dam) just thirty miles from the St. Vegas railway station.

The dam needed workers and the workers needed rest and relaxation. Las Vegas seized its moment. Nevada had not only a beautiful climate in terms of sunshine but also the most relaxed climate for gambling anywhere in the country, and it was soon licensing gaming houses (and turning a blind eye to other related "businesses") to cater for workers to whom, wrote one historian

> the prospect of a night on the town in Las Vegas was more welcome than a bucket of ice water . . . On pay-days they bolted out of buttoned-up Boulder City as if it were on fire and headed straight for the bawdy, brightly lit Fremont Street or the clubs on the outskirts of town, where they crowded two or three deep round the tables, cheerfully emptying their pockets in exchange for a few hours of sinful release.[12]

As far as Las Vegas was concerned, the dam became the equivalent of the silver and gold mines that had created the boomtowns of the old West. There were not only the workers; visitors came from all over the country to see the dam being built and based themselves in Las Vegas. Many never made it to the dam at all. With Prohibition ended, with almost every other vice acceptable to Nevadan law and with even divorce and marriage made easy, Las Vegas had "discovered the immense potential for profit in America's forbidden desires."[13]

Work on the dam was coming to an end in the mid-1930s, but there was no end to Las Vegas's luck. First, it was decided to develop Highway 91, the road between Las Vegas and Los Angeles. This created fresh interest in the rising resort. Then the area was chosen for some major defense installations. More people, more money, more gambling.

The Second World War came and went and, as it ended, what had been a tiny settlement at the beginning of the century had grown substantially and was on the verge of take-off. It had the climate. It had a rising population. It had the most liberal laws in the country. All it needed was the people with energy, resources, and ruthless determination to drive it forward.

It was at this moment that Benny Binion, his timing impeccable as ever, came to town.

Benny built his base in the area still known as "downtown"—in Fremont Street, the Glitter Gulch. It's said that its lighting and signage can be seen from space; it is so bright that, like the Arctic in the season of the midnight sun, it is always daytime on Fremont Street. Benny felt more at home there than up the other end of Las Vegas Boulevard, where what was to become known as The Strip was still largely a dream in Bugsy Siegel's eye. (Siegel, a Mob psychopath, came to Las Vegas the same year as Benny and went on to build the flamboyant Flamingo.) Benny began with the Las Vegas Club. He himself described it as "not the most beautiful place you've ever seen. It was an old, rundown kind of a place." That was soon sold and with his share of the profits he then built a place called The Westerner. He sold that to buy up another rundown place called El Dorado: "It had an $870,000 tax loss, which was very attractive. So I took it and built it from there."[14] He re-named it the Horseshoe and was immensely proud that it was the first casino with a carpet. "I put the first carpet on the floor that was ever downtown . . . The carpet was $18,000 and the fellow that put the carpet in, well, he was a player, and the first night he played. I won $18,000 exactly. So I won the carpet."[15]

Benny is so associated with the growth of poker in Las Vegas that it is surprising to discover that for his first twenty-five years in town he had little to do with it. In the early days the casinos did not see poker as a profitable business, because players competed against and paid each other instead of the house. Benny only really became centrally involved in poker with the launch of the World Series in 1970. In the intervening years he ran the Horseshoe as a no-frills but no-limit gambling joint. Not for him the cabarets and big-name stars; instead he offered generous odds and even more generous helpings of food at low prices. "If you want to get rich," he said, "make little people feel big—give 'em good food cheap, good whisky cheap, and a good gamble." And it worked. Binion's Horseshoe became a popular and highly profitable business.

I first went to the Horseshoe in the mid-'70s; despite the glamour of the citadels of hedonism further up The Strip—Caesars Palace, the Dunes, and the rest—I was drawn to the Horseshoe because everyone seemed to be having fun. It was gambling without the pretensions. It was smoke-filled, a bit scruffy, and noisy. I didn't see Benny, but he was everywhere—on the menus and napkins, the cards and the chips, on matchbooks and slot machines, and in blazing lights all over the outside of the building. The coffee shop served Benny Binion Texas Chili and the Benny Binion Breakfast. And on the top floor it had a steakhouse that today, some thirty years later, is still serving food the way Benny liked it. And, to be fair to Benny, when it came to beef, what he liked was fine.

Life was a lot easier for Benny by now. Instead of holding together a wide-ranging and unruly crime empire, he could spend much of the day in a corner seat in the casino coffee shop. This was his office and almost his home. In addition to his six-acre estate and ranch-style home in Las Vegas, and a flat above the casino, he purchased a huge ranch in Montana where, a caller noted, "even the cook wore a pistol." In Las Vegas he cultivated his newly created image as the kindly, fair provider of gambling to both the ordinary punter and the high-stakes gambler, and he seemingly had no preference for one or the other. In Montana he lived the life of the cowboy, trading horses just as his father had done in Texas all those years ago.

A leading Las Vegas journalist of the time, A. D. Hopkins, describes him:

> The first thing you noticed about him as he entered from the parking lot was his white cowboy hat, worn cocked forward like the gunfighters sometimes wore them to make sure the sun was not in their eyes when it counted. From under the brim gazed piercing blue eyes, locked in a sizing-you-up squint. He carried his head unusually erect, and on his round face he wore an almost-permanent cocky smile. Not particularly tall, he was pudgy but powerfully built in the chest and shoulders, with the short sturdy neck that resists auto accidents and uppercuts. He wore Western-cut suits of grey and other conservative colors, but the buttons on his shirt were made of real gold coins. His favorite overcoat was of buffalo hide with the fur on. He did not like neckties and he did not shave every day.
>
> His eyes never seemed to stop moving, darting about the casino as he walked through, darting about the casino's restaurant as he sat alone, sometimes for hours, drumming his fingers on the table.

But had Benny really changed? Not according to Denton and Morris, who claimed:

> Beneath the public confection, his present was, if anything, more brutal, brazen and corrupt than his past. In Binion's Horseshoe the police were rarely called for suspected cheats or security problems; instead hired thugs mercilessly beat or even killed the accused . . . meanwhile Binion blatantly paid off US senators, governors, judges, and other politicians and officials.[16]

One senator who spoke for Benny when he was applying for his gaming licence said that Benny's only limitation was his unbounded generosity.

But even Benny Binion's luck had to run out sometime. A zealous district attorney in Dallas called Henry Wade was determined that the former crime boss should not be able to leave Dallas behind without paying a price. He initiated a prosecution for tax evasion. It took five years and five grand juries, but eventually the case came to trial. Benny fought to have it dealt with in Nevada, where, helped by his connections, he escaped with a suspended sentence and a small fine. But Wade wouldn't give up and reputedly went to Washington to recruit Federal assistance. Finally Benny went back to Texas with a lot of money, believing that he could pay the tax, pay some fines, pay a bribe or two, and rid himself of the problem once and for all. He surrendered himself to his old buddy Bill Decker. Binion was furious when the bribes were rejected and he was ordered to pay around $800,000 in back taxes and $20,000 in fines, and sent to Leavenworth Prison. He spent three and a half years there. And from the day he was released for the rest of his life, he became obsessed with getting a presidential pardon. But despite making campaign contributions and offering all sorts of "help" to six presidents over thirty years, it never came. One contribution was $15,000 to Ronald Reagan's campaign; Benny never forgave Reagan for his failure to respond. He was close to a pardon once after he helped influence a Senate vote, but then he blew it; a former Mafia hit man claimed that Benny had hired him to kill someone and, instead of just calmly denying it, Benny said, "Tell 'em I don't need to contract out a killing—I'm capable of doing my own killing." His defense was not well received!

This meant that he could no longer have a gaming licence and he turned the running of the Horseshoe over to the family, notably his wife and his sons, Jack and Ted. He remained in his corner seat of the coffee shop, telling stories and "advising" employees on the running of the place, but he had no formal link. No one cared; as far as Las Vegas was concerned, it was still Benny's place.

And some things had never changed. "Good ol' Benny" remained his own lawman. He never called the police. His security guards were uncompromisingly vicious. Anyone who cheated or stole was taken to a dark place and brutally beaten. They never returned. As Benny himself stepped back from the business, the tradition was carried on by other family members. In the 1980s there was a series of unsavory incidents. One backfired. Two blackjack players accused of cheating were beaten and robbed. Unlike most of the Horseshoe victims, they went to the police. Now, this coincided with a growing view in Las Vegas that the city needed a more family-friendly image; this kind of behavior and the headlines it attracted were not helpful. Not only did the Binions have to settle a lawsuit by paying $675,000 to the two players but Benny's grandson, Steven Binion Fescher, and two security guards were also charged and later convicted of assault. Fortunately for them Benny had imported to Las Vegas his talent for making influential friends and the district judge overturned the verdict, but the law enforcement authorities were not happy.

On June 21, 1987, the *Las Vegas Sun* reported: "The Binions are facing a monster crisis . . . they've become the target of a massive three-pronged investigation by Metro Police, the Nevada Attorney General's office, and the FBI into allegations the family has a long-standing policy of allowing its security guards to beat up patrons."

The paper reported a high-ranking law enforcement officer as saying: "The Binions are going to have to learn that they can't run the casino in the '80s in the way they did in the '60s."

It took some time but the incident came back to haunt the family. In 1990, after Benny's death, the *Las Vegas Review-Journal* reported:

> The son of Binion's Horseshoe owner Benny Binion and seven others were charged with a federal indictment Friday with robbing, kidnapping and beating "undesirable patrons" including poorly dressed and "aggressive looking" blacks. Former casino executive Ted Binion, 47, whose father built the Horseshoe into a Downtown landmark, leads the list of defendants charged in the racketeering indictment . . .
>
> Authorities also charged that former Horseshoe manager Steven Binion Fescher, 35, a grandson of Benny Binion, instructed the casino's security force to carry out the beatings.
>
> Ted Binion and Fescher both are accused of participating in the violence.
>
> The indictment charges that "it was the policy among the security personnel and the owners and managers of Binion's Horseshoe to encourage the kidnappings and beatings of 'undesirable patrons' to foster the image of the Horseshoe as a place which meted out its own justice, and send out warnings and messages that certain persons would not be welcome at the casino . . . Ted Binion and the other defendants administered their own brand of punishment to certain patrons rather than rely on Nevada's judicial system to address their concerns."

An FBI officer was quoted as saying: "These robberies, kidnappings and beatings took place on Horseshoe property—often in the security office, the alley behind the Horseshoe, or in other places hidden from public view."

The Binions' ability to influence proceedings continued. The charges were dropped in 1992 because of what were described as "insurmountable" problems with evidence. As always with the Binion family the witnesses had faded away.

One of Benny's proudest boasts was that he had grown a tightly knit and happy family. Once more the facts intrude.

To begin with, he was unable to transfer his hatred of drugs to his children.

One daughter, Barbara, developed a drug addiction and committed suicide.

His son Ted was a one-man disaster area. The files of local newspapers vividly record the decline and fall of Ted. A play-boy with a special liking for strippers, Ted in 1986 lost his gaming licence after allegations about involvement in drug trafficking; it took him five years to regain it and then he lost it a second time after the Nevada gaming authorities cited a twelve-year drug habit and his connections to leading under-world figures. In 1997 he was arrested after threatening a service station attendant with a shotgun. By now he had become involved with a young woman called Sandy Murphy and had bequeathed her his $900,000 home with its contents and $300,000 in cash. On September 17, 1998, Murphy called for an ambulance, but when it arrived at the house Ted was dead. Two days later police found Murphy's other boyfriend, Rick Tabish, opening a vault in the desert floor a relatively short drive from Las Vegas. In it were 48,000 pounds of silver bars, bullion, and coins that Ted had asked Tabish to bury there for safekeeping. Tabish was charged with stealing it. After Ted's funeral the police concluded Ted was murdered. Murphy and Tabish were charged; their trial in 2000 was the most sensational Las Vegas had ever known. They were found guilty and imprisoned for life. But they achieved a retrial and this time were found not guilty.

As for Ted, he was described after his death by Vegas lawyer Oscar Goodman as "one of the best guys I ever met." Shades of Steve Wynn talking about Benny, except that the kind of guys Goodman met included his Mafia client Tony Spilotro, who was said to have killed one competitor by putting his head in a vice and squeezing his eyeballs out before he slit his throat.

Doyle Brunson spoke of Ted more ambiguously: "He had the whole package—the personality, the looks, the talent, the guts and the money. He had some problems, but he was one of a kind." We have to hope the ambiguity was deliberate.

Still, the family troubles were not over. After Benny's death, followed by the death of his wife, what was left of the family fell apart. One of Benny's other daughters, Becky, had married a man called Nick Behnen, a former Horseshoe dealer, and whether or not it was under his influence (as other family members claimed in newspaper interviews), Becky decided that Jack was proving a failure as head of the Horseshoe and began a two-year war to take it over. She cited a collapse in earnings of $100 million in one year and promised to nurse it back to health. Jack spent at least a million dollars in lawyers' fees trying to stave her off but in the end capitulated. He told the *Wall Street Journal* he was exhausted by the battle: "I'm just walking away because I'm just tired of listening to the bullshit!" he said. He and Becky didn't speak for years.

While the Binion children were demolishing Benny's vision of himself as the patriarch of a united and happy family, Las Vegas had been changing. More and more imaginative resorts were being opened at the other end of Las Vegas Boulevard—spectacular hotel-casinos like the Bellagio, the Mirage, and the Venetian. The attractions of Glitter Gulch could no longer match those of The Strip. Under Becky's management, the Horseshoe became run-down, a shadow of the dynamic "gambling hall of the people" that Benny had created. Finally she sold out to Harrah's, who probably felt that paying for the Horseshoe was worth it to capture the real prize—ownership of the World Series of Poker. The World Series was removed to the Rio. The Binion name was removed from the Horseshoe. It was goodbye Benny.

Only one member of the Binion family comes out of the whole story with a reasonably clean sheet—the oldest son, Jack.

He proved that criticism of his casino management skills was totally unjustified by making a fortune from a number of casinos in other parts of the United States, most notably the Horseshoe in Tunica, Mississippi, where he established the Jack Binion Open each January as the first big poker event of the year. In 2006 Steve Wynn persuaded him to become chairman of Wynn International, with responsibility for building up its Asian operations. Jack does not have any of the arrogance or aura of violence of his father and brother Ted. He is approachable and cheerful. While the rest of the family lived in some style, Jack has always lived relatively modestly. Back in his Horseshoe days, the *Wall Street Journal* found him working in "a windowless office, upstairs in the Horseshoe. He and the former Horseshoe cocktail waitress he married live in a small house with worn carpeting and a clothes dryer on the back porch."

You don't build up a gambling empire without being cynical and a tough character, and, truth be told, there are no angels in the gambling business, but Jack appears to have emerged from it all with few enemies. He is liked, not feared.

Two things have placed Benny Binion, his family, and the Horseshoe at the center of poker history. First is the World Series. As the years went by and it became world famous, stories about it and the Horseshoe dominated the emerging poker books, and features and pictures appeared in newspapers and magazines all over the world. Second, Benny quickly established himself as the players' friend. Together with Jack, he made the players welcome and was always open to helping them when they went broke, as even the best did. Johnny Moss leaned heavily on Benny in his latter years, living at the Horseshoe for free and being bankrolled by Benny. As a result the Horseshoe became the game's home.

With Benny restricted by not having a licence and Ted too irresponsible, Jack was heavily involved in both the Horseshoe and the World Series from the start until fifteen years or so after Benny died when Becky took over. The World Series achieved its pre-eminence and survives today because of Jack's enthusiasm for it; he fully deserved to be added to poker's Hall of Fame in 2005.

But back to Benny. In 1989 he was at his Montana ranch and gave his last lengthy interview, to a Texan journalist, Mark Self. Now a sick man, he was still raging that he had not been given a presidential pardon. "Listen, I paid 'em every nickel . . . Hell, I been out of jail since '57 and I ain't violated a law. By the constitution if you don't do anything in five years, you're supposed to get a pardon. The pardon would restore my freedom. There's so many things I can't do. You can't do this. You can't do that. You can't borrow money. You can't do nuthin'."

But he didn't need to borrow money.

"I know it. But what if I did? . . . You can't vote. You can't have guns."

But he had guns.

"Yeah . . . but don't nobody know it."

Later in the interview he returns to the subject. Self writes:

He sits on the side of his bed swatting flies and cursing his tormenters . . . a host of lying lawmen and presidents who, he says, accepted his campaign contributions but denied his pardon.

The cursing!

The accusations.

The old trailer shakes with Benny Binion's rage.

It was an ambition that was never fulfilled, a rage that was never stilled. Later that year, on December 18, he was taken to the Valley Hospital in Las Vegas complaining he felt ill. He died on Christmas Day, his wife and son Jack at his side. Over 1,000 people attended the funeral service. His white cowboy hat was placed on top of the coffin. The preacher said that Benny's "faith in God was little known." He said Benny would be remembered "for his love of family, his closeness to friends, his sense of humor, his charity, and his deep feeling for religion.

"Sometimes he was gruff and grizzly, but inside he was soft as a lamb . . . He was a man for all seasons." Turning to the casket, he said, "We loved you in life and we'll miss you now."

The seemingly inevitable Steve Wynn said, "I never met anybody who met Benny Binion who didn't like him within two minutes and who didn't respect him within five minutes."

The casket was carried in a stagecoach pulled by six black horses to a memorial park to the north of Las Vegas Boulevard, where Benny Binion was laid to rest.

So what do we conclude about Benny Binion?

Is it enough to say, as he did repeatedly, that hard times make hard people? Maybe it is, but millions of Texans and millions more across America experienced those hard times. They needed food and water and clothing and a home, too, but they didn't become gangsters and killers.

Did he change when he came to Las Vegas—become a reformed character? It's not easy to make that case. The culture of violence around the Horseshoe emanated from him, politicians and policemen were still bribed; every now and then the mask would drop and Benny's ruthlessness would re-emerge.

In Las Vegas in 2007 I find myself in a room at the university listening to a voice. It is a dead man talking. It is the voice of Benny Binion, recorded on tape in 1976: "If anybody goes to talkin' about doin' me bodily harm . . . I'm very capable, thank God, of really takin' care of 'em in a *most* artistic way . . . I don't have to hire nobody to do my dirty work."[17]

"*A most artistic way.*" The man is dead, but this voice from the grave still has the power to send a chill down the spine.

Yet it would be wrong not to note that he had many admirers, even many who loved him. A. D. Hopkins wrote in *The Nevadan*:

> What was most appealing in Binion was his essential fairness. Even the most sinister stories of him smelled of justice . . . Balancing the rough, dangerous side of Binion was the fact that if he gave you his word on something, anything, it was better than a cashier's check.

The *Las Vegas Review* devoted an editorial to him:

> Binion was a man of substance, a man to be reckoned with and sometimes a man to be feared. Yet he remained one of the people. Holding court in the casino restaurant, he could be approached by anybody for any reason. He constantly gave free meals to vagrants and jobs to old cowboys down on their luck. For all his success, power, and dangerous sense of justice, he died a widely loved man.

There *are* positive things to be said about him. He *did* eschew any involvement with drugs or prostitution all his life. It may seem ludicrous to talk of principles in the case of Benny, but this does suggest some. He *did*, especially in his later years, help a lot of people when they were short of friends. He *did* shake up gambling in Las Vegas by introducing a fairer kind of casino . . .

Andy Bellin was probably right when he concluded:

> He was great at running a game and the reasons for that were pretty simple. First, he was known for being an honest criminal. And he brought that reputation to his game by making sure it was run as fairly as possible. The other thing he did was set higher table limits than anybody else around. That's it. That's

been the not-so-secret ingredient to Benny Binion's success his whole life: let people gamble as much as they wanted. And deal a straight game.[18]

And, of course, as far as poker is concerned, he *did* launch the World Series, the event that has held the game together and enabled it to develop over the years to the huge international recreational activity it is today.

Benny Binion's story is a classic case of how time and vested interest can change history . . . in his case, the Dallas days seem far-off now, the behavior of the time excused by graphic memories of the effects of Prohibition and the Depression. As for vested interests, those of Las Vegas politicians and power brokers, of gamblers and poker players all converge around the cozy figure in his cozy corner of the Horseshoe coffee shops, with his friendly smile, his folksy stories, and his $100 million in the bank.

It also has to be said that it takes a remarkable personality to have led the life he did, act as he did, survive what he did, and end up with so many friends and supporters—a pillar of the community, even if the community was Las Vegas.

Some argue that his story is relevant to more than the world of poker, that it's relevant to the history of his country. As Denton and Morris wrote:

The Binion story offers a sombre reflection on the sociology of knowledge in American history—that crude and illiterate thugs, however decisive their role, seldom get the serious attention (apart from their celebrity) given more culturally preferable villains, tyrants seen as worthy of their subject. It is no mere nuance; the omission can conceal an essence of national experience. Only a handful of authors have seen the embarrassing reflection and importance in Binion's life as an archetype . . . [19]

"Poker Alice" Tubbs
(courtesy Adams Museum, Deadwood)

James Butler "Wild Bill" Hickok
(courtesy Adams Museum, Deadwood)

Deadwood promotes its greatest asset – the legend of Wild Bill's death

The Earps and Doc Holliday (second from right) . . . not the real thing but a group pictured at the 125th anniversary of the Gunfight at the OK Corral

George H. Devol
– riverboat poker
hustler

Mississippi steamboat in the 1880s

Thomas "Amarillo Slim" Preston – on his ranch in Texas, 2006

**Johnny Moss –
the first Texas road gambler**
(Ulvis Alberts)

**Sailor Roberts –
poker's ultimate hedonist**
(courtesy Gambler's Book Shop)

Jack Straus – a chip and a chair
(Ulvis Alberts)

T.J. Cloutier – the greatest tournament player not to win the World Series
(courtesy Poker Images)

**Bobby Baldwin –
1978 world champion**
(courtesy Gambler's Book Shop)

Crandell Addington – always immaculately dressed
(courtesy Poker Images)

Benny Binion – the Godfather
(Ulvis Alberts)

Stu Ungar (center) with Doyle Brunson and Jack Binion
(Ulvis Alberts)

**Jack Binion, with a clearly disappointed Bobby Hoff (center)
and a bemused Hal Fowler after their 1979 final**
(courtesy Gambler's Book Shop)

Major Riddle – was he poker's biggest loser?
(courtesy ULV, Special Collections)

Andy Beal – a central figure in the biggest game ever
(Amy Calistri)

Terry Rogers – introduced hold'em to Europe
(courtesy Gambler's Book Shop)

Puggy Pearson – the hustler
(courtesy Gambler's Book Shop)

Doyle Brunson – early days in Las Vegas
(Ulvis Alberts)

Doyle Brunson – today's poker Godfather
(Michael Vu)

Phil Hellmuth – has a record 11 World Series gold bracelets and a record 61 World Series "cashes"; he was youngest main event winner in 1989 – at 24

(courtesy Poker Images)

LEFT: Tom McEvoy – the first satellite qualifier to win the World Series main event, 1983
(courtesy Tom McEvoy)

ABOVE: Tom McEvoy – today
(courtesy Poker Images)

Chris Moneymaker – the first Internet qualifier to win the World Series main event
(courtesy Poker Images)

Sam Farha
(courtesy Poker Images)

Gus Hansen
(courtesy Poker Images)

HIGH-STAKES PLAYERS IN BOBBY'S ROOM

Phil Ivey
(Michael Vu)

Daniel Negreanu
(Michael Vu)

Mike Sexton – the "Ambassador of Poker"
(courtesy Poker Images)

Chip Reese – the greatest all-round player?
(Michael Vu)

Howard Lederer – "the professor" of poker
(courtesy Poker Images)

Mike Matusow – the man they call "the Mouth"
(Michael Vu)

**Chris "Jesus" Ferguson – built
his game on maths**
(courtesy Poker Images)

**Men Nguyen – the
Vietnamese "Master"**
(Michael Vu)

**Noel Furlong – winner
in the "year of the Irish"**
(courtesy Paddy Power)

**Johnny Chan – winner of ten
World Series gold bracelets**
(courtesy Poker Images)

Annie Duke
(courtesy Poker Images)

Jennifer Harman
(Amy Calistri)

Kathy Liebert
(Michael Vu)

Cyndy Violette
(courtesy Poker Images)

Jerry Yang – 2007 World
Series main event winner
(Michael Vu)

Tuan Lam in the 2007 World Series
(Michael Vu)

Heads-up – the climax of the 2007 main event
(Michael Vu)

Play at the 2007 World Series

(Michael Vu)

Benny had his own view of his critics. On the tape recording I listened to, he says: "These people walkin' around all rared back and writin' up and raisin' hell about this, that, and the other, to me, they just don't mean nothin'. I just don't pay no attention to them because I know they're gonna go away. Don't mean nothin'."[20]

I will leave the last word on Benny Binion to a friendly voice . . . to Jim Gatewood, who concludes his biography: "You could say he was the last one left standing. He had hustled, fought, schemed and connived to stay ahead of the smartest, meanest and most treacherous men of his time and was the last to leave the table."

six

The Godfather—Part II
Texas Dolly—the living legend

It's 2006, a warm July night in Vegas. I slowly make my way up The Strip, hampered by the crowds of animated holiday-makers on their way to dinner, or to hear Celine Dion at Caesars Palace, or to hit the blackjack tables and slot machines. The sports-betting crowd at the major casinos are by now well settled in front of arrays of cinema-size screens showing live coverage of baseball from San Francisco, horse racing from New York; at their feet discarded betting slips, in their heads the next bet; another game, another race . . . always another game, another race. At the Rio, over 1,500 players are absorbed in a super satellite for the World Series of Poker main event. As for me, I'm headed for a ballroom at the Bellagio to what is, in effect, *The Godfather: Part II*—another party for another star.

No, there are not the 18,000 that Benny Binion attracted, more like 350, but this is still the hottest ticket in town; everyone who is anyone in world poker is here: money men such as Jack Binion and Bobby Baldwin, television-poker performers Mike Sexton and Gabe Kaplin, veteran players Chip Reese and Dewey Tomko, and a host of today's stars including, on the platform, Phil Hellmuth, Barry Greenstein, and Todd Brunson.

This is poker's A-list. The elite. If you're in this room, then in poker you've made it.

Only you haven't made it as much as the star has made it. He sits in a big leather chair, close to the lectern, facing the audience. He wears as big a Stetson as you will ever see and he's doing his best to keep smiling as he's subjected to that uniquely American experience—The Roast. Poker is celebrating its living legend . . . Doyle Brunson, the man they call Texas Dolly, the man who, in terms of influence, is Benny Binion's successor as The Godfather of the game.

"Doyle, I suppose I should thank you for giving me a free copy of your instructional book all those years back," begins Gabe Kaplin. "Trouble is, since then it has cost me at least $38 million." The room rocks with laughter.

Chip Reese tells a story about the two of them travelling the country, trying to put a business deal together. They ended up in a motel watching a local beauty contest on television and, unable to resist a bet, decided each would back one of the two finalists. One was beautiful, the other relatively ugly. Chip was amazed when Doyle chose the ugly one, and even more amazed when she won. "How the hell did you know she would win?" he asked. "You don't understand local politics," said Doyle. "If she's got this far, there has to be a reason— either there's a lot of money on her or she's related to someone powerful in town. She wouldn't be in the final if it isn't a fix."

So the jokes and stories continue, until Brunson climbs unsteadily to his feet and walks slowly to the lectern to reply. He's leaning heavily on a stick. Everyone rises with him, clapping and cheering. He speaks poorly, stumbling over words written for him by someone else because, truth be told, he's not at ease . . . this is not his scene; he would much rather be at a corner table playing poker. But it doesn't matter that he's not a public speaker, no one in the ballroom this night is in any doubt . . . this is *the man*.

A couple of days later he is honored a second time, and in a way more impressively. He has just been knocked out of the World Series main event. Looking every one of his seventy-three years, he hobbles slowly from the table, picking his way down the aisle between tables of kids with iPods and baseball hats, many of them not even born when he turned fifty. As he does so, all of the 2,000-plus players in the room for a moment abandon their cards and their dreams of World Series glory and stand to clap and cheer too. No one in this giant card room is in any doubt . . . yes, this IS *the man*.

But does this man—this great survivor who has diced with death more than once, who has stayed at the top as a gambler and poker player for fifty years, who was once an outlaw and now enjoys worldwide fame and respectability, who has made and lost fortunes betting on sport or playing golf for $100,000 a hole, who at this time is one of three who share the record for the most gold bracelets won in the World Series (ten), virtually bald under the Stetson, with the face of an old bulldog—deserve this adulation? Can he really have achieved what he has and have still been straight? Is there a hard man behind the friendly facade, the familiar grin? Who really is Doyle Brunson?

I decide to follow his tracks from the day he was born in a tiny hamlet in West Texas all the way to his pre-eminent place in poker today. It is an extraordinary story . . . one even he, the ultimate gambler, would bet could not happen to anybody if he had not experienced it himself.

I start in Longworth, West Texas. I've driven down from Amarillo, first on Highway 70 and then on half-forgotten country roads, passing farms with collapsing barns and rusty machinery, towns that have seen better days. Despite its wealth, initially from cattle ranching and cotton farming, and later from oil and natural gas, Texas always had its share of rural poverty and I'm seeing it now in Fisher County. At first I can't find Longworth. Then I realize I've driven down its main street and yet not even seen it. I backtrack. The main street is on the main road, Plum Creek and Farm Road, south-east of the town of Roby. The town—if you can call it that—was apparently named after the old F. M. Long Ranch and I can be forgiven for missing it because Longworth is more or less a ghost town. Just after the war a couple of hundred people lived in it, but now there are only a few survivors, and in the hour I spend strolling around it I don't see one of them, just a couple of dogs and a few goats. The church and school are closed, and many of the houses (including the one the Brunson family of five owned) are now ruins. The best-kept place is the cemetery on a nearby hill; perhaps that's as it should be, because the dead now far outnumber the living.

I *know* what life was like for the Brunsons in that four-room house with an outhouse at the back because I, too, was raised in a small house with no central heating to warm the winters, no air conditioning to cool the summers . . . and an outside WC. I can sympathize with Doyle, who, when he was a kid, swore that if he ever made some money he would move the plumbing indoors. It can get cold out there at night. I *know* what life was like—coming home to find your mom working . . . always working, knitting, sewing, cooking, washing, and waiting to welcome your dad home from a day's hard labor . . . never being far away from the comforting smell of home cooking, huddling in front of the fire in winter, listening to the radio until being sent off to shared bedrooms for the night—and yet I also *know* it was OK for Doyle, as it was for me, because small-town kids know of no better life than the one they have. And, anyway, a kid always has his dreams. I even *know* what Doyle's dreams were like, because they were the same as mine. We both wanted to be a sports star. Only he had the talent, and I didn't.

Years later he was to write of his father:

My dad was perhaps the calmest, most even-tempered individual I've ever known. Nothing ruffled him. I can't remember ever seeing him get angry. When things went wrong he'd take it in his stride, smile, and say that setbacks were only temporary things. Tomorrow would always be better.[1]

Without father or son knowing it, Doyle was being imbued with the ideal philosophy for what was to become his chosen profession.

I turn off the main road and drive up a half-hidden lane, and there I find what was once a schoolhouse. This is where Doyle Brunson, born in this tiny hamlet in 1933, was taught to read and write. There were so few pupils that kids from several grades all shared the same classroom. When it came to high school, he went to nearby Sweetwater. There were no cars or bicycles in the family, so Doyle ran. He ran everywhere. He would run eight miles to the nearest swimming hole. As a result he became a winning runner, the top high-school mile-runner in Texas; he ran a mile in 4.38. (When you think that the four-minute mile was not cracked by the best runners in the world until the 1950s, this gives some idea of that performance by a schoolboy.) But at high school he was proving an all-round sports star. It appeared effortless. He shone at baseball, but he was especially hot at basketball. He and two friends from Longworth became the outstanding performers on the school team. Known as the Longworth Triple Threat, they helped the school win a place in the state championships (it took over fifty years for the feat to be repeated). Doyle was identified as one of the five best high-school players in the state. Inevitably the offers of university scholarships flooded in. His choice says a lot about the closeness of his family and the values he had inherited from his parents: instead of a more glamorous college, he chose Hardin-Simmons in nearby Abilene, because it was close to home and was affiliated to the Baptist Church. The college also had a reputation for developing teachers and sports coaches, and Doyle saw this as the way to go. (Despite his worldwide celebrity, Doyle has never been elected to his old college's Hall of Fame—his ultimate choice of occupation has been deemed inappropriate.)

He began brilliantly at Hardin-Simmons. Quickly his reputation spread. He was named as one of the top-ten college basketball players in the country and was beginning to be approached by professional teams. The Minneapolis Lakers, in particular, were keeping a close eye on him. Then disaster struck.

Doyle was staying at home for the summer and earning money by working in the gypsum factory down the road. One day he was told to load a stack of sheet rock onto a boxcar for shipping. As he took the sheets off the pile, one by one, he felt the stack begin to slide. Instead of jumping aside, he tried to steady the stack by leaning on it. More than 2,000 pounds of sheet rock came crashing down. As it enveloped him, he felt his right leg crack. In fact it was broken in two places. It was a life-changing moment. He hobbled with his leg in a plaster cast for two whole years, always hoping that when it eventually came off he would be fit to resume his sporting career. But it was not to be. As an athlete he was finished. He would limp forever. It was a crushing blow . . . physically and psychologically.

Doyle then realized he had to make his living with his intellectual skills rather than the physical ones. Many would have had their will broken by the accident, but he had the character not to give up; he worked hard at his studies and achieved a Master's degree, but when he began applying for work all that was available was the position of basketball coach at a small-town high school for $4,800 a year. This posed a problem—because Doyle was already winning more than that at poker.

He had taken up the game at college and, even winning the little that other students could afford to lose, he had paid his way. So he decided to apply to be a business-machines salesman in Fort Worth, calculating he could play poker in the evenings. His first day was to prove fateful. He had been told that, with commission, he could build up to a salary of $25,000-plus a year. But what commission? He found himself being turned away by one potential customer after another. This didn't look good. Discouraged, he headed for a poker game instead. Playing seven-card stud, he won what would have been a month's salary in three hours. On his way home he asked himself: "What am I doing trying to sell machines I don't care about, to people who don't want to buy them, when I can play poker and make ten times the money in a sixth of the time?" The answer was, to him, obvious: he would play poker full time. Thus began the poker-playing career of Doyle Brunson.

What was it that motivated him at this time? He knew his parents, whom he loved and respected, would be horrified. He knew he was choosing the life of an outlaw. He knew that most of the men he would spend his time with were cheats and crooks. And he couldn't have chosen a harder place to start. Exchange Street in Fort Worth was as amoral and violent a place as you would find anywhere in the United States. The main game he played in was run by a gangster who boasted of having killed half a dozen men in his time. At least five were murdered on Exchange Street while Doyle was frequenting its back-room games.

To someone of his ambition and imagination, one motivating factor would have been the depressing nature of the work that was available to him with the handicap he now had.

Another was that he had discovered that he was more than just a skilled poker player . . . somehow this son of a God-fearing mother and a hard-working father had been born a gambler. *Doyle was a gambler*: destined to gamble, and ultimately unable not to gamble. At some point this unstoppable drive—to gamble—was bound to emerge, and, initially at college, but especially now in Fort Worth, it did.

Then there was a third factor: Doyle was exceptionally competitive. He was many years later to say to me, "As long as there was a contest, any kind of contest, even if it was marble-shooting, I wanted to be part of it." That's what the sport had been about. But now those sporting days were over, poker provided another arena where his competitive instincts could be expressed.

So all in all, if this day had not come in Fort Worth it would have come somewhere else at some other time.

Soon he was fadin' the white line—a Texan road gambler armed with a .357 Magnum. As he travelled he got to know the road-gambling crowd and he extended his wagers from poker to sports betting, pool, and even, despite the limp, golf. And he loved it all. If he couldn't star at athletics or basketball in front of cheering crowds, he could set himself the toughest of challenges on the gambling circuit, and given that he had never been that enamored of cheering crowds anyway winning was satisfying enough.

While on the circuit he met Sailor Roberts, and then Amarillo Slim, and so began the poker-playing, sports-betting partnership described in Chapter Four. They had their ups and downs, both as friends and as winners and losers, but on the whole they won more than they lost and they had a lot of fun.

In 1960 Doyle fell for a pharmacist called Louise. For two years he tried to persuade her to marry him; understandably, given his profession, she was cautious but marry him she did, in 1962, and then four months later Doyle faced disaster for a second time. He woke up one day with a sore throat and a little knot on his neck. His doctor prescribed antibiotics. After three weeks the knot had increased in size and he decided to consult a cancer specialist, who took one look and decided to operate on what he hoped was a non-malignant tumor. Instead they found he was riddled with cancer. Five specialists were consulted; they were unanimous. He was a walking tumor. There was no point in operating. He was done for. He had four months to live. This he accepted sadly; he even made a list of pall-bearers for his funeral.

After weeks in the hospital he went home for a day before flying to Houston for further treatment. More than two hundred family and friends came to say goodbye. No one expected to see him alive again. The following day he went to Houston to the M. D. Anderson cancer clinic. He knew he couldn't be saved, but Louise was expecting a baby and he hoped he could win a bit more time to see the child before he died. He spent eight hours in surgery. He woke up to news of a miracle. The cancer—every bit of it—had gone. Disappeared. Vanished. It wasn't possible . . . but still it happened. To this day no one has been able to explain it. Its effect on Louise was to confirm her belief in prayer. She was to become active in the Church. Its effect on Doyle was to eradicate from his gambling any fear of losing. He was dead, but he was alive. He had achieved the impossible. He was indestructible. How could he lose? How could he be beaten at poker? He began playing with fresh confidence and he began playing better. "My brush with death had apparently triggered innate abilities that had never surfaced before," he later wrote. He proceeded to win fifty-five consecutive sessions.

But the effect of the "miracle" was greater than that. Under pressure from family and friends he had been thinking about giving up gambling and earning instead what they described as "an honest living"; the "miracle" convinced him otherwise:

> I discovered my true vocation. I had finally dispelled any doubts about what my chosen profession in life was going to be. I was never going to be a working stiff, nor was I going to have a boss. I was going to make my way through life my own way.[2]

He continued on the road in Texas for a time, albeit with increasing numbers of trips to Las Vegas each year, and then in 1973, three years after the World Series was established, he moved to the Nevada resort and has lived there ever since.

Doyle arrived in Las Vegas with a young family. He had to make a reliable living and do it in an unreliable profession. He combined sports betting with his two favorite activities, playing golf and playing poker. He became one of a small number, including Johnny Moss and Puggy Pearson, who formed the nucleus of a high-stakes poker game that has lasted, with a changing cast, for nearly thirty-five years. In that time it has moved around from the Horseshoe (during the World Series) to the Aladdin, the Dunes, the Silver Bird, Sam's Town, and, more recently, the Bellagio. Sometimes it has just been a group of friendly rivals playing each other, but the ideal has always been to have a producer, or "live one," in the game. Over the years some of these producers have helped Doyle and Chip Reese and a few others to become wealthy men with beautiful homes in the more exclusive conclaves of the city.

Things were a bit murky in the early Las Vegas days. With poker players not deemed profitable because they were playing each other instead of the house, the casinos would take their cut by leasing space to people to run their own games. Sometimes the poker room "managers" also played. Johnny Moss ran a number of poker rooms over the years. Doyle Brunson and Eric Drache ran the Silver Bird poker room together. Since the casinos' reputations and standards were not at stake, there was little supervision, and there are all sorts of rumors about what was happening. There's no evidence, however, that Doyle was acting in an underhand way; he has survived on the front line of poker for fifty years while maintaining a reputation for being straight—it's doubtful he could have done that unless he was.

Doyle didn't take the World Series itself too seriously at first, welcoming it mainly because of the cash games on the side. As we will see (in Chapter Seven), he had concerns about the notoriety that winning it would create. But he did win it, twice in a row, in 1976 and '77. In 1976 he beat an old Texan rival, Jesse Alto, in the heads-up and won with a hand that has become associated with his name: ten-two. (For non-poker players, I should stress that this is a really bad hand; you and I would be right to throw it away whenever we see it.) Years later, Doyle told me: "I had about 75 percent of the chips and Jesse was steaming. I knew Jesse from years back and he was a hell of a steamer. He raised and I called him with ten-two. I picked up another ten on the flop. Of course I didn't know it, but he had ace-jack and the flop paired both cards, so he was well ahead. Anyway, Jesse bet and I called him with my two tens. The turn card was a two and I moved in. Then I landed a ten on the river for a full house."

"He must have been as mad as hell," I said.

Doyle grinned. "He wasn't too happy."

And then it happened the following year?

"Yep, I was heads-up at the end of the main event with a man from Nevada called Bones Berland. I had ten-two and he had eight-five, and the flop came ten-eight-five. We both checked. The turn card was a deuce. I bet and he moved in on me and I called. The river card was another deuce, so for the second year in a row I won with a full house with ten-two."

He has not won the main event since, but he has won ten World Series gold bracelets in all, a feat equalled only by Johnny Chan and, in 2006, by Phil Hellmuth. (This is even more impressive when you consider Brunson boycotted the event for a number of years out of loyalty to his friend Jack Binion, when he was being driven out of the Horseshoe by his sister, Becky.) But he's still a contender at the top level, as he proved as recently as 2004 by beating 600 top professionals in the *World Poker Tour* Legends of Poker event, winning over $1,173,000, and then winning that tenth WSOP bracelet the following year in the $5,000 no-limit short-handed Texas hold'em event.

Away from poker, Doyle was even happier on the golf course, albeit playing less as age and physical handicap took their toll. Not that the gambling stopped at the first tee: on the contrary. Doyle has played for sums of money that would make even Tiger Woods blanch—sometimes there would be $50,000 or $100,000 at stake on one hole. He played off a low handicap, but his strength was his ability to turn it on under pressure; his partners always knew that when the big money was on the line and Doyle had to sink a putt, he would sink it. Of course, he didn't always win. In his book, *Super System: A Course in Power Poker*, he describes playing a millionaire. They finally had $180,000 riding on one hole. The millionaire scored a par, Doyle one-over.

One of the more enjoyable hours I spent while researching this book was listening to Mike Sexton describing to me one of the most famous poker-golf games ever, involving Doyle and himself against former poker champion Huck Seed and the "Professor" of poker, Howard Lederer.

"Somehow they talk Doyle into a game. He hasn't played for a couple of years and I haven't played for a couple of years and they are playing all the time, but they persuade him to play in a game that could cost $100,000 if it's lost. Somehow he suckered me into being his partner. Doyle says to me that he has forgotten more about golf than they will ever know, but as far as I'm concerned the only good news is that they will play from the back tees and we will play from the ladies' tees.

"So the day after they make the bet they bump into Doyle in the poker room and they're joking about how he has no chance. Well, Doyle being Doyle, he says, 'OK, if that's what you think, we'll double the bet.' So now we can lose $200,000.

"He and I decide we'll have a round and find out what we can score. Now, the game is to be a scramble, where we each hit a drive and then play the best ball from there on, and in this round we hit 76 and Doyle is upset. He figures we're going to get beat bad. He tells me, 'We have to find a way to get out of this bet.' I tell him I will improve, but no, he wants to get out of the bet, so now he finds them and tells them his knee is giving him trouble and he doesn't think he can play. Well, of course they say he's just running away from the bet . . . Well, Doyle is Doyle, and he says to them, 'Well, if that's what you think, we'll double the bet again.' So now we can lose $400,000.

"So I say to Doyle, 'Look, I think I should fly down to Florida and put in a couple of weeks of golf with my friend [one-time British Open winner] Harold Henning before we play this.' So I do that, and when I come back someone sees me play and tells Doyle that I'm playing well and that these guys have no chance. So what does Doyle do? He goes back to Howard and Huck and he doubles the bet again . . . Now we're playing in a match that could cost us $800,000—for one round of golf.

"Everyone is now talking about this game and half the poker world comes out to watch. We're followed everywhere by about fifty golf carts. Well, we're two-up after five and Doyle is telling them they don't know how to play and everyone is loving it, and Howard and Huck are looking more and more tight-lipped. By the fifteenth hole it's all-even, and that's a real easy hole but we both miss the green with our drives and bogey it, and they're now one-up and now Doyle is in a state. We come to the sixteenth and we're all over the place . . . I hit a wood and it looks like it's headed for the pin, but it hits a bank and falls into the water. Doyle blows his shot completely and I then put it fifty feet from the hole. The putt is near impossible—not just fifty feet, but with a break of about ten feet. It looks like it's all over, but you have to understand that it's in positions like this that Doyle becomes unplayable. He hits this putt and when it's still fifteen feet away he's shouting, "It's in, it's in!" . . . And it was. An unbelievable putt. Well, the guys on the golf carts, a lot of whom had money on the game, go wild.

"We're still only even, but Howard and Huck are broken. They lost both the last two holes and Doyle, whose bet it was, wins what I think is the biggest bet there's ever been on one game of golf."

Today the Gambler's Book Shop in Las Vegas carries hundreds of "how to play poker" books, but the first major one, and still one of the best-selling, was Doyle's *Super System*. First published in 1978, it contains chapters by some of the best players in poker history, with the chapter on no-limit hold'em written by Doyle himself. He spent $400,000 getting it together and self-publishing it, advertising it widely and selling it for $100. It's believed to have sold nearly 250,000 copies, and in 2006 he followed it with an update, *Super System 2*. Ironically this venture received mixed reviews from the game's veterans. "What the hell are you doing, giving away our secrets?" complained one. "You're destroying our living." Doyle admits there have been times when he wondered whether he had been wise, but he doesn't regret it a bit.

But people don't get beyond seventy without bad days as well, and Doyle has had a few. The worst was when his daughter, Doyla, died at only eighteen. He writes about it movingly in *Super System*:

> We knew she had a valve problem with her heart, but it wasn't supposed to be serious. They say it was taking too much potassium that took her from us. It was so unexpected, it was like being kicked in the gut so hard you don't think you can ever stand up again, breathe again . . . I remember Doyla every day, and the shock and sadness of losing her will never end.[3]

Then there were some business disasters. Doyle clearly has some outstanding qualities but choosing what to invest in is not one of them. He even persuaded Chip Reese to invest with him in some religious television stations. Clearly even God didn't like them because they failed. His biggest mistake was to turn down the chance of investing in the *World Poker Tour* when it was launched; its founder, Lyle Berman, reckons that decision cost Brunson $50 million. He was to complain (about himself) later that he lost a lot of money investing in things he knew nothing about and, then, when he had the chance to invest in poker, he blew it.

Over the years he has become the doyen of the game, cheered every time he appears in the World Series, honored at functions, interviewed on every radio and television program about the game, and now fronting an Internet poker room, *Doyle's Room.* He looks old and, as he limps around on his stick or drives himself around the Rio and other poker palaces in his electric scooter, there's no mistaking he's seriously handicapped. Sometimes, when caught unawares at the table, he looks tired, even bored, and yet, when his competitive juices are flowing, his energy can be amazing.

So is his ambition. While the main event was being played out in 2006, I was competing in one of the last remaining gold bracelet events, a $1,500 buy-in no-limit hold'em tournament. I was amazed to see both Doyle Brunson and Phil Hellmuth playing. Surely this was not in their league—what were they doing? Then I realized: they were now equal, ten bracelets each. Both wanted another. Both wanted to be undisputed King of the World Series. Fair enough for Phil, still relatively young; but isn't it eloquent testimony to the competitive instincts of Doyle that he was still there, determined to prove he was the best, at seventy-three?

Mike Sexton once said that if there were Halls of Fame for the following, Doyle would be inducted into all of them on the first ballot:

- Those who have overcome odds
- True competitors—people with heart and a determination to win
- High-stakes golfers and sports bettors
- Guys who create action

But what is the Doyle Brunson balance sheet—compared with poker's first Godfather, Benny Binion?

He shares two things with Benny Binion: dislike of drugs and love of family—although while Binion's family became bedevilled by drugs and fell apart, Brunson's family has avoided drugs and remained close and united.

Both have been outlaws, but, unlike Binion, Brunson hasn't, as far as I know, ever bribed anyone, directly robbed anyone, or killed anyone. In this respect he's a gambler in a way that Binion never was. Binion loaded the dice; he did whatever was necessary to win and at whatever cost to others. That wasn't gambling—it was crime. Brunson, on the other hand, has the gambler's ability to enter a contest fully accepting he can lose and knowing that at least sometimes he should expect to; he faces defeat with equanimity, even good humor.

Insomuch as they came together, it was because for both of them poker became their business, Binion as promoter of the World Series, Brunson as player. Brunson has never made the same money, because he wasn't driven by money in the way Binion was. For Brunson the money has always been a way of keeping the score—of course, he had to earn to keep his family, but deep down the contest was the thing; satisfying his competitive instincts was the driving motivation.

Is he an angel? No way . . . and I doubt he would claim to be. There are bound to have been things done in Texas he would rather forget. He's turned a blind eye to the character of some of those he's associated with over the years—Benny Binion being one; he's also played poker and golf with men like Jimmy Chagra, whose drug dealing has caused untold misery and who deserved the prison sentence he received. And he spent much of 2005–2007 living under the shadow of a Securities and Exchange Commission inquiry into the propriety of an offer he made to buy the *World Poker Tour*—an offer he later withdrew. No mistake about it, he is a tough customer. But playing to win, fighting fire with fire, and accepting whoever is at the table, no matter how disreputable, is and always has been part of the game he took up in tougher times in Texas.

The fact is when people referred to Benny Binion as The Godfather, they did so with an element of fear. When people talk of Brunson as The Godfather, they do so with respect and affection.

He deserves respect for his stamina and his longevity as a top-class competitor; for what he's put back in the game; for his record of achievement—the ten bracelets, the two World Series main event titles, the extraordinary ability to still win in these much more competitive days; for the competitive drive he has, even in his seventies; and for his physical courage—who knows how much pain he endures?

He deserves respect because day in and day out over fifty years he has been THE enduring star of a difficult game, put himself and his reputation on the line time after time after time, and has always behaved in public with good humor and sportsmanship.

In poker the word "respect" means everything. When one player concedes to another, he is said to be "giving respect." In the world of poker Doyle Brunson has *everyone's* respect. That's quite something.

seven

The World Series of Poker

... the mystery surrounding the most famous game in history: did Johnny Moss ever play Nick "the Greek"? ... the truth about how the WSOP began ... the final that was fixed— and other classic confrontations

The most famous poker story by far concerns a game said to have taken place in 1949 between Johnny Moss and a renowned gambler called Nick "the Greek" Dandolos. It is widely assumed, and often "authoritatively" stated, that this game gave birth to the World Series of Poker. However ... I am not persuaded. As Anthony Holden says in his book, *Bigger Deal*, it is a "curiously undocumented episode."[1]

As the story is usually told, Dandolos asked Benny Binion to find him "the biggest poker game that this world can offer." Binion set up a game with Johnny Moss, insisting that it be played in public at the Horseshoe in Las Vegas. Moss had just been playing for four days in Texas, but he immediately set off for Vegas, sat down, and the game began. There were some huge pots; in one hand of five-card stud, Dandolos won $500,000 by drawing a jack on the river to match the one in the hole and beat Moss's pair of nines. They played for three or four days at a time for six months. After Moss had taken the Greek for over $2 million, Dandolos finally rose wearily to his feet and said, "Mr. Moss, I'm going to have to let you go."

This story is so ingrained in the fabric of poker history that it seems sacrilegious to question it, but while at the 2006 World Series I first hear someone question whether this Horseshoe match ever actually took place. I decide to investigate.

Before I can, poker author Michael Craig sticks his own head above the parapet, raising the issue on his website:

> . . . The earliest accounts of the game are 25–30 years after the fact. More contemporaneous sources that should have mentioned it, if it took on the dimensions and significance described, said nothing about [this] marathon poker game . . . [Jon] Bradshaw's book *Fast Company* was published in 1975. Jenkins's book on Moss in 1981. Why didn't this story come to light earlier?
>
> . . . In May 1973, just two years before Bradshaw's published account, Benny Binion gave an interview to . . . the University of Nevada Oral History Program. I have read the transcript carefully . . . Benny Binion talks about several pivotal moments in the early days of the Horseshoe. He talks about Nick the Greek in connection with the Horseshoe back then and in later days. He never mentions (a) Johnny Moss; (b) a poker game between Moss and Dandolos; (c) any big poker game that drew spectators to the Horseshoe; or (d) any poker game from that era having anything to do with the start of the World Series of Poker in 1970.
>
> Let's go further back in time. Dandolos died in Los Angeles at Christmas in 1966. He was buried in Las Vegas and SUN and REVIEW-JOURNAL both reported it on the front page. (Hank Greenspun, publisher of the SUN, was one of the pall-bearers and delivered a eulogy.) The REVIEW-JOURNAL story says: "The Greek was an attraction here for many years. Local gamblers enjoyed pointing out the legendary 'Aristotle of the pass line' to gaping tourists." There is no mention, however, of poker, Moss, the Horseshoe, Benny Binion, or the legendary game.

The SUN's obit described many tales about Nick the Greek . . . isn't it odd that among all these stories, the game with Johnny Moss isn't mentioned?

Let's go back still further, to 1954. *Colliers* published a massive profile, "Nick the Greek—Fabulous King of the Gamblers," stretching over 2 April, 16 April and 30 April issues . . . if that game took place just three or five years earlier, wouldn't it have merited a mention?[2]

By now I'm convinced this needs looking into, and I become even more intrigued when I read Cy Rice's authorized biography of Nick the Greek, published in 1969.[3] It details all of the famous gambler's high-stakes poker games, but there is no mention of the game with Johnny Moss. Why not? I then read a book by Stephen Longstreet.[4] He knew Nick the Greek personally and devotes a whole chapter to him. He, too, makes no mention of the Moss game. Why not? It seems extraordinary that, if the game was as big as described by Moss, both these friends of his independently chose not to refer to it.

If this match took place, there would have been some reference to it in local newspapers at the time. I explore the clippings libraries; I cannot find one story about it. Nor do I find any reference to it in "the Binion Collection," a filing cabinet of records from the Horseshoe now housed in the local university library.

As I read all the references to the game, it strikes me that every story I have read, including the lengthy account of it in Al Alvarez's book, appears to come from Moss. Nick the Greek never seems to have spoken about it. And none of those who have described it in books were actually there.

Did Moss invent it? He was known as an embellisher of stories, but he spoke about the match so often and in such detail that it seems highly unlikely that he completely invented the game. He clearly believed his own story. After studying all of the Moss-inspired accounts of it, I begin to come to a conclusion. It is that Moss *probably* did have a match with Nick the Greek, it *probably* was set up by Benny Binion (who would have staked Moss), and it *probably* lasted some time—*probably* on and off, rather than continuously. But, also *probably*, it was not as big a game as legend has it, and this explains why Dandolos never spoke of it and why his friends and biographers (either in books or in magazines) never referred to it. Nick the Greek was old and dying when he talked to Cy Rice for his biography. He had never covered up his setbacks when he was fit and well and a player: why should he become shy about this particular game when he had little to lose by describing it?

Could it be that Dandolos didn't talk about it because it simply didn't figure as a major event in his gambling career? Whereas for Moss playing and beating the famous Nick the Greek *would* have been a major event; hence his frequent repeating of the story and the likelihood that, as time went by, he exaggerated until it became the confrontation of historic proportions that poker folklore suggests.

Even more questionable than whether the match took place is the assumption, indeed the constantly repeated assertion, that this match at the Horseshoe led to the founding of the World Series of Poker.

Even the best of poker writers—authors of the game's classics—have said it. It began with Al Alvarez. After describing the Horseshoe game, he wrote, "In 1970 the Binions decided to re-stage [this] battle of the giants."[5] This, he suggested, was the beginning of the World Series. Many other books have made the same link. There are also scores of references in other books, in newspaper and magazine articles, and on the Internet to the relationship between that game and the founding of the World Series of Poker.

In my view it is a false assumption. If the Horseshoe match took place, it did *not* inspire the launch of the World Series.

Consider the timing: if it took place, the Horseshoe match was in 1949, and the first official World Series event was in

1970, no less than *twenty-one* years later. If that match had inspired Benny Binion to launch the World Series, he would hardly have waited twenty-one years to do it!

What kind of "inspiration" takes twenty-one years to engender action—especially in the head and heart of a man like Benny Binion?

So what really inspired the World Series? It has its origins in an event in Reno in 1969. Tom Moore, the Texan who had with Slim Lambert been one of the San Antonio boss gamblers, had moved to Reno and taken over the Holiday Casino there. It was intended that Crandell Addington would be a partner, but, because of delays in obtaining a gaming licence, Addington never did join up. Instead he played in Las Vegas, where Moore contacted him with an idea. In order to publicize the casino, and perhaps hoping to establish it as a base for the high-stakes poker players now gathering in Las Vegas, he wanted to invite all his old friends, the top road gamblers, to a "Texas Gamblers Reunion" (it was at one point more formally described as a "Gaming Fraternity Convention").

Crandell Addington says: "Tom said he wanted to concentrate it on the top high-stakes players. I said, 'Yes, that will work, why don't you get the best players and we'll have a game.' And I said, 'Let's try and get some producers, too,' and he said, 'Perhaps some bookmakers will play.' And a bunch of them did show up. We even had Minnesota Fats show up and we had the infamous murderer, Woody Harrelson's dad, Charles. Johnny Moss was there, and so were Doyle Brunson, Amarillo Slim, Sailor Roberts, Jack Straus, James Roy, Bill Boyd, Puggy Pearson, and Corky McCorquodale . . . the top players in the country were there. And Benny Binion was there, too. We played a variety of all-cash games including hold'em, Kansas City low-ball draw and razz."

The high-stakes event was a success. Everyone had a good time, but Benny Binion, always with an eye for the angle, saw its greater potential. He asked Moore whether he could buy the idea off him and transfer it to the Horseshoe. Moore said he didn't want money for it: "Just go ahead and do it."

The group re-assembled at the Horseshoe in Las Vegas in 1970. After a few days' play it was decided they would elect a world champion. According to legend most voted for themselves, so they had to choose a "second best" and it was these votes that led to Johnny Moss being crowned. The title World Series is usually credited to another Greek, Jimmy "the Greek" Snyder, who played a key role as publicist and promoter of the event in its early days.

Thus began the World Series of Poker. There was no relationship between the Horseshoe match and the launch of the World Series.

Still not convinced? Well, there is one more witness . . . Benny Binion himself.

Michael Craig is right about the Binion tapes. I find them in the special collections section of the university and review them myself. When Binion is asked how the World Series started, he replies: "Well, there was this fellow by the name of Tom Moore started it in Reno . . ." and he then tells the story about the Texan Gamblers Reunion and how he took it on from there. He then goes on to talk about the World Series at length, but not once does he refer to the match between Moss and Nick the Greek at the Horseshoe. Not once!

I rest my case.

The World Series does not need make-believe stories to capture our imagination; it *is* a remarkable story, with its growth from that handful of refugees from outlawed card rooms of Texas playing each other in Reno in 1969 to an entry field of several thousand buying in for $10,000 each today. Over the years it has been the arena for many great games of poker . . . heads-up confrontations full of controversy and drama, triumph and despair, with not just the world title at stake but also increasing sums of money, climaxing in the record $12 million first prize in 2006—a higher purse than the four golf majors and the Wimbledon men's and women's singles tennis titles all added together.

It began in a corner of Binion's Horseshoe and stayed there until Harrah's took it over and moved it to the Rio in 2005. It built up slowly, dominated at first by the Texans and then gradually attracting others, many of whom initially came for the high-stakes side games rather than the main event. It took over ten years to exceed one hundred competitors. Then gradually it began to catch on. The Alvarez 1983 book, *The Biggest Game in Town* (extended from an article for the *New Yorker*), did a lot to put it on the map, as did Anthony Holden's *Big Deal* in 1990. Support tournaments were added so that it became a longer event, offering a variety of opportunities for winning what was becoming a coveted winner's gold bracelet. By the turn of the century, entries exceeded 500 and it had become what it is today—the Olympic Games of poker, the greatest prize, the ultimate test; winning it is now every poker player's dream. Throughout, there have been some constants: the $10,000 buy-in for the main event, and the fact that anyone—anyone at all, you, me, the guy next door—can play if we can come up with the money. But what has changed is the route to victory.

In the early 1980s Eric Drache, who was director of the event for a number of years, had an idea: "I was wandering around the Horseshoe trying to drum up some more competitors and I saw these guys playing with about $10,000 on the table. I said to them, 'Why don't you play a freeze-out for the money and the winner will be able to enter the main event?'

"So they did. And so for the first time we had a satellite."

Later, as the Internet poker sites began to compete for players, they started their own satellites and these became so popular that in 2006 the *Poker Stars* site alone produced 1,750 main event players. A *Poker Stars* qualifier won two years in a row. The Internet sites began to produce players from all over the world; for instance, in 2007 Ladbrokes in the UK took one hundred competitors across the Atlantic. In 2007 the event lasted six weeks and involved fifty-five events.

A lot of poker is played and money won in the build-up events, but the real drama comes over the last two weeks as the Internet qualifiers arrive for the main event, ambitious, excited, geared up to go. The fields for the support events grow, some to well over 2,000 players. There are lines for the cash games; the Rio itself is packed, its bars and restaurants overflowing, and other casinos in Las Vegas hold their own tournaments to create opportunities for the thousands of visitors to play. Las Vegas goes poker crazy.

Then comes the first day of the event—actually spread over three or four days because there simply is not enough space for up to 9,000 competitors. So each day begins with 2,000–3,000 players and is reduced to a few hundred who will continue on to the "official" second day. The huge specially created card room contains over 200 tables. Spectators crowd behind the ropes. Poker writers and television crews squeeze their way between the players.

What would the ghosts make of the way the game they played in back alleys has developed to become this show and spectacle, with the prize money for the main event up from $100,000 in their day to over $60 million in 2007 and to $160 million for the whole six weeks? How the ghosts at the table would look upon the scene and wonder.

Strangely, as the main event proceeds, day after day, and thousands are eliminated, the event becomes quieter. The Internet players begin to fly home, their big adventure over; the poker tables are removed one by one and the arena becomes smaller. This means less for spectators to see and thus smaller crowds, until on the final night the last few players come face to face on a specially built television set before an audience of a few hundred. The corridors, packed with enthusiastic, excited players and observers for weeks, are now empty. The exhibition stalls are packed away. By the last night this huge public spectacle has become almost a private affair. Except that it's being followed at home by hundreds of thousands, glued to computer screens, and will eventually be watched on television by millions.

Like the Olympic Games itself, the World Series has its famous moments and its legendary stars. Two players—Johnny Moss and Stu Ungar—have won the main event three times, an achievement never likely to be equalled because of the sheer size of today's entries (in fact Moss was awarded it the first year, so Ungar is the only man to have truly won it three times).

Prior to the 2007 World Series, three players—Doyle Brunson, Johnny Chan, and Phil Hellmuth Jr—had each won ten World Series gold bracelets, a remarkable achievement. Apart from Ungar, to whom we shall return, these have been the outstanding personalities in World Series history.

Unlike Brunson (whom we have already met), Johnny Chan was not born in Texas, but when his family travelled to the US from Hong Kong in the '60s they settled there, in Houston. At twenty-one Johnny abandoned plans to work in the family restaurant business and instead took off for Nevada to become a professional poker player. Despite winning the World Series in both 1987 (the year he turned thirty) and 1988, he really became famous for appearing in the poker film *Rounders*, with Matt Damon and Edward Norton. This made him the best-known poker player in the world, and that was fair enough because he was one of the best players in the world. A man of moods, he is a big money-earner outside of poker. In 2007 he was promoting his own online site and was owner of a diner in the Stratosphere hotel in Las Vegas, as well as maintaining his profile by playing regularly on television programs such as *Poker Superstars* and *High Stakes Poker*. He was an advisor to Jamie Gold, winner of the 2006 main event, but says he was not on a percentage.

Having won the World Series main event two years in a row, Chan's position was eclipsed in 1989 by a kid from Madison,

Wisconsin, called Phil Hellmuth Jr. At twenty-four, he was the youngest-ever winner of the main event (and still is). Hellmuth drew level with Brunson and Chan on ten gold bracelets in 2006, and in 2007 took the lead by beating the biggest field he has ever faced and winning the $1,500 no-limit hold'em event, a truly remarkable achievement, celebrated amid emotional scenes, including a presentation of the bracelet by Brunson and Chan. Hellmuth is the John McEnroe of poker, capable of some spectacularly childlike behavior when he suffers a bad beat, or when he thinks he's been knocked out by an inferior player (and that means just about everyone). As a result he's controversial. His nickname is Poker Brat. Humility is not a word he can even spell; he once said on television: "If luck weren't involved, I'd win everything." However, if you look beyond this, there's a lot to recommend him. First, he is, as the record shows, a superb poker player, winning around $10 million so far. His strength is hold'em (he has won all eleven of his World Series gold bracelets at this form of the game). Second, away from the table, he is a friendly and likeable character who puts a great deal back into the game with books, magazine articles, videos, boot camps, and so on, and is one of the first to respond to appeals to the poker community to contribute to charities or other causes. There is no doubting his love of poker and desire to share it with others. Provided he's not just lost a hand or a game, he can take a joke. In 2002 he was commentating on the World Series and said that if the recreational player Robert Varkonyi won, he would have his head shaved. Varkonyi did, and Hellmuth was shorn live on television. At the Doyle Brunson roast in 2006, Hellmuth told a rambling story about golf and kept saying, "It's a true story, it's a true story." When he sat down, the abrasive MC, Brad Garrett, said to him, "Phil, let me give you an advice. No one gives a f**k whether the story is true, but it *is* supposed to be funny." The audience fell about, but, to his credit, Hellmuth joined in the laughter. Finally, he's a shrewd businessman. Front man for Ultimate Bet and involved in a variety of other business activities, he said in a television interview that he could earn up to $400 million away from the table. Even allowing for Hellmuth hyperbole, he is undoubtedly a rich man. And clever. He is also a devoted family man and, despite his wealth, still lives with his wife and two children in the house they bought together in Palo Alto, California, in 1996.

So the World Series has produced some extraordinary characters and occasions, but of all the thirty-eight final tables since 1970 eight have been especially memorable for one reason or another, and now, in Las Vegas for the 2007 World Series, I find myself re-living them with the winners and losers, or those who were as close to the action as it was possible to get.

1972: The main event is fixed

It's hard to credit that the main event of the World Series of Poker could be "fixed," but in 1972, the year that Amarillo Slim "won," that's what happened.

As I look around the huge poker room at the Rio, at the thousands who contest it today, it's also hard to imagine what the main event was like in its pioneer days. It was really just a gathering of a small number of friends, albeit the best poker players on the planet. In 1972 only eight players were willing to pay the $10,000 buy-in, including the former partners from the Texan road show, Amarillo Slim, Doyle Brunson, and Sailor Roberts. This was the year when Johnny Moss had to pass on the crown. It was Brunson who struck the fatal blow, picking up a third ace on the river to beat the old man's three deuces. That left only two for Brunson to beat—Amarillo Slim, who was low on chips, and Puggy Pearson, the extrovert gambler from Nashville, Tennessee.

Puggy was what's known as a "character." They say beauty is in the eye of the beholder . . . well, so are characters. Depending on what you know about them—or maybe just your sense of humor—you can love them or hate them, take them or leave them. Maybe because the poker world is partly built on pretense—pretense at the table—it tends to revere rather than reject its characters. To reverse the words of Shakespeare, in poker the good that men do lives after them, the evil is oft interred with their bones. In the eyes of history this enables them to get away with murder—in Benny Binion's case, literally. When Pearson died, he was the subject of good-natured obituaries all over the world; his notoriety justified them, but Pearson was a beneficiary of poker's blind eye.

I saw him at the World Series in 2005, shortly before he died. He was wearing a black top hat and reminded me of the old comedian W. C. Fields. (In fact Fields could have been Puggy; when famously asked in one of his films, "Is poker a game of chance?" he replied, "Not the way I play it.") In other years he had turned up as a Viking and an Arabian sheik. But this was no comic. There were similarities with Amarillo Slim: both began as pool hustlers, both loved the limelight (Puggy was also a golf hustler). And, like Moss and Binion, he came up the hard way. Admittedly he could play—he won the World Series main event once, albeit in 1973 when there were just thirteen entries—but he was also a cheat.

Like poker itself, Pearson created his own mythology. Like Moss, he went on the record claiming to be whiter than white. In a book by the late David Spanier, he makes the same point Moss would make: "You can beat a guy, just beat him and beat him and beat him, and he'll keep coming back . . . but you screw him out of just one quarter and he'll never come back."[6]

Another author, Michael Kaplan, tells it differently:

Puggy surreptitiously scooped chips out of pots and short-changed players when he made his bets . . . One of Puggy's more enduring moves, employed when he had a hand that was not necessarily the best one, was to call a final bet and push his chips to the pot, but not release his hand from the chips. Assuming that Puggy was in, the other player would reveal his cards. At that point, if Puggy had the stronger hand, he removed his fingers from the chips, showed his cards and raked in the pot. If beaten, he pulled the chips back and insisted that he hadn't intended to call the bet, that the other player had misread what Puggy was doing and should never have turned up his cards prematurely. Mayhem routinely ensued, but Puggy was a master at diversion and diffusion, and he insisted (rightly) that so long as his hand remained on the chips, no bet had been made.[7]

T. J. Cloutier acknowledges that Puggy was a cheat, but says, "His cheating wasn't like other people's . . . it was a kind of gamesmanship. He was a hustler, he couldn't help himself. It was second nature to do whatever it took to win. He had more moves than a mongoose." Tom McEvoy, who played with Puggy many times, says he was a notorious cheat. But he uses the same phrase as T. J.: "Puggy couldn't help himself."

Of course, Puggy wouldn't call it cheating. To him the game was about winning and if you had a few moves of your own to do that . . . well, that's what it's all about. He wouldn't criticize anyone else for trying too. A classic Pearson "can't help himself" story arises from a golf match Doyle Brunson had set up with the drug dealer Jimmy Chagra. Doyle told Puggy, "We can't lose—we can make a lot of money. So, whatever you do, don't cheat, because if anyone is caught cheating they'll forfeit the game." Well, the way Doyle tells it, they were about $250,000 up and heading for a big payday when Puggy's ball ended up in the rough and he kicked it out. A bodyguard saw him and the game was forfeited and the money lost. Doyle was furious. "What the hell did you do that for?" he roared. "We were winning easily—you didn't need to do that." Puggy replied, "I'm sorry, Doyle . . . I just couldn't help myself."

Like Moss, he could be unpleasant to dealers. Once a female dealer took off her stilettos and began hitting him over the head with them, forcing him to leave the table in disarray.

But to be fair to Puggy, he had a lot of talent and was utterly fearless. He was a big-time gambler, would bet $10,000 a hole on a round of golf, $50,000 on the result of the Super Bowl. From time to time he went spectacularly broke, but he always made the one crucial bet that got him back on track. He was a major Las Vegas figure for thirty years. Yes, a character. Take him or leave him . . .

And now, at the 1972 World Series, Puggy found himself close to breaking the Texan grip on the World Series. With Doyle Brunson in the lead and Puggy not far behind, Amarillo Slim was the short stack. Then the final took an unexpected turn.

The Binion publicity machine had been at work, and the players were suddenly surrounded by reporters with note-books and even by television cameras. And Doyle Brunson didn't like it. Brunson had been an outlaw most of his life. He was especially sensitive about the illegality of poker in many states. To protect his family from any fallout, he had always kept a low profile. "I had three children," he says, "and I didn't want my family treated like second-class citizens because of what I did." He also had another concern; he didn't want the tax authorities to know the kind of money that was being won and lost. As he looked at the reporters, he began to fear that after twenty years or more earning his living in the shadows, he was about to be exposed to the sunlight and there was a real danger he would get burned. So he called a time out and met with Jack Binion and Puggy and Slim, and told them, "I don't like this; I don't want all this publicity. I don't want to win this thing."

Pearson, who had mixed views about publicity—he loved the limelight but also liked to keep his dealings private—was impressed by Brunson's reasoning. He announced he didn't want to win either. Not so Slim. Slim was the opposite of Doyle Brunson; he thrived on attention, loved publicity, wanted to be champion. So when the others said they didn't want to win, he said, "Well, I do."

Brunson takes up the story: "We said to Slim, 'We'll let you win it; we'll just count our money now and keep the money we've got.' At that point Slim had almost no money. So we went back and started to let Slim win, but he couldn't help himself and began to act up to the media and the spectators as if he was winning on merit and he made such a fool out of himself that it was embarrassing. I finally beat him in a pot just to stop him."

Watching all this, Jack Binion was horrified. Having attracted the media, he saw the whole event was in danger of being discredited and its reputation ruined. Doyle says: "He called us over and said, 'You guys can't do this, it's going to ruin the whole thing, you've got to play.' So I said, 'Jack, I don't want to play,' and he said, 'Well, you can withdraw; just keep your money and withdraw and let them play.' So I withdrew and took my $40,000." It was then announced that he had an upset stomach and he went home.

At this point the stories about the game diverge. Doyle believes that Pearson still wanted to win—that he tried his best but was beaten fair and square. Surprisingly it is Slim who acknowledges that the result was a fix. Slim introduces a new factor. He says that Binion and his publicists, having captured the media's imagination for the first time, wanted a suitable winner and that he, with his flair for publicity, was the obvious man.

I ask Slim about it when I'm in Amarillo and this is what he says. "It was never cut and dried what we were going to do until the last thirty minutes. Then, they decided—Jack Binion and his publicity guys—that if I won it, it would get some notoriety. That wasn't me talking, it was them."

But was Puggy trying to win right to the end?

"No. But he was trying right up to the last thirty minutes of it. That's when it happened. They knew they couldn't get any publicity out of it if Doyle won it . . . and that's not putting Doyle down . . . Doyle just wasn't a talker in those days. And Puggy wouldn't have been a good choice because about half the people he had screwed over the years were bound to say a few things. So I was the pick for winning it."

Did Puggy say he intended to lose or did Slim just instinctively know?

"No, I just knew they had all got together and decided it would be a lot better for poker if I won it."

Who persuaded Puggy that he shouldn't win it?

"I think it was Jack Binion, because me or Doyle wouldn't have [had] any power over him . . . we couldn't have persuaded him."

It is easy to believe Slim is telling the truth because he, more than anyone else involved, has a particularly strong reason to cover the deal up . . . namely that it makes a mockery of his claim to have been a world champion.

Slim is not ashamed of it because, he says, it wasn't his idea . . . and the decision was not his. He believes, or has persuaded himself to believe, that it was done in the best interests of poker.

Brunson is not ashamed of it because he publicly withdrew, and was not, therefore, involved in the sham ending.

As for Pearson, he's not around to be ashamed.

Perhaps the one man who *is* ashamed is Jack Binion. That would explain why 1972 was the one year in the whole history of the World Series when a gold bracelet was not awarded to the winner.

1978: Addington v. Baldwin

Puggy Pearson only had to wait a year for his turn. He won it in 1973. The following year Johnny Moss made a comeback, beating Crandell Addington in the heads-up. It was to be his last year in the spotlight. In 1975 the second member of the Texas team of Doyle–Sailor–Slim, the fun-loving Sailor Roberts, had his day, and then in 1976 Doyle Brunson, apparently no longer publicity shy, made it a hat-trick for the trio by winning it for the first of two consecutive years. So we come to 1978 and one of the most memorable one-on-one encounters the World Series has known, pitting two Texas hold'em specialists against each other: the veteran Texan Crandell Addington and the brilliant young "honorary Texan" Bobby Baldwin.

We have already met Crandell Addington, in San Antonio: older than Baldwin, genial, immaculately dressed, but don't let him fool you—tough and shrewd as they come. Baldwin is best described as a forerunner to the whiz-kid players of today. He came down to Texas from Tulsa, Oklahoma, in his early twenties and quickly established a reputation as a brilliant player of no-limit Texas hold'em. Unlike the older road gamblers, whose education came from their experiences travelling the circuit, Baldwin had learned the game by reading every book on poker he could find; he was a kind of poker intellectual but with a terrific sense for what cards other players had in their hands. Then he added to his intellectual grasp real experience on the road. He played in the Briscoe game at Denton and in all the poker towns from Dallas to Corpus Christi in the South, making so much money that he could afford a driver to steer his Lincoln from game to game.

The confrontation between the good-natured but determined veteran Crandell Addington and the intense whiz-kid Bobby Baldwin in 1978 in Las Vegas was always bound to be a classic. Addington, already runner-up twice and aware time was running out, desperately wanted to win the world title and as he approached the heads-up was convinced this was his year. He respected Baldwin, whose talent was beyond doubt, but he believed his experience would make the difference.

I talked to both of them about the game, Addington in his skyscraper office in San Antonio and Baldwin in his palatial pad in Las Vegas (he is now president of the Bellagio), and this is what happened, in their own words:

Bobby: "Well, it was about eight o'clock on the fourth day and Crandell and I were in the heads-up. He had been beating me up for several hours and he had about $275,000 worth of chips and I was on $145,000. Then we were asked by the television crew to take a break; I don't think Crandell was too pleased about this because he said it was like stopping a heavyweight title fight when one of the boxers was on the ropes, but I decided to use it. I have often compared it with the guy in *The Hustler* who was always tidying himself up because he felt it gave him a psychological lead. So I went to my room and had a shower and changed into a kind of tracksuit. I decided that when I went back I would try and play faster and knock him out of the conservative mode that he was comfortable playing in. I wanted to knock him out of his rhythm. Obviously there was a downside; I could get eliminated quickly. But I decided it was the best strategy for me."

Crandell: "For years I've been trying to remember what I was holding in the famous hand that followed the break. I think it was seven-eight. Anyway, the blinds were $3,000 and $6,000 and I made what was really a token $10,000 pre-flop raise, and he called. The flop came queen of diamonds, four of diamonds, and three of hearts . . . this was no help to me. And he then bet $30,000 and I called immediately; I figured he was looking for information with his bet and I wanted to show strength. I could have thrown my hand away, but I didn't have enough information about his hand yet, so I decided to take the turn card with the intention of playing his hand, not mine, on the turn. My hand was irrelevant; I could have been playing two unprinted cards, because I didn't have a hand and I was not on the draw.

"In heads-up play, you must outplay your opponent—that's why it's called poker and not just catching cards. If you want to know what to do in these positions, read the books written by field marshals and generals because no-limit poker is crystallized aggression and you have to be willing to sacrifice some troops in a battle to win the war. Most people are unable or unwilling to do that and that's why they're not good players. In this case Bobby was sacrificing troops to glean information about my hand and I was sacrificing troops to demonstrate strength."

Bobby: "I had the nine and ten of hearts. But when he called I decided he was weak—probably playing a low drawing hand. Then came the ace of diamonds on the turn, so three diamonds were showing. To me, that was a perfect bluffing situation. If he had diamonds in the pocket, he would not have just called on the flop. So if I was right and he was trying for a low straight, he would fear a flush. So I bet $65,000 on the turn. That put nearly all my chips in the middle."

Crandell: "You hear people all the time talking about the importance of position in poker and, yes, the man behind often has the advantage . . . but not always. I like to be in front—it's where I play most of my hands from. In this hand Bobby was able to act in front of me and of course I couldn't call that bet. So I folded, and then he threw the ten-nine of hearts on the table in front of me to show he was bluffing. Some would have been offended at that, but I wasn't . . . it was just a gambit. But I was not happy with the outcome of the hand because it gave him the lead in the game."

Bobby: "I intentionally showed him the hand, not to be discourteous but to unsettle him. I was trying to knock him out of his rhythm. Actually it's become famous as a bluff, and in a way it was, but as I put him on what could be a worse hand than my own, it was really about getting my chips in first. Given the cards on the board, plus the fact that I felt he was weak, I knew I had him on that hand."

For Crandell the moment had passed. Whether it was the break being called when he was in command, whether it was Bobby's change of pace, whether it was the blow of that particular hand (still, rightly or wrongly, recalled as one of the great "bluffs" of the World Series), or whether it was just that the cards deserted him, he quickly dropped back until he had only $50,000 worth of chips to Bobby's $370,000. At that point he found himself looking at pocket nines.

Crandell: "I only called the blind. Some believe I was feigning weakness, but I wasn't. It's absurd to move all-in with two nines, or for that matter any other two cards, before the flop under the majority of circumstances. Someone calls with ace-king, how can you hope to win that pot? There's only one way . . . The only way you can win if you move all-in pre-flop is if you're ahead after five more cards come out. That's not about skill; that's a gamble. But if you take a flop, there are two ways you can win—you can either have the best hand or you can outplay your opponent, and outplaying your opponent has to be the primary strategy of no-limit hold'em. The game was designed to be played after the flop, not before it. With this hand, I preferred to play after the flop."

Bobby: "As it happens, his decision was irrelevant. I had pocket queens and was going to bet them either way. When he called, I raised $10,000, hoping he would consider that a fairly moderate bet and sense weakness."

Crandell: "The position had now changed. To call him was going to take a fifth of my chips, but I had no choice but to continue with the hand. First, there was a real possibility he was reacting to my call with an attempt to steal the hand and, second, there was no way I was not going to play the nines. As I've explained, I like playing from the front, so the position had changed . . . if I was to take control of the hand, I had to make a substantial raise and, given our respective stacks, I decided it now did make sense to go all-in. This is the equivalent of changing strategies on a shifting battlefield.

"Normally I would have been more than pleased with the flop—there was a nine to give me trips. Problem was, there was a queen to give him trips too."

The last two cards were an ace and a ten. Bobby Baldwin, with the higher three-of-a-kind, had become world champion.

In doing so he had demonstrated in spectacular fashion that you don't have to have a big hand to win even the world title, just the judgment to know when to make the big move. And the nerve. Above all, the nerve.

1982: A chip and a chair— the most amazing comeback in poker history

There is a saying in poker that "all you need is a chip and a chair." It dates back to the 1982 World Series final and the most amazing comeback performance in the history of the game.

The man at the heart of the story was six feet seven inches tall. No wonder he was universally known as Treetop. This was another of the Texan road gamblers, Jack Straus. In a magazine article written to commemorate Straus's posthumous admission to poker's Hall of Fame in 1988, Al Alvarez described him at the poker table as

> sitting slumped low, as though to disguise his enormous height, his big head, with its curly grey hair and curly grey beard, hunched into his shoulders . . . His eyes missed nothing. They were extraordinary eyes, dark blue, full of life and wit, and they seemed to slant from right to left. The left eye always slightly closed, like a marksman taking aim.

Carl McKelvey says that "he looked like he was made out of spare parts."

Straus has been described as the gambler's gambler. He couldn't resist a bet. He once went to a race meeting with inside information that guaranteed him two wins. The tips proved right, but he still left a loser because he couldn't resist betting on every race.

He was totally fearless. Once he lost all but $40 at poker, so went and stuck it on a blackjack box. When he won, he kept the money there until it reached $500. He then returned to the poker table and increased it to $4,000. Back he went to the blackjack table and increased it further, to $10,000. He then put the lot on the Kansas City Chiefs in the Super Bowl and turned it into $20,000. And as Al Alvarez wrote: "The point of the story is his refusal to compromise. Each time he bet, he bet all the money he had, from the first $40 to the final $10,000. He had an all-or-nothing courage that very few of us could ever emulate."

Of course this meant he often went broke, and even friends acknowledge he was not above a trick or two to win the money back. He was no angel. But he was huge fun, full of heart, and he could be kind. Phil Doc Earle tells of the day an amateur sat down at a table where nearly all the top Texans were playing. "He quickly got cleaned out of chips and went to the cashier to get more. While he was waiting in the queue, a huge man from the table he had been playing at walked past, then paused, and came over and whispered to him that the guys he was playing with included three world champions. 'Give it a miss,' he advised. Jack Straus could have joined the others and profited from the man's innocence, but he didn't have the heart to do it."

In later years Straus loved to describe how he was summonsed to court on a tax charge. While he was waiting at the back for his case to be heard, he listened to another man pleading for time to pay his debts. Paying it all at once would, he told the judge, destroy his family. Straus couldn't bear it any longer. He rose to his feet and called out, "Judge, just stick it on my tab."

Straus played in the World Series from day one, in 1970. He was on the final table three years in a row, from 1971 to 1973. He was particularly strong playing short-handed and heads-up in tournaments; in ring games he was more vulnerable. His friend Carl McKelvey says that in a ring game he was often the fish. T. J. Cloutier says, "In a ring game, you would love to play him, but heads-up he was probably the toughest that ever lived . . . Everyone knew that in a ring game he wasn't worth a dime because he didn't have the patience for it, but in heads-up he could really fire those chips."

For a while it looked like the 1982 World Series would be a disaster for Straus. It was hardly under way and he pushed all his chips in, only to lose the hand. Then he noticed that there was still one $500 chip left (it had been obscured by a napkin). Fortunately he had not actually called "all-in" when he put his chips in, so he was able to sit back down and play that chip. From there he began an incredible comeback. He immediately went all-in, won that hand and then set about attacking everyone else at the table, bluffing outrageously and pushing every reasonable hand as strongly as possible until he had not only come back all the way from the dead but taken the lead.

With nearly twice as many chips as anyone else, he now began to boss the competitive final table, raising almost every pot and eliminating one opponent after another. Doyle Brunson says they called the seat immediately to the right of Straus "the electric chair" because anyone who sat there was executed.

It all came down to a heads-up with the amiable Dewey Tomko and they were soon involved in the biggest pot the event had ever seen. There was just under a million dollars—$967,000, to be precise—on the table. Tomko, with ace-four of diamonds, opened for $100,000 and Straus, with ace-ten unsuited, raised him $180,000. Tomko then went all-in. The flop of six-five-four gave Tomko the lead in the hand, albeit with only a pair of fours. The turn card was a queen, no help to either player. Then came the river card, a ten, and Straus had come back from having one solitary chip to win $520,000 and the world title.

As a comeback it has no equal. As evidence that you're never beaten until the last chip has gone and they drag you kicking and screaming from your chair, it remains an inspiration to poker players everywhere.

As for Jack Straus, it was to be the climax of his gambling career. He never made another final table in the World Series main event and died of a heart attack in the middle of a game at the Bicycle Club in Los Angeles in 1988.

1983: The man who came from nowhere: the World Series' first satellite winner

There's a restaurant at the top of the old Horseshoe with a stunning view of Las Vegas, from downtown all the way up The Strip. There was a time when the poker giants would be there every night, but once the World Series moved uptown to the Rio, it lost most of that celebrated and colorful clientele. But not Tom McEvoy; he still likes to go back, and only partly because it gives him a chance to look at his picture on the cardroom wall with the other world champions. He likes its steaks, too, and while disposing of a couple of them, we re-live his historic triumph in 1983—historic because he became the first satellite winner to win the main event.

Tom was born in Grand Rapids, Michigan, and lived in the area for nearly thirty-five years. Such fame as he achieved locally was as a table-tennis player. He won over 200 trophies and it was as a table-tennis competitor that he first went to Las Vegas. He liked the place and, bored out of his mind with his work as an accountant, he persuaded his family to move there. He walked into the Horseshoe just in time to see Bobby Baldwin win the world title. From that moment, winning the World Series became his goal. He soon became a regular at Caesars Palace, the Golden Nugget, and the Stardust; in particular the Golden Nugget, where he could always be seen in the $10–$20 limit hold'em game.

He also played countless tournaments. Now, he tells me: "I probably had more tournament experience than anybody in the World Series field, just playing cheap tournaments around town, playing lots of them to help my tournament game and develop strategies. And when I came to the World Series, I was totally fearless. I was determined that no name player like Slim or Doyle Brunson or any of them were going to push me around."

Tom's experience in 1983 explains a lot about the market trading, the wheeling and dealing that goes on behind the scenes of the World Series. "It was a nine-handed satellite at the Horseshoe. One of the guys approached me and asked me if I wanted to go partners on a satellite, so I said 'yes' . . . It was about $1,100 approximately, nine-handed, and I put my name down on the list for a one-table satellite. Then I saw Johnny Chan was on the list for the same satellite. At the time I was friends with Johnny Chan and I went up to him and said, 'Johnny, I want to play this next satellite.' He knew it was my dream to be in this main event, and had been from the beginning of my poker career. I said, 'I would appreciate it if you don't play, but if you do want to play I will sit out and play another one, because I don't want to play against you.' He said, 'No, go ahead,' so I sat down and I saw two other guys in the satellite who I thought were good players and who I was on good terms with at the time. One was a guy named Jimmy Dolman and the other was David Sklansky. So I said to both of them, 'Do you want to trade 5 percent in case one of us wins it?', and they both said yes and it got down to three players: me, Dolman, and Sklansky. So there were the three of us heads-up, and Sklansky has the lead and I'm in second, and at that point Johnny Chan comes over to the satellite and he says, 'I'll give you $1,000 for 20 percent of your action.' Now, don't forget, I hadn't won the satellite yet and Sklansky had the lead and there were still three of us left, so I said to my partner,

'Well, I think I should take it, because if I lose we can at least do another one,' and we'd be getting almost all our money back. It sounded like a reasonable deal, so we took it and I went on to win. So now the percentages are redistributed. Johnny Chan now has 20 percent and the other two guys have 5 percent each and that was 30 percent gone. That leaves me with 35 percent and my other original partner with 35 percent, so my percentage has declined dramatically. And then before it started, I traded 1 percent with two more guys that I was friendly with. So by the time the smoke cleared I had 33 percent of myself in the main event."

Another friend of Tom's also won his way into the main event via a satellite. His name was Rod Peate. He was a good enough player to make the final table for a second time in 1990, and he and Tom had played in the same cash games for some time. Now the two of them confounded everybody by making the final table and quickly eliminating their opponents, including Carl McKelvey, until there was only them and Doyle Brunson left.

"Doyle then made a terrible play against Rod Peate, an absolutely horrendous play, and got himself broke. What happened was that Doyle, who had been playing particularly aggressively, called a $9,000 raise by Rod. Rod had a pair of nines and Doyle had the jack-nine of diamonds. The flop gave Rod a third nine but also had two diamonds, so Doyle had a flush draw and two nines. Doyle checked and Rod bet $15,000, then Doyle committed suicide. He went all-in with more than half a million chips. He totally over-bet the pot in a spot where he was either going to win a small pot or lose everything unless he gets real lucky, because Rod isn't likely to call him unless he can beat Doyle's hand. It's true Doyle had top pair, but how many times does top pair get beat? A lot of times.

"We had a long dinner break, somewhere between three and four hours, and came back around 7 p.m. to go heads-up. I'd been very aggressive all of the tournament, but I believed my best shot against Rod Peate was to kind of grind him down because when Doyle got busted Rod had a little over 60 percent of the chips.

"At the start this wasn't working. Rod kept beating me, a little here and there, and pretty soon he had over $800,000 and I had about $280,000, so I knew I had to change gear. When he next raised, I looked down and I've got king-queen, so I raised him back and the flop gave me top pair, but he had two clubs with two on the board. He could have got a fifth and won and it could have been all over in less than an hour of heads-up play. But he didn't get the flush and I doubled, and now the chips were equal and we see-sawed back and forth and I went back to my original strategy and I ground him down. It lasted seven hours . . . seven hours of heads-up play.

"Mike Sexton said later that I set poker back ten years because we bored the television people to death and they didn't come back for a number of years.

"I hadn't had one big pair all day, but finally I looked down and I had pocket queens. The blinds were now $8,000–$16,000, which at that time was a record and stayed a record for several years even though there were more players. It was now nearly quarter to two in the morning and he raised going in and I just moved in on him. He had a king-jack of diamonds and he called me real fast, and I could see he had cracked. I wanted to win it more than he did. He had it in the palm of his hand and I just took it away. He managed to catch a jack but that wasn't enough help, and the queens held up and that was it."

After that incredible show of patience—seven hours, a record World Series heads-up that remained until Chip Reese and Andy Bloch exceeded it in 2006 in the H.O.R.S.E. event—Tom finally let go, leaping onto his chair, arms in the air.

In the exhausted crowd Johnny Chan smiled quietly to himself. He not only had 20 percent of McEvoy's prize, but he had also negotiated 20 percent of Peate's action. He won more than either of them.

At about 3 a.m. Tom walked across the road to his daily stamping ground, the Golden Nugget. "The card room was full and they had been watching it on closed circuit and I went quietly up to the rail. I was wearing my Stetson and Western wear. Then all of a sudden people noticed me, and for a couple of seconds you could hear a pin drop, and then everybody stood up, including the floor people, and I got a standing ovation, and that was the most touching moment of my life . . . because it was like one of theirs had done it."

Quite so. One of us, we ordinary players, we who can't afford $10,000 to buy in and depend on satellites, we who, before Tom showed the way, were only bit players in the drama . . . One of us had done it.

Beaten the best in the world.

Won the World Series.

From now on it would be a possible dream.

1997: Stu Ungar's return— and the $500,000 he had to give to a man called Billy

On the outskirts of Las Vegas, not far from the airport, there is a community the millions of tourists never see. It's hidden behind high walls and the gates are manned by security guards. Behind these walls are expensive ranch houses and haciendas. Water sprinklers keep the grass outside these homes green all year round; swimming pools keep their owners cool. The cars parked outside are the best. It's peaceful and it's exclusive and it's where Billy Baxter lives, down the road from Robert Goulet and Wayne Newton.

I find Baxter there on a quiet day during the 2007 World Series, but not a quiet day for him. Two computer screens light up his dimly lit study, aided by a $10,000 satellite dish. The phone rings constantly. Billy, who comes from Georgia and moved to Las Vegas after a spell in a "correctional institution" for illegal bookmaking, has been sports betting for over thirty-five years.

He's one of the country's biggest operators and has made a lot of money at it, hence this beautifully decorated house. He actually began as a pool hustler but then became a quality poker player who would win seven World Series gold bracelets, all in his speciality, low-ball games. There's not much he doesn't gamble on; he even bets on life and death—he bet $18,000 that his first child would be a girl; she was (some time later one of the losers, Doyle Brunson, asked him, "When are you going to take the dress off that boy?"). And he bet $10,000 a local casino boss would reach eighty; this time he lost. The man died at seventy-nine.

Popular, with the appearance of a prosperous lawyer or business executive rather than a poker and sports betting hustler, he is a highly respected figure in Las Vegas, and famous for two things.

The first was his one-man battle with the IRS, leading to a historic court case (*William E. Baxter* v. *the United States of America*).

Now he tells me about it:

"When I came to Vegas, where gambling was legal, I completely legitimized myself. I paid a lot of income taxes from gambling winnings because I won quite a few poker tournaments back at that time. All of this money was documented. So now here comes the IRS. At that time the maximum tax bracket was 50 percent and I'd already paid the 50 percent, but now they said my gambling money was unearned income, like dividends and interest, meaning the maximum tax could be as high as 70 percent. They said you owe us another 20 percent on this money, and that kind of set me back. I mean, 50 percent was brutal but 70 percent was a killer. It would have cost me another $178,000.

"So I said I'm going to test this out. I rang my tax accountant and he advised I pay the money and then sue for a return, so that's what we did. We paid the taxes and the other 20 percent and we sued for a return of the money.

"First thing it did was go to the court in Reno, like a district court in Nevada. And the judge said, 'I find the Government's argument to be completely ludicrous' . . . that was the word he used. We used the analogy that if Jack Nicklaus won a golf tournament, his money was earned income, yet if I won a poker tournament this was unearned income. So we said, 'There's something wrong here somewhere . . . poker is also a game of skill and I'm making this money because I'm talented in this area.' The judge not only accepted that but he also said to the IRS lawyer, 'I just wish you had some money and could sit down and play a little bit and I think you'd find out that there's a little more to this game than just luck' . . . and he tossed them out of court.

"Well, the Government wasn't satisfied. They went to the US Circuit Court of Appeals in California and they got bounced out again. I won. Now they go all the way to the United States Supreme Court, but by now they were trying to make all sorts of deals with me, thinking I would cave in. They finally just gave in because they realized they couldn't win. It took me about five years to get my money back, the interest and penalties and all, but I finally got it back. And it's in all the law books now, *Baxter* v. *the United States of America*."

As a result of Baxter's fight, poker players would now pay taxes only on earned income, could deduct expenses and losses, and could create pension funds; it was part of making the game respectable and was enormously helpful when the big money came into the game later.

In 1997 Billy Baxter played in a satellite for the World Series main event. He didn't need to be doing that, he could afford the buy-in, but what the hell . . . and he won it. As he was leaving the card room, he was accosted by a man in his early forties. It was Stuey Ungar, the man who had won back-to-back World Series titles in 1980 and '81, and he looked like death warmed up. In their brilliant book on his life, Nolan Dalla and Peter Alson describe him thus:

He had once been dubbed in print the "Keith Richards of poker" both for his rock-star aura and for his spindly little-boy body and mop-topped boyish good looks . . . [now] those who knew him were appalled by what they saw. Up close the boyishness was gone. Stuey's face was sickly white, ravaged by years of hard, careless living and drug abuse. One side of his nose was collapsed from snorting too much cocaine. His skin was papery and looked as if it would rip at the slightest touch. More disturbing, in a way, was the way he had let himself go. He was unshaven. His fingernails were long and dirty. His clothes looked slept-in. And he smelled.[8]

Billy Baxter was shocked and when Stuey asked him to buy him into the main event, he declined, embarrassed to be rejecting a friend and someone he had backed before but convinced Stuey would never last four days and would be humiliated.

Poker as theater has its full share of comedies and dramas, its soap operas and its thrillers, and it also has its tragedies, and Stu Ungar is its greatest. He was a genius. Mike Sexton, a loyal friend through good times and bad, has described him as "the greatest gladiator in poker history. He took command of every table he played at and dominated his opponents heads-up . . . When it came to cards, he had no equal . . . the greatest no-limit hold'em player ever to have played the game." And the record speaks for itself: in his short career he won ten major no-limit tournaments (with a buy-in of over $5,000), including both the Super Bowl of Poker and the World Series main event three times each.

As a kid in New York, the son of a bookmaker, Stuey developed an astounding skill at gin rummy. Adopted as protégé and friend by the crime boss Victor Romano, he was backed to play all-comers and demolished them all. At that time a Canadian called Harry Stein (but better known as Yonkie) was believed to be the best in the world. He was enticed to New York to play the young upstart called Stuey Ungar and lost every one of their twenty-seven games.

Stuey ran out of opponents. He was also being harassed by bookmakers to whom he owed money. So he moved to Las Vegas, where he added poker to his repertoire. In 1980, in one of his first-ever tournaments, he beat Doyle Brunson in the heads-up to win the World Series for the first time. In 1981 he repeated Brunson's feat of winning it in consecutive years. But his character couldn't match his talent. He gambled away every dollar he won; he won and lost at least $10 million in his career—won it with skill, lost it with a supreme indifference to its value. He lost astronomic sums on the golf course. The first time he went to a course he found himself on the putting green with Jack Straus. Within a few minutes the two of them were putting for $500 a hole and within two hours Ungar had lost $78,000—without ever leaving the putting green. He once lost $1.8 million gambling on football over a weekend. He turned to cocaine and even harder drugs. The thriller that was his earlier years had become tragedy.

Billy Baxter had backed Stu in 1990 and, disillusioned, had sworn it was the last time. But now, seven years later, in 1997, he was driving in his car when his phone rang. It was Stuey, still begging for help—begging for money, begging to be put into the main event.

Billy now tells me: "Everyone was kind of down on him, and I didn't want to stake him either, because he'd kind of gone off at the deep end on the drugs, and so when he came to me at the Horseshoe I said to leave me alone and that he could find someone else to stake him. This will tell you why I didn't want to stake him: many years before I'd staked him several different times and one time I had him staked in one of the big tournaments in the Horseshoe and he was the chip leader at the end of the first day. The next day he didn't show up. We called the Golden Nugget, where he was staying, and there was no answer. So I sent security up to his room and they found him passed out on the floor and took him to the hospital. Now, don't forget, he's got the chip lead in this big tournament. I get in my car and drive to the hospital and he's so small they had him in a cot; he was in the corridor and hadn't been admitted to a room yet. I go up to him and I shake him, and this doctor taps me on the shoulder and says, 'Sir, what's going on here?' and I say, 'This guy is a friend of mine who's playing a poker tournament and I'm trying to get him up,' and he says, 'I've got some bad news for you, then, because he's not getting up for a day or two; we've just given him a shot and he's going to be down for a while.' He still actually got in the money even without being there because he had so many chips, but of course we would have won a great deal more. So I told him from that point on: 'Stuey, don't ask me about staking you any more because you can't stay in your chair even when you get winning.'"

But Stuey begged and Billy relented. The deal was he would pay the $10,000 buy-in and any money Stuey won would be split 50–50. The field had grown to over 300 that year, but on the second day Stuey found himself on a table with some of the best players in the game—Brunson and Baldwin, Phil Hellmuth and Berry Johnston, all of whom had won the title at one time or another—and if there was any doubt he had retained his skills, it was soon dispelled. He played brilliantly and soon everyone was tipping him to win.

Come the final day, they moved the table outside into the sunlight. There, in view of a bigger crowd than had ever watched a poker game before, the sun warming his fragile frame, Stuey Ungar really turned it on. Typical of his play was a sensational bluff when confronting the fourth-place finisher Ron Stanley. The flop was showing ace-nine-six and both checked. The turn card was an eight. Stanley, who had nine-seven in the pocket, now had a pair of nines and an open-ended straight draw, so he bet $25,000 and then called when Ungar raised the pot by $60,000. The river card was a king. Stanley had failed to get his straight but still had his nines, but Ungar bet a stunning $225,000 and Stanley folded. Ungar then showed queen-ten . . . he had nothing.

Ungar had provided this theater of poker with its greatest scene—a dazzling performance that took him to his third title. It had been a comeback beyond belief.

There was another winner, too. Billy Baxter. His act of compassion and friendship for the man who had so let him down in the past was repaid with a return of at least $500,000 on the buy-in of $10,000, his share of the prize money making him the biggest-ever winner of a poker game without even making the final table.

As for Stuey, eighteen months later he was found lying face down on a bed in a sleazy flophouse motel . . . the kind of cesspool that has only porno movies on the television set, burned holes in the carpet, seedy drapes, and a cockroach to the square inch, where you risk your life just breathing in the air. Only Stuey wasn't breathing. He was dead at forty-five.

1999: The year of the Irish

The World Series was thirteen years old before a non-American voice was heard for the first time at the final table. The first to make it was Donnacha O'Dea, the son of a famous Irish theatrical couple, Denis O'Dea and Siobhan McKenna. A former Olympic swimmer, now a professional gambler, Donnacha came sixth behind Tom McEvoy in 1983 (he also came ninth in 1991 and eventually won a World Series gold bracelet for pot-limit Omaha in 1998, beating Johnny Chan in the heads-up). It was not until 1997 that someone from England made a serious challenge, former hairdresser Mel Judah, coming in third. He was followed by fellow Londoner Ben Roberts, a stalwart of "the Vic," who came sixth in 1998. Then in 1999—well, this leads me to another extraordinary story from the World Series final table.

Poker began to flourish in London in the 1960s. It was mainly played in unlawful clubs called spielers. These tended to be ethnic—there were Greek spielers, Cypriot spielers, Polish spielers, Jewish spielers, and so on. They were mostly in dimly lit basements, with threadbare carpets, peeling wallpaper, and the minimum of furniture. Most had a professional dealer, and if you picked the right game, it was honest. Usually the game was five-card stud.

The spiritual home of British poker in those days was a corner of an upstairs chess club on The Strand called En Passant, run by two huge men, Boris Watson, a Russian, and Ted Isles, a former London policeman. The game was ideally positioned to attract actors from the West End, barristers from the Law Courts, journalists from Fleet Street, barrow boys from Covent Garden, and chancers and low-life from all over town. There you could play with Jake the Waiter, Vile Oats, Accordian John, Maurice the Lawyer, and a player who was rumored to make his living by attracting homosexuals to hotel rooms, beating them up, and robbing them. It's said that he often paid for his poker chips with blood-stained banknotes. Eventually there was a fire at the club and it was declared unsafe. The game moved to the Victoria Sporting Club, and the Vic has been the home of British poker ever since.

The other center of poker in England was in the Midlands, in particular the Rainbow Casino and a couple of spielers in Birmingham. One of the spielers was run by Derek Baxter, as tough a player as you would not wish to meet, and a man called Barry. This game at Barry's was at the time one of the biggest in the UK; it attracted a list of players who were to become internationally competitive, including World Series finalist John Shipley, World Poker Tour winner Dave Devilfish Ulliott, and two who later became European number ones, Dave El Blondie Colclough and Mickey Wernick. Lucy Rokach, one of the top British women players ever, was another regular. The game was built around a wealthy builder who lost well over a million pounds there.

There was a lot of interaction between Irish and English poker, with players like Donnacha O'Dea regularly flying from

Dublin to the Vic, and in fact it was not from England that the first major European assault on the World Series was launched: it was from across the Irish Sea.

Hanlons Corner is a working-class area of Dublin, about half a mile from the city center. There, on a busy, dusty thoroughfare called Old Cabra Road (or, in Irish, Sean Bhothar Na Cabrai), there's a butcher's and a mini-market, and between these two there's a betting shop with a freshly painted blue-and-yellow sign saying *Terry Rogers—Bookmaker*. Beside it there is a permanently locked door; no one ever appears to go to whatever lies behind it. But they did once—almost every name in Irish poker went there. It was a place where legends were made. From behind that door came three men who would all make the final table at the World Series of Poker in the same year. That was 1999—the year of the Irish.

That door led in the 1980s and '90s to the stairway to a poker club located on two floors, with a kitchen where players down on their luck could count on getting a meal. This was the Eccentrics Club, founded by Terry Rogers, a one-man powerhouse who turned Ireland into a major force in world poker. Having seen it in Las Vegas, he introduced Texas hold'em to Europe, and he built up the Eccentrics Club into the place where you learned the hard way, laughing away the hours while simultaneously honing your skills and doing your best to send the others home broke. As Padraig Parkinson says, "The treasurer couldn't count, the secretary couldn't type, the owner [Rogers] had rows with everyone, but if you could win there, you could win anywhere—everyone was a top-class player."

There was *Donnacha O'Dea*, of course—a polished aristocrat compared with some of those who had come up from rougher backgrounds, a cool and relatively cautious player by Irish standards, but the first European competitor the Americans came to fear.

There was *Jimmy Langan*, a small, skilful player, who became the first to win the Irish Open twice, and also performed well in the WSOP. Like Tom McEvoy, he was a brilliant table-tennis player. Langan made a lot of money from his furniture business and was renowned for generosity to anyone experiencing hard times.

There was bookmaker *Liam Flood*, cohort of Terry Rogers, who was to become a consistent winner in European events for twenty years and a highly respected tournament director. Liam won the Eccentrics Invitational on the Isle of Man in 1984 by beating the then world champion Jack Keller. (Liam had no money and so had to sell himself to Rogers and others; when he arrived back in Dublin he was handed an empty briefcase by Rogers and told to wave it at the photographers and smile. "I have nothing to smile about," he said.) He and Rogers were also to achieve the almost impossible feat of being arrested in Las Vegas on a gambling offense and were briefly locked up.

There was *Colette Doherty*, who in 1980 became the first woman to win the Irish Open and who repeated her success eleven years later. She was one of the first women ever to play in the World Series main event.

There was *Frank Callaghan*, who was to become a wealthy businessman, who still puts that wealth to good use, i.e., paying buy-in fees at major tournaments all over the world.

There was a guy called *Dave Jackson* who played so tight that he only had to reach for a chip and everyone seriously considered folding.

There was *Scott Gray*, who was to come fourth in the 2002 World Series and was for years a partner of Padraig Parkinson, both of them playing off the same bankroll.

And holding the whole thing together was the extraordinary personality of Terry Rogers: abrasive, difficult, egocentric, but also capable of great generosity. Frank Callaghan says, "When you got to know him he was a likeable man, but it was hard to get to know him. He was always roaring and shouting and if you didn't know him it was easy to take offense. If you think of the most abrasive man you could possibly meet, you think of Terry Rogers." He was convinced that others were always looking for an opportunity to rob or cheat him. At the races he took to wearing a jacket with a note pinned to it, saying, "This jacket has been stolen from Terry Rogers." He put heavy pressure on dealers to cut the deck in a way he believed prevented cheating and would declare a hand null and void if it wasn't dealt that way. He was very superstitious; for instance, he would never play with a mirror in a room. He was often falling out with players; he and Padraig Parkinson once didn't speak for nearly two years. But Padraig says, "He could be great and he could be terrible, but it was all part of the package. At times I got on great with Terry and at times we hated one another, but that was the normal relationship people had with him. He had run-ins with everybody. It was all part of the deal. But he was a lot more good than bad and, I have to confess, I liked the man." And that probably sums up the view of all the Irish players; such was his generosity, his enthusiasm for the game, his honesty, and—despite appearances—his well-disguised good nature that, while they all acknowledge his eccentricity and his occasional impossibility, they all speak fondly of him. "Terry was Terry," they'll say, and then launch into yet another story about his antics.

Scott Gray tells a story that sums up Rogers and the way the Eccentric Club worked. "Dave Jackson's cards were accidentally pulled in by the dealer, but they didn't hit the muck. Jacko lost his head, so Terry was called in to make a ruling. 'That hand's dead. You should know better; put a chip on your cards to protect them.'

"Dave replied, 'I don't have a chip. I was all-in.'

"Terry said, 'Well, put a lighter or a box of matches on them, then.'

"Dave said, 'But I don't smoke.'

"Quick as a flash, Terry said, 'Then give the man back his cards.'

"Now anywhere else but the Eccentrics Club there would have been a riot over that contrary ruling, but there everyone just cracked up laughing and got on with it."

Terry Rogers first went to Las Vegas in 1979 and fell in love with the Horseshoe and with Texas hold'em, and from then on, year after year, he would take a team over for the World Series. Rogers ran a book on the result of the main event with such attractive odds that many of the top Americans bet with him.

But Rogers was not just in Las Vegas to run a book on the World Series; he was there to mastermind an Irish takeover of the world title, and in 1999 he pulled it off.

Fast forward to 2007. I'm at the Paddy Power Irish Open in Dublin and, as I hoped, I find there three men who were part of the Rogers assault on the world title in 1999. Two of them are seventy years old now, and the first, *Noel Furlong*, says he has retired from poker. In fact he was never a professional; he made millions from his business activities, notably carpets. But every now and then he would make a foray into poker, with devastating results. A highly aggressive player, even by Irish standards, because there's a lot of gamble in the Irish game, he won the Irish Open three times and in 1989 made the World Series final table. Padraig Parkinson says Furlong would have succeeded in any career he chose: "His brain is always working, he's always looking for angle and he's a very good judge of people. He's proved you don't have to have thousands of hours under your belt playing Texas hold'em to be a good player. In a game of two-card chicken, the guy that's fearless and can read the other guy can make up for lack of technical skill. And Noel was fearless with a capital F." George McKeever says that Noel either had a mountain of chips in front of him or none. He tells of one event they were both playing in: as he walked past at an early break, while Noel was still completing a hand, George thought, "How on earth did he get so many chips so quickly?" Less than thirty seconds later he was in the Gents and Noel arrived. "How did you get all those chips?" George asked him. "What chips?" replied Noel. He had lost them all in those few intervening seconds.

The second, *George McKeever*, has also made serious money in business—in forestry and timber, and from a hotel and golf resort. Like Furlong, he played at the Eccentrics Club from time to time.

An unassuming, self-effacing man, George tended to be underestimated by other players. They did this at their peril. Padraig Parkinson points out, "He was in the money at the World Series four times in five years; if he was an American, everyone would know that, but because he was an unassuming guy from County Derry nobody noticed." George didn't play a lot of hands in his top days, but when he did he played them hard. He never entered a pot with a call, always a bet or a raise; he won whole tournaments without calling a bet once. But it wasn't aggression as it's defined in poker today; it was the employment of a judicious strategy to maximize playable hands.

Padraig Parkinson is about twenty years younger than the other two and probably the most popular Irish poker personality. A player who loves to talk and has done more than his bit for the drink industry, and blown a number of potentially big moments as a result, he is described by poker writer and commentator Jesse May as "a hard man . . . One moment you're watching him play the game, and the next moment the game's on you. He's a one-man wrecking crew of how great the game can be and how weak we all are. And in the midst of it all breathes a poker player, a master of a rare art." Like anyone else who is fortunate enough to find him propping up the bar, I find him friendly and helpful. Of these three men, Padraig Parkinson is still the most highly competitive and as recently as the 2006 World Series came a well-paid third in a gold bracelet event.

There were 393 players in the main event in 1999, but few people know that it was nearly 391. Noel Furlong and Padraig Parkinson nearly missed it. In fact when the cry "shuffle up and deal" set the main event in motion, Padraig was not there and not on the entry list. George McKeever noticed this and asked Liam Flood, who was on the rail, where Padraig was. Liam explained that he was in his room, having decided not to play. What none of them knew was that Padraig was suffering withdrawal symptoms from giving up a five-packs-a-day smoking habit. He was a bundle of nerves and didn't fancy sitting at a poker table for any length of time, let alone with a $10,000 buy-in at stake. George told Liam that he and a friend were going to put Padraig in the event and sent Liam to his room to collect him. But George had forgotten one small matter: he didn't have $10,000 on him. So he went to Donnacha O'Dea, who was already playing, and Donnacha, always the gentleman, temporarily abandoned his cards and went to the cage and paid for Padraig to play. By this time Padraig had arrived downstairs to find the event well under way. "But I don't want to play," he told George.

"Never mind that," said George, "I've put you in. So sit down and play cards."

Noel Furlong nearly wasn't there either. He had decided not to travel to Las Vegas and only changed his mind when Terry Rogers telephoned him at the last moment and told him there was a first-class ticket waiting for him at the airport and that he was coming, whether he liked it or not. And he didn't buy in with his own money either: he won a satellite the day before. In fact, such was his form, he entered another satellite and won that too.

So now the three of them were in there, with Terry Rogers and the Irish crowd urging them on from the rail.

Padraig Parkinson immediately repaid George McKeever's generosity and faith in him by attacking George's blinds without mercy. (This, together with the fact that Furlong was to knock them both out, proves that when the chips are down, there's no complicity in top-level poker . . . especially Irish poker. It really is every man for himself.)

George himself got into a difficult hand at one point. He had 90 percent of his chips in a pot when he came to the conclusion that he was going to lose on the river. So he folded.

Some of the Irish supporters in the crowd criticized him, saying that with 90 percent in he had no choice but to go all-in. He was pot-committed. George replies: not if he was going to lose. And he proceeded to fight his way back. "It just shows," he says, "how important it is to stay in the tournament. At all costs."

So came the penultimate day and all three were still there. While the final table consisted of ten players, only six would play on television on the last day, and George was in seventh place with a problem. He had never expected to make the final table and had his plane ticket all lined up and reasons to fly back to Ireland on the final day. So he decided that as soon as he got a good hand all his chips were going into the pot; if he won he would be so well placed at the final table that he would be justified in reorganizing his life; if he lost, he would catch his plane. He found himself with the ace and queen of clubs and, with the blinds $10,000–$20,000, opened the pot for $70,000. Huck Seed (champion three years earlier) called, but Noel Furlong, with two kings, raised $1 million. George then went all-in with his remaining $300,000, and Huck Seed folded, but the kings held up and George went out on "the bubble," leaving six players for the final day. Alas for George, had he folded, Seed with nine-nine would undoubtedly have called and been eliminated and George would have made the final six.

On this penultimate day Furlong and Parkinson were seated on either side of Huck Seed. This enabled them to frustrate Seed by raising and re-raising him so that his usual bluffing game became highly precarious. This undoubtedly affected his play and was probably still doing so on the final day with what was to become a much-debated hand for years to come. Seed had doubled up in the first ten minutes and was on $800,000 when he called a big blind of $20,000. Noel raised it to $100,000, then Seed called all-in. Noel immediately called. Huck turned over jack-eight of diamonds, and Noel ace-three of hearts. Now it is a widely held view that both players had lost their minds . . . that neither had a hand that justified the bets they were making. Phil Hellmuth is one who reads it differently. He points out that Noel had been on Huck's left for three days and had never given him a chance . . . a confrontation was inevitable. And Huck had correctly read Noel for a weak hand. On that—I repeat, *correct*—judgment, Huck had played it well. But not well enough: Furlong stunned everyone by calling and his ace-high stood up. Huck Seed was out.

Why did Noel Furlong call $700,000 with a weak hand himself? In Dublin these many years later I ask him. He replies: "Because I had a tell on Huck. I didn't *think* he was bluffing—I *knew* he was bluffing."

What was the tell?

He just smiles.

Phil Hellmuth defends Furlong as well as Seed.

Give Noel a lot of credit. He knew Huck was bluffing . . . Huck is a great player who won't give many openings . . . why not just be a 3-to-2 favorite over Huck for all his money and perhaps get rid of him right there and then? Thus, I believe Noel Furlong made a great call.[9]

Now there were only the two Irishmen and a New York player, Alan Goehring, left in the event. Padraig had been having a bad run of cards and decided to play queen-ten off-suit. Noel called and two diamonds came on the flop. Padraig, believing that the flop had not helped Furlong, decided to bluff that he was on a flush draw and went all-in for more than

$600,000. Noel, for the first time, really hesitated, thinking for over three minutes before calling with an ace-high of diamonds; it was he who had the flush draw. He did not land another diamond, but he was rewarded with a second ace on the turn, and Padraig, who paired on the river, was out.

In the crowd Terry Rogers was in a right state. One of his team had demolished the other two. But Noel, a childhood friend from the same small seaside village of Dun Laoghaire, was still there, now in heads-up with Alan Goehring. What was to prove the last hand began quietly. Furlong, with five-five, limped into the pot from the button and Goehring, with six-six, flat-called. Both players checked the flop, which was queen-queen-five, and then Goehring checked on the turn. At this point Furlong, with his full house, decided he had to make a move if he was going to get any money out of the hand, so he bet $150,000, and Goehring, with a pair and also four for a flush, decided he had the chance of a big win and raised $300,000. Furlong promptly went all-in and Goehring called. The New Yorker failed to get a six on the river but did get a flush, which, of course, was not good enough, and Furlong became the first (and still the only) Irishman to win the World Series.

On the rail Padraig Parkinson, Scott Gray, Donnacha O'Dea, and the others from Ireland went wild.

At the Chicago airport, George McKeever, in transit on his way home, heard it on the radio and made for the bar and a celebratory drink.

Back at the Eccentrics Club in Dublin the cards were abandoned in favor of Guinness.

For a brief moment the Irish had taken over the Horseshoe ... and the poker world.

As for Terry Rogers, it was a dream fulfilled. What more was there to live for?

He died in 1999 and so was gone by the time an Irish player, Andrew Black, came fifth out of 5,619 in 2005 and won a staggering $1,750,000, and when in 2007 the Irish Open, with 708 competitors, become the biggest-ever European tournament.

Still, wherever you go in Irish poker, you can feel Terry's presence. If he isn't there, his ghost surely is . . . he is Ireland's ghost at the table.

2003: A money-maker called Moneymaker . . . the winner who changed the face of poker

He just had to be called Moneymaker. No other name fits the story.

Chris Moneymaker was born in Nashville, Tennessee, the son of a motor-fleet manager who still proudly follows his poker-playing son from event to event. Despite a near-addiction to gambling, he trained as an accountant and, at twenty-seven, was the financial controller for a restaurant. He was also a poker player with one advantage: he had an amazing memory. (He was later to co-author a book on his 2003 World Series, describing almost every hand from memory.) In 2003 he paid $40 to buy in to a *Poker Stars* satellite for the World Series. By winning it he qualified for a $600 satellite the following week and won it and the $10,000 final event entry fee. He sold half of it to his father and some friends and headed for Las Vegas, perhaps the least likely in a field of 839 to win.

At the end of the first day he was in eleventh place with 60,475 chips. On the second day he moved up to 180,000 chips but then fell back to 100,900 and twenty-sixth place under pressure from two other notable players at his table, two-time World Series winner Johnny Chan and the rising star Phil Ivey. On the third day he found himself on the televised table with Johnny Chan, Paul Darden, and Howard Lederer and that's about as tough as it gets. He could not have made a more embarrassing start, forgetting to actually fold a hand he had decided not to play. So he sat there, studying Chan and Lederer, wondering why they were not making a move. Three minutes went by, then Chan said, "You know it's up to you, right?" The young Nashville player went several shades of red and folded to much laughter—all on national television! The other players looked at each other. This guy was a fish. Except he wasn't. Before the day was out he had knocked out Chan, moved ahead of Lederer and was in sixth place with 357,000 chips. By the dinner break on day four he was still lying sixth, but with 516,000 chips. By then there were only twenty-two players left, with most of the big names gone. Then that night, after dinner, things began to happen.

Moneymaker found himself on the button with three-three and called a $40,000 raise by Dutch Boyd. The flop came nine-two-five. Moneymaker bet 100,000 and then was shaken to the core when Boyd went all-in. For two or three minutes Moneymaker fretted over the hand. He was convinced Boyd was bluffing, but the stakes were about as high as they could be.

> The easy move would have been to fold, I would still have had a healthy chip position, but the better move, the bolder move, was to call. I may have been outplayed to this point in the hand, but I could change all that with one call . . . I took my glasses off, I rubbed my eyes, I stood and paced. There was nothing to shield at this point. I was torn with indecision, and it didn't matter if Boyd knew it. He had played his hand and now it fell to me to play mine. I CALLED.[10]

The last two cards were a four and an ace and he had a straight. It was one of the great calls in World Series history, and now Moneymaker was in the lead with 1.2 million chips. By the end of the night—actually around five in the morning—he was leading the World Series with 2,344,000 chips.

On the final table he found himself with only three survivors, and the other two were great players, former world champion Dan Harrington and the experienced and cunning Sam Farha. But Harrington was first to crack, and so the unknown from Nashville was now in a heads-up for the World Series main event.

At this point Chris began thinking seriously about the money. This was life-changing. Shouldn't he try to take home as much as he could? So during a break he suggested to Farha they split the first and second prize money and take $1.9 million each. Farha said no—he may have had the shorter stack but he was not short of self-belief and he expected the younger man to crack under the pressure. He was wrong. Having made one of the greatest calls in World Series history, Moneymaker now made one of the greatest bluffs, going all-in with king-high, i.e., nothing. Farha folded and Moneymaker now had a huge lead.

The climax came shortly afterwards. Moneymaker had five-four and called a $100,000 bet by Farha, who had jack-ten. The flop came jack-five-four and Farha, with his two jacks, bet $175,000. Moneymaker, with two pairs, raised another $100,000 and Farha went all-in. Moneymaker called and a five on the river gave him a full house and a remarkable victory.

And it didn't just change Moneymaker's life: it changed poker. This was the first Internet qualifier to win. It was to inspire others. Nolan Dalla, media director that year, says, "We were all spinning with ecstasy that he had a name like that. We knew immediately that we could not have written a better script . . . we could not have invented a more marketable name or personality to light the fuse that set off the poker explosion."

And explode it did. Fueled by what became known as "the Moneymaker effect," poker began to take off.

The fourth age of poker was about to begin.

eight

Bobby Hoff's bad beat

. . . and Hal Fowler—the champion who vanished

I'm in California, because I have one other World Series story to explore. I want to solve one of poker's enduring mysteries: *what ever happened to Hal Fowler?*

But, first, I have to find Bobby Hoff, because when Hal Fowler came from nowhere to win the World Series of Poker in 1979 he beat Bobby Hoff heads-up in the greatest upset in the history of the event.

The fact that Fowler was from California and that this also became Bobby Hoff's adopted state is no coincidence. By the 1960s and '70s California was replacing Texas as the breeding ground for top poker players (producing a stream of champions, including Johnny Chan, Chris Ferguson, and in 2006 the biggest World Series money-winner of all time, Jamie Gold, whose $12 million first prize may never be matched).

Poker arrived in California with the Gold Rush in 1848. Portsmouth Square in San Francisco became a forerunner to Las Vegas, packed with sumptuous gaming houses, the most famous being the El Dorado. (Some were less salubrious; outside one rough-and-ready saloon hung the sign: *"Five free drinks if you find any of the waiter girls wearing underwear."*) Poker, however, was only a minority sport in those days . . . it takes time and thought to play well and the Gold Rush gamblers wanted action. So faro prevailed at first, and poker didn't really take off in California for another twenty years or so, when it became the scene of some serious high-stakes poker, much of it at the Baldwin or Palace hotels or the Pacific Club in San Francisco. There you would find such exceptionally wealthy men as William C. Ralston, president of the Bank of California, James C. Flood, who made a fortune from silver mining, and Nevada senators William Stewart and William Sharon.

Sharon is said to have won $1 million playing poker at the Pacific Club—that would, of course, be worth almost $10 million today. This was the predecessor of the Las Vegas *big game* described in my next chapter. There were frequent pots of $50,000 and even occasionally $100,000. The most famous hand played at the Pacific Club involved Sharon and Ralston, who found themselves alone in a pot with $150,000 on the table. Sharon raised it $50,000 and Ralston re-raised for a further $150,000. There was a stunned silence, and then Sharon tossed his cards into the muck and said "I quit." Ralston then turned over two tens. Sharon made no comment, nor did he until after Ralston's death. He then revealed that he had been holding two jacks.

A more gruesome California story involves an encounter between one of the lively Chinese gambling community, Ah Tia, and a Native American called Poker Tom. No one knows what upset the Chinese player, but after the two had played poker heads-up he killed Poker Tom, cut him into pieces, cooked him, and then invited Poker Tom's friends to dinner. The stew he served was much appreciated until sometime later the truth emerged. At that point Ah Tia was murdered in revenge but, fortunately for his friends, the killers did not hold a return dinner.

For much of the twentieth century, poker was illegal in California. Then someone noticed that the Penal Code outlawed "any game of faro, monte, roulette, *stud-horse poker*, twenty-one . . ." but it did not mention *draw poker*. So one or two clubs were opened for draw poker only, the Attorney General at the time, one Ulysses Webb, refusing to close them down when pressed, stating there was no law forbidding the game. By the late 1960s there were hundreds of licensed clubs in California. First to see the potential of all this was Gardena, a small former market-gardening suburb of Los Angeles; it confirmed the legality of draw poker in 1936 and became for thirty years and more the poker capital of the world. When I went there in the early '70s, there were six huge poker palaces: the El Dorado (previously the Embassy), Normandie, Horseshoe, Rainbow, Monterey, and Gardena Club. I still have the Monterey's leaflet in a desk drawer, full of pictures of its thirty-five tables, offering games from as low as $1 to whatever level you wanted to play. You could play with doctors and lawyers, laborers and truck drivers, and an array of colorful characters with such names as Toothpick Vic, Suitcase Sam, The Arm, the Mad Russian, Mike the Cop, Joe the Jinx, and Whacky Jackie. One of the most famous in the '60s and '70s was Lakewood Louie, a proposition player who was one of those who was to be wiped out in the 1979 WSOP main event by Hal Fowler (trip queens on the river to beat two aces). Fowler himself must have played there frequently. Poker players came from all over California to Gardena; others came from across America or, like me, from other countries.

The games were tough and there was an epidemic of cheating, so bad that the *LA Times* ran a series about it. One began: "High-stakes poker players expecting a square game in Bell and Gardena casinos are being fleeced by professional cheaters whose activities are known to casino management."

The then manager of the Rainbow was quoted as saying, "These aren't Sunday schools, you know." Another club manager was said to have claimed: "In the top-stakes games it's really just a cheating match. All you can do is try to keep the honest players from getting caught in the middle."

Still, poker players were not deterred and enough of them avoided being robbed for many engaging stories to emerge from the Gardena heydays. Rex Jones, a well-known California poker player and writer, wrote about a happening at the Normandie:

> A player was seated with his back to the emergency exit. Suddenly he was dealt a pat straight flush. He had not seen a hand worth playing for days. He leaned back in his chair holding up the hand for further study and toppled backward and out the door, head over heels. The door slammed on him. It all happened so fast that nobody knew what to do. Then the front door burst open and in ran the jubilant player holding up the hand for all to see, only to get a ruling from the floor man that it was unplayable.[1]

In the 1980s the law was reinterpreted even more liberally, and games like Texas hold'em became legal. Poker really took off in California and by 2006 *Card Player* magazine was reporting that it had the most poker rooms in the country. Poor old Gardena, having done so much for poker in California, now found itself with giant Los Angeles competitors, in particular the Bicycle and the Commerce, each quickly building to over 170 tables. As the Gardena card rooms began to fade, these newcomers grew rapidly and became world-famous, packed every day and hosting major televised events.

It's to the Commerce that I'm headed now. I'm told Bobby Hoff is a proposition player there. On my twenty-minute taxi ride up the freeway from the airport, I pass its rival, the Bicycle, now an impressive complex in Bell Gardens. At the Commerce I thread my way past table after table, with a game to match every bankroll . . . past a multitude of dealers, floor managers, waiters, and, of course, players. Eventually I find myself in a far corner of the room. Here the game is $20–$40 no-limit and the table is about as multicultural as it can get—blacks, Hispanics, whites—but all in their thirties or younger, except for one guy at the end of the table. He stands out from the crowd. Probably in his mid-60s, he has thinning hair, glasses, wears a white shirt and cotton jacket, and has a canvas bag hanging on the back of his chair. He looks like an academic; he could be a university professor. While I watch, he gets a king-high flush. Another guy has a jack-high flush in the same suit. The "professor" raises the pot, card by card, and finally wipes him out, picks up a tray of chips, and heads for a door marked VIP. This is Bobby Hoff, a poker player for nearly fifty years, a regular at the Commerce for at least seventeen years and a guy you definitely don't want to meet when he's got a flush higher than yours.

Later he tells me that when he came to Los Angeles, he did indeed begin at the Commerce as a proposition player (meaning he was paid by the card room to help get the games started). In Bobby's case he chose the best hold'em game there was and was paid $30 an hour to play in it. For the first time in his life he was, in effect, working for someone, and as a result got a social security number and became a citizen. However, he does so well at the game that he doesn't need the $30 an hour anymore and prefers to come and go as he pleases. He has won $3,000 today. "I make a reasonable living. But my expenses are quite high." All believable; the car we're in is expensive, and he takes me to dinner at one of the more fashionable restaurants in LA.

I know that Bobby is one of the generation of Texan road gamblers who began after players like Slim, Doyle, and Sailor had already been on the road for ten years. Now he tells me the story:

"I had a golf scholarship at the University of Texas in 1959. I was a fair golfer, but when I went to university I fell into what really was quite a big poker game . . . pot limit, seven-card stud . . . and that was it; it was all I did. So I was thrown out. But I had won forty times in a row and I had $8,000 in my pocket. I went back home to where I lived in Victoria. This was a town of about 50,000 population, with at that time more millionaires per capita then any other town in the United States. Some big ranch owners, who were already wealthy, discovered oil and gas on their property and became some of the wealthiest people anywhere. Several families had hundreds of millions of dollars back when that was real money. And there was an Air Force base there as well. There was a lot of illegal gambling. There were three clandestine casinos and there were poker games all over town, around the clock, mostly pot-limit and no-limit games.

"One of the casinos was right across the street from the Air Force base and one of them was on a hill on the outside of town. They paid off everybody—the sheriff and the Texas Rangers and guys at the Liquor Control Board, and I think they had a couple of judges that they had to pay, too.

"So I came back home to Victoria, thinking I was the best poker player in the world, and I started playing in these clandestine games and I got broke at first, so I started working in the casinos. They paid me every day in cash, and I would go straight from work to the poker game and I would play until I either got broke or it was time to go back to work.

"Then a friend and I read a book about blackjack called *Beat the Dealer* and we learnt to count and play. I spent most of the '60s doing that in various places, until by about 1969 I had built up a bankroll of about $50,000 and so I went to Las Vegas and started playing no-limit hold'em.

"I was playing against men like Doyle Brunson and Sailor Roberts. I'd met Sailor Roberts a little bit before that, when I was playing blackjack, but we really hadn't become friends until I started playing poker and then we became really close friends. Well, anyway, I lost all my $50,000 blackjack winnings in those games, but I learnt how to play and Sailor started staking me to play.

"I was thirty-one years old and it was then I started to play serious poker. I remember I made a big breakthrough. I started making plays in my head and I could see they were working . . .

I won $80,000 just like that. And every time I saw a possible play to make, I would make it, and that's how I got started in the big time.

"And Sailor was a big help. Sailor was so special I just don't know where to start. He was probably the most generous man I've ever known. He never learnt to say no to anyone. And he was such an honorable man. His word was his absolute bond.

"We both had a lot of the same weaknesses, alcohol and drugs, partying and things like that. And he loved women, oh my God did he love women. He was a little guy with a big belly, but he had a lot of money, and he always had the girls hanging off him, and I always thought that if this poor guy ever gets broke these girls would leave him just like that. Not true. I saw him get completely broke and one day we were sitting in a coffee shop, yet most of the women came over and gave Sailor a hug. They knew how much he loved them, and he loved them dearly. Sailor always knew the right thing to say, the right way to feel about things, not to mention the fact that he was a great poker player and a terrific bookmaker. Very smart and very good at mathematics. An absolutely cold-blooded gambler. I mean, he bet it all."

His partnership with Doyle Brunson and Amarillo Slim at an end, Sailor joined up with Bobby and Carl McKelvey, and thus began the boozing, cocaine-sniffing, poker-playing rampage that ultimately killed Sailor and has damaged Bobby's health for the rest of his life. (Before we got out of the car at the restaurant, he downed a bottle of strange-looking liquid—a health drink of some sort—and a handful of pills.) Bobby sunk to such a low that he was eventually found holed up in a cheap motel in Las Vegas, broke, and all but out of it from drug-taking. He was saved by his old friend Carl McKelvey, who dragged him back to Texas and helped him sort himself out.

The tragedy was that if Bobby had kept to poker, there's no telling what he would have achieved. McKelvey, who has seen them all, says, "Bobby in the 1970s played the game on a different dimension from the rest of us. He was way above the other players of our generation." T. J. Cloutier says that Bobby Hoff would be one of the first he would choose for a planetary team to play Mars. "He's as good as anyone when he plays it the way it's meant to be played. Bobby is probably the best heads-up player I ever saw. He is a fabulous heads-up player. You don't get a breath; he keeps the pressure on you all the time. Every minute you're sitting at the table with Bobby, you're under pressure."

So we come to 1979 and the $10,000 buy-in main event at the World Series of Poker. Bobby remembers every detail:

"There were fifty-five players and I remember that I had $5,000 before the tournament started, so I sold 50 percent of myself. I went in with two $20 bills left in my pocket. I started the last day and I guess we were down to eighteen players and I was very short of chips . . . I had about 1,500 . . . and I got two aces on my first deal and doubled my chips, and then I went right on to the last table.

"The final table was fearsome. They were all good players. There was Johnny Moss, Bobby Baldwin, Crandell Addington, Sam Moon, Sam Petrillo, George Huber—all professionals— and then there was this one other guy, a man called Hal Fowler. No one had seen him before. He was a complete unknown. He definitely was not a professional . . . we couldn't understand how he made the final table, because he didn't seem to know what to do. I remember one pot, where he had a lot of chips af-ter some miracle draws, and Sam Moon bet out . . . this was really quite a big pot. And then it was up to Hal and he was completely lost. He didn't even know it was his turn to play, but Sam didn't realize that, and he said, 'Hal, throw your hand away, you know you're not going to call,' but Hal looked down at his hand and said, 'Oh yeah, I'm going to call it,' and he had jack-ten off suit and he put all of his chips in the pot and the flop came ace-queen-king . . . a straight. And he shouldn't have been in the hand."

So it came down to Hal Fowler and Bobby Hoff, both, it has to be said, under the influence of drugs. With Hoff, it was cocaine, taken as "breakfast" every day before play began. With Fowler, it was Valium, taken throughout the day and evening.

Crandell Addington says, "I sat right next to Hal and he had his pills out there on the table. Of course a lot of guys used to get up and go sniff and snort in the bathroom in those days, but he had some Valium and also some amphetamines, the real strong ones, and he actually put these on the table by his chips. I really believe that much of the time he didn't have a clue what he was doing."

As for Bobby Hoff, he admits, "Oh yes, I was taking cocaine during that tournament and I probably played as well if not better on cocaine. I would put two lines of coke by the bed every night and take it when I woke up. And I would have some cognac as well. It's like any drug that you're used to, like coffee or an alcoholic drink . . . it was no big deal, except I was affecting my health long term."

So back to the game: "It got down to just the two of us, me and Hal, and we were about even in chips, probably about 250,000 apiece. And I thought I was a big favorite to beat him because he was playing way too tight. Then I raised with an ace and a ten, and he called me with a six and a four. And the flop came ace, king, ten, three suits. He checked and I bet, and he called and the turn card was a jack. Any queen and I was the nuts, and he bet 250,000 all-in, with the six-four he had; it was one of the worst plays I had ever seen. I mean, he could have found out exactly the same thing for 30,000, because if I had the queen it's over. Well, I threw my hand away and he showed me the six-four, and I remember thinking, this is going to be a lot tougher game than I expected . . . I just don't know what this guy is going to do.

"And then we played several pots on, and I remember one we played where I started bluffing at the pot on the flop and I picked up a flush draw on the turn, bluffed again and on the river made the king-high flush and, would you believe it, he had made an ace-high flush and won the pot.

"And then we had a pot when I finally had him short on chips. I had been grinding him out on small pots, because he was throwing away a lot, and I had him short on chips. I raised the pot with a queen and a six; I'm not even sure if I had looked at them or not. And he called me with a king and a jack, and the flop came up a queen, a five and a deuce, something like that. And I checked and he checked and the turn card was a jack. We both went all-in (but I had more than him, so I still had 150,000 left over) and he caught a jack at the river to stay alive. It just seemed that no matter what I did, he landed the card he needed.

"He kept taking these Valiums and he was really getting pretty stoned and pretty tired and we were playing a long time, maybe eight or ten hours, and it had escalated and the blinds were ridiculously high. And finally he said, 'Let's call it off and come back and play tomorrow,' and I said, 'I can't make that decision, it's not up to me.' They had television going and that sort of thing. And so he said, 'OK, I'm just going to move in every hand,' and then he did. This meant that I had lost any control of the game I may have had. It was a nightmare. Finally I caught two aces and I made a big raise before the flop, and he called me with a six and a seven and then came a jack and a four and a three, and I bet half my chips and he called me and a five came on the river. I bet the rest of my chips, but, of course, he had a straight and I was dead."

T. J. Cloutier says, "No one—and I mean NO ONE—could have beaten Hal Fowler that day. Not even God. He was just getting the cards and that was that."

Bobby Hoff was devastated. "I can't tell you how sick I was. I thought when the tournament started that I was playing for the money, but I realized before the tournament was over that I wanted to win so bad that I would've given all the money for the title, even though I only had $40 in my pocket,

I would've given all the money to win and I didn't know that about myself.

"I never felt pressure like that before and it is the only time in my life that the palms of my hands were sweaty. And I thought I played very well; I might have made one or two mistakes, but I thought I played very well.

"It really bothered me for a long time. I dreamed about it for a couple of weeks and I've thought about it in the daytime ever since, because, like I say, I didn't realize how much I wanted to win. It was such an honor then, I wanted my picture up on the wall with my friends and those other great players."

But it is over twenty-five years back. Surely he's got over it by now?

"No, I haven't got over it, it still bothers me."

It was the greatest upset in the history of the World Series. It was not only Bobby Hoff who was stunned. The whole poker world was. Bobby Baldwin, who watched the whole heads-up, says, "Bobby Hoff was a very good player and a very aggressive player and he looked up for it, but Hal Fowler was paying no attention at all to what Bobby was or wasn't doing in a particular hand. He was just betting in a pattern that made no sense whatsoever. So Bobby was a huge favorite to beat this guy, but the guy was making all sorts of inexplicable moves at just the right time and it was impossible for Bobby to know what he was doing. Hal Fowler bluffed him a couple of times where, if Bobby had had one particular card, he would have broken him there and then, but it just turned out that Bobby was bluffing too, on the same hands, and so he had to fold. But it was one crazy game . . . a freak game and a freak result."

Tom McEvoy says that Fowler had taken so much Valium that after he won he just sat there expressionless, as if he didn't know what had happened. "He looked totally out of it."

So it was over and Hoff had missed his best chance.

Now a strange thing happened.

Hal Fowler disappeared.

He never came back to the World Series to defend his title . . . in fact, never came back to Las Vegas. If it were not for a video recording of the event and a few photographs, and one or two unconfirmed reports that he had been "sighted" playing in California and in Reno, it was as if everyone had been hallucinating—that he had never actually been there.

I have asked everyone who is anyone in the poker world and no one knows where Hal Fowler is. Some say he's dead.

Amarillo Slim casts a particularly sinister light on it: "I asked Benny Binion one time, 'Did you kill Hal Fowler?' and he said, 'Let's not talk about it,' and that's all he ever said."

How can someone conquer the world and then disappear? I can't stop thinking about it. I become obsessed with Hal Fowler's fate . . . and I begin to feel sorry for him. He is described on one website as an "unpopular" champion. But why? Because we all like a popular favorite to win and he stole the show? Sure, he got lucky—but that's poker. Yes, he was taking Valium, but, unlike Bobby Hoff's cocaine, it *was* a legal drug. And the pressure on this loner finding himself heads-up for the world title must have been tremendous.

Obviously the World Series had been the high point of Hal's life . . . did he then go on a rampage somewhere and lose all the money? Did he turn to drink and drugs, and end up on skid row?

I *have* to know.

I *have* to bring him back.

I *have* to get the world of poker to remember him one more time—and to recognize his achievement. Because, when you think about it, Johnny Moss, Bobby Baldwin, and Crandell Addington were on that final table as well as Bobby Hoff. He beat them all. Luck or no luck, that was a hell of an achievement.

But where to start? What do we know? Only that he came from California and was engaged in some kind of advertising or public-relations work.

I decide the way forward is to hire a private detective. According to the movies, California is full of them—Philip Marlowe, Sam Spade, Jim Rockford, that sort of guy. Now, I've never hired a private detective before. How does one do this? I surf the web and find Jeff Banks (private investigator CA licence 21501), who is a former Marine and policeman who claims to find people and carry out debugging, surveillance, undercover operations . . . the sort of thing we would all be doing if we had the time. I phone him and, after being assured it won't cost a fortune, I put him on the case. I am now a private eye's client!

A few weeks pass and little happens. Jeff assures me that he's detecting away, even after my humble retainer runs out. But it is clearly proving more difficult than I imagined. However, while Jeff is doing whatever private eyes do, I am raising questions about Hal in *Poker Pro* magazine and, by sheer coincidence, the day I hear from Jeff that he may have tracked Hal down, I receive this email from a man in Fort Wayne, Indiana, who had picked up the magazine in a card room in Detroit:

> My profession is the location of missing persons, mostly with respect to probate matters. I read your article asking what happened to Hal Fowler. I can probably find him, if he hasn't already turned up . . . let me know if you want my help. No charge. Steven Richard

I put Steven in touch with Jeff, and now things really begin to happen.

To Des from Jeff
    I have found a reference on a poker website to Hal Fowler coming from Vermont. Have you come across any reference to Vermont?

To Jeff from Des
    No. I have only references to California.

To Des from Steven

We may have solved the case!

I talked with Jeff Banks. You know he found a reference on a website to Vermont, he says he has located a Harold Fowler buried in San Joaquin National Cemetery in California who was from Vermont. He thinks this might be the guy.

I searched the type of historical records that I use in my business and located a Harold A. Fowler born in Vermont. He would have been the same age as Hal Fowler and the same age as the man buried at San Joaquin Cemetery. He was one of five sons of an Ernest and Iva Fowler. I then discovered the widow of Eugene Fowler, one of those sons who lived all his life in Vermont. She confirms she had a brother-in-law named Harold Fowler. She told me that nobody in the family had heard from Harold Fowler in more than 50 years.

To Des from Steven

I have now contacted the public library in Harold's home town of Rutland, Vermont, to obtain details of Eugene Fowler's obituary. It refers to another brother living in Brandon, Florida. As a result, yesterday I spoke to that man's daughter. She confirmed she had an Uncle Harold who disappeared around 50 years back, but she has a family photo album that apparently includes pictures of him. She is going to check the Internet for pictures of Hal Fowler, the poker champ, and compare it to family photos. She will also show it to her father, who she visits daily in the hospital.

I made a few phone calls and did some additional research of Californian records available on the Internet. I discovered that a power-of-attorney was filed in Tulare County for the Harold Fowler from Vermont. It was given to a lady living in the same complex as Harold Fowler; apparently she and her husband were friends of Harold's. Jeff Banks will follow this up.

To Des from Jeff

I believe I have located the lady Steven refers to. It appears that she and Hal Fowler lived in the same seniors' complex. Am on my way there now . . .

To Des from Jeff

It's him!

The lady confirms that the Hal Fowler who lived in the complex was a former world champion poker player.

In the best traditions of Marlowe, Spade, Rockford, and the rest, Jeff, with help from Steven, has found our man.

Jeff and I talk on the phone. The seniors' complex had been extremely cautious but finally contact had been made with the lady in question. It was she and her husband who took Hal to the hospital the night he died in November 2000. According to his death certificate, Harold Arthur Fowler died of hemorrhagic shock due to upper gastro-intestinal bleeding. He had a duodenal ulcer and cirrhosis. The certificate confirmed he was seventy-three; his parents were indeed from Vermont. His occupation is listed as public relations. He was divorced.

He had left a number of possessions with his friends in the complex.

One was a small gun.

Another was a video recording of the 1979 World Series of Poker.

By now I myself have made contact with Hal Fowler's niece, who lives in Florida. She tells me a remarkable story.

Apparently Hal's father took off when the boys were small and left Hal's mother to look after them alone. Hal and the brothers all worked to help her—by the time Hal was four, he was picking berries and selling them. He left high school after just two years and went into the Service at eighteen, just when the Second World War was ending (everyone is vague about where and when he served). He returned to Vermont some years later, but, after only twenty-four hours with his family, he suddenly said he had to leave—and they have never seen him since.

At one point they made strenuous efforts to contact him and nearly did . . . but instead of replying to a message from them, he let it be known they should communicate via his attorney and that he would reply in the same way. When Iva Fowler died, they sent the details of the funeral to Hal's attorney, but Hal never showed up. His niece said the family never did understand it; there had never been a family row—indeed the brothers were close. The reasons for his self-inflicted isolation were a complete mystery.

So, 1979—the year of his World Series win—was not the first time that Hal Fowler had chosen to disappear. He had done so when he left his family thirty-four years earlier. But why? And why insist he could only be reached via his attorney?

Could it be that when he came back from the Service he had cause to hide from someone? That he knew if he stayed with the family in Vermont he would be found? Or that he would put them in danger? Could it be that after winning the World Series—probably to his own surprise—he, for the same reason, became concerned about the publicity and that is why he left the poker world so quickly to live in relative obscurity in California? Was he living in fear of somebody or something? This may seem far-fetched—it probably is—but how else can his behavior be explained?

As no one in the family had a clue what had happened to him, I found myself having to break the news to the Florida branch that he was dead.

By now my private eye friend, Jeff, has put me in touch with the lady who, with her husband, was closest to Hal over the last ten years of his life.* This is what she told me:

_____

*In order to preserve the privacy of the women I spoke to, I am not disclosing their names.

"We met Hal about twelve or so years before he died. We became friends at a senior citizens' residential place. We loved Hal. We were so close that when we moved to another low-income seniors' complex in the county of Tulare, California, he moved there too. We were always pleased he did—it was as if he had chosen us to be his family for his last years.

"He never talked much about his real family or past life . . . it was sad he didn't have any dealings with them . . . I wondered whether he kept out of touch because he was ashamed of the way he let himself go. I know that at one time he was well off, operating as a promoter of rodeos and things and working in public relations, and he had a lot of money and a beautiful home, but he lost it all. He gambled—he had a poker table in his home and I think they played for big money—and he drank a lot and he liked the ladies. I think he lived a fast life and he paid for it, because it affected his health and he ran out of money.

"For the last ten years of his life he had no money. He lived on social security. He was proud of winning the World Series—he had a newspaper clipping about it—but I believe he had to sell his gold bracelet and, when I helped him with some money, he wanted to give me the two beautiful boxes of chips they gave him with his name on.

"Towards the end he was suffering a lot from a huge inoperable ulcer and he was almost totally blind; he couldn't read or even see the television. He had to use a 'walker' to move around. All he could do in the evenings was sit outside his front door and chat and tell stories with his neighbors. And, you know, he had a lot of friends here—he was a lovely man; he was kind and he was mellow and he just loved to talk, and he remained cheerful up to the end.

"We spoke every day and I often took him food. One day I phoned him and he didn't answer. My husband went over and found him bleeding badly. By the time they got him to a hospital, he was in a coma. He died that night. They were giving him blood transfusions, but he had told me that when this happened he didn't want to be helped to stay alive, so I told them to stop. Anyway, he did not die alone—we were there with him . . . I was holding his hand when he passed away."

Then she told me a strange thing. "He told me he didn't want anyone to be told he had died . . . not until at least two years had passed. He was emphatic about that. So I never did tell anyone."

So, for a third and last time, Hal Fowler had decided to disappear. Even in death his whereabouts were to remain a mystery. Why?

It was an extraordinary final chapter to an extraordinary story.

His grave is in a veterans' cemetery in a peaceful corner of the Californian countryside. It is marked by a simple white stone. In fact, apart from the bare details upon them all the stones are identical. His says:

Harold Arthur Fowler
Army 8/13/1945 to 12/12/1945
Air Force 10/23/45 to 10/12/50

And that is all it says. No passer-by could ever know that under that stone lies a man who was once the poker champion of the world . . . *the man*. His achievement, like his secrets, was buried with him.

As for Bobby Hoff, he's still playing at the Commerce. At the end of the day, when he's won enough—and he *does* win—he drives in his expensive car to his comfortable home in Long Beach . . . to have dinner with the woman who has been for many years the love of his life. Afterwards he will read, or watch a little television. He will sleep well. Despite the ups and downs of his life, he is today a happy and healthy man . . . a survivor.

Bobby Hoff may have lost a game of poker to Hal Fowler, but there's a bigger game out there.

It's called life.

And, in that game, it's Bobby, not Hal, who has been the winner.

That has to be better than a gold bracelet.

nine

Million-dollar hands
. . . the world of high-stakes poker

It's summer 2007 and I'm playing in a $5–$10 no-limit cash game at the Bellagio. At the table with me are a man in his sixties wearing an Army veteran's cap and the kind of camouflage fatigues they wore in the Vietnam jungle (and who I wipe out with four deuces to three queens full—poker's equivalent of a napalm attack); a heavy-breathing, overweight lawyer from Detroit who fancies himself as a player but doesn't know his aces from his ankles, and is the fish in the game (assuming, of course, that the others don't think it's me); a kid with sinister shades, earphones, and baseball cap who tries to look and play like Phil Ivey but without the moves; two men in their forties or fifties who I suspect play here for a living every day, who only enter a pot if they have two aces and a promissory note for two more; an attractive blonde with a stare that would stop a charging rhinoceros in its tracks; a friendly bespectacled guy from London, who is here on a poker holiday and claims he's $5,000 up but borrows ten from me for a hot dog; and a Texan, complete with Stetson, jeans, and drawl.

I've been playing for a couple of hours when Doyle Brunson comes in. Because of his disability he drives a motorized scooter. Does he steer it gently between the tables? He does not. He drives it at breakneck speed. I have a vision—thank God, so far only a vision—of him losing control and crashing into a table, scattering players and cards in all directions. Fortunately he's not heading for my table but a room directly in front of me—one with glass walls from floor to ceiling. While I wait for a playable hand, I observe it closely. Were it not for the glass, providing a full view of its plush interior, it would be a completely private card room. There are two beautifully brushed and polished poker tables. There are two television sets, showing sports. There are expensive leather sofas and armchairs, and on the walls are photos and paintings of some of the world's top high-stakes players, including, of course, Brunson himself.

I realize that what I am looking at is Bobby's Room.

Bobby's Room is a club we can all join. In fact we're all welcome. All we have to do is wander in and place at least $100,000 in $100 bills on the table (about twice the annual income of most Americans) and have enough cash, or credit with the other players, to be able to lose up to a million dollars before going home (it can be more than a million, but the players are partially "protected" by a $100,000 cap; that is to say, no player can lose more than a mere $100,000 in any one hand!).

What takes place in Bobby's Room is the famous *big game*— they say that once you've played in it, you will never be happy playing anywhere else. This will never be my problem, especially when I discover that this particular evening they're playing Omaha with limits of $4,000–$8,000. To me, the stakes are terrifying. The most I ever took out of a session was $6,000 when I won a 161-player $100 buy-in event; these top professionals are tossing more than $6,000 into the pot as a blind bet before each and every hand begins! If there are ten players at the table and, say, six call the blind bet, there's $60,000 on the table before they become seriously involved in the hand. This is another world. Even highly experienced and world-class professionals keep their distance; one is two-times runner-up in the World Series main event Dewey Tomko, who says, "If you hit a losing streak, it could cost you $20–30 million in a year—that is life changing."

Life changing? Words like calamity, catastrophe, disaster, and ruin come to mind . . . closely followed by gun, single bullet, and suicide!

World Poker Tour host Mike Sexton, who is a top player himself, tells me, "Every day someone can win or lose a million dollars—half a million, for sure. You're talking about $150,000 in a pot—and it's pot after pot after pot. The first time I played in that game I had $100,000 in front of me and I quickly lost that, and Phil Ivey, who was in the game, shoved me $200,000 more and said, 'Here, come on,' so I played that, lost, borrowed another $100,000, lost that . . . so I'm like a $400,000 loser in an hour. So I borrowed another $100,000, and now I struck it lucky and I ended up by winning $60,000 . . . I was down $400,000 and then won it back and up $60,000 in three or four hours. That shows just how fast it is."

The big game, as it's universally known, has over the years become a poker tourist attraction, making it difficult for the players to concentrate or relax. That's why Bobby Baldwin (the Bobby of Bobby's Room) decided to protect this special corner of the card room with walls of glass. It doesn't need a closed door; the $100,000-plus buy-in is the barrier. As I watch, Lyle Berman arrives and begins to play heads-up with Sammy Farha: Berman has the assurance of a billionaire to whom $100,000 is pocket money, Farha the confidence of a poker gambler who, according to Todd Brunson, "would make a suicide bomber look like a coward." Shortly afterwards tiny Jennifer Harman throws down her stack of $100 bills and climbs onto a stool, tucking her legs under her. Jennifer, the only woman player with the nerve and skill to compete over time at this level, is followed by Danish-born Gus Hansen, whose dinner arrives simultaneously on a trolley loaded with silver platters. Mike Sexton wanders in to watch but not play, followed by

Chip Reese, wearing a red shirt and jeans. Then there's Chau Giang, one of an army of Vietnamese who make a living from poker. (Chau was one of the Vietnamese boat people. He worked as a chef before becoming a winning player.) Finally, for now, David Benyamine arrives.

The whole poker world is talking about Benyamine. He is a French player who is rumored to be the big winner in the game at this time—he is said to be $15 million up on the others.

Obviously the money tends to move around the table when the game is restricted to the usual suspects, but I know that every now and then they land a fish. One in recent years has been Jay Bachman, a man who made a lot of money in business and didn't mind losing some of it playing poker. Todd Brunson, who writes about the big game in *Card Player* magazine, publicly stated that Jay loved stud high-lo but never really got on top of it and "pumped a lot of money into the big game."

Another business figure who "pumped" money into the big game was Howard Mann, but it was not only by playing poker. Whenever he came to the game, he would talk about a stock he and his father supported. He was so convincing about its growth potential that all the players (except Doyle Brunson, who, as usual, made a bad business decision) went out and bought it. They soon discovered that Mann knew what he was talking about; the shares went up forty times. At least a dozen of them made over $1 million and one is said to have made $10 million.

What qualities do they need to play and win in this game?

Obviously they have to be outstanding all-around players. (Rarely are they playing straightforward hold'em or stud poker; more likely it's one of about a dozen variations on the standards, with pot-limit Omaha, limit Omaha split, no-limit deuce to seven, and seven-card stud hi-lo the more popular games. They need a good understanding of each of these games.) They require the mathematical skill to estimate the odds on landing any particular card and an instinct for how to handle any situation. They need the self-awareness to eliminate "tells," the discipline to avoid going on tilt, and the patience to ride out particularly bad runs of luck. And they need physical and mental stamina.

But there's a lot more to it than even that. Above all, they need nerve. Call it courage or call it madness, they have to have it because there's no point entering Bobby's Room unless they're utterly fearless and that means that money simply must not matter. To them, money is merely a tool of the trade. They need it to buy the chips, and the chips are the way they keep the score . . . and that's it. All of them have been big winners at poker over the years, and sometimes big losers; they have lived daily with ups and downs involving hundreds of thousands of dollars. But they know—they don't think it, they *know*—that if they lose, there's always another game, and another, and another, and one day they'll win the money back.

And that is where we come to the other necessity: self-confidence on a major scale. They've conquered this game. They've lived with its ebbs and flows. They know they can handle it. They know if they lose it will be because of an uncharacteristic error, or because the cards are just not falling their way this day or this week, and that they just have to stay in there and all will be well. Their peers know it, too; that's why they feel able to lend each other substantial sums—hundreds of thousands—without so much as a receipt.

As I look on and fantasize about playing in the big game, I note that the regulars playing tonight—and the cast appears to change from time to time—span the last three of my four ages of poker. (Oh, how the stars of the first age—Wild Bill, Doc Holliday, Dick Clark, and the rest—would have loved to be there.)

From the second age—the days of the Texan road gamblers—there is, of course, *Doyle Brunson*, The Godfather.

Next to him, from the third age, there is *Chip Reese*, Brunson's close friend and occasional partner, who many believe is the best all-around poker player ever, and who proved it in 2006, when the World Series for the first time included a $50,000 buy-in tournament known as the H.O.R.S.E. This required the players to compete in several forms of poker within the same event, the aim being to discover who could prevail as an all-rounder. Despite the size of the buy-in, it attracted all the big names . . . both the veterans and the young guns. It concluded with a titanic heads-up battle between Chip Reese and Andy Bloch, with Reese emerging the winner.

Reese, who with his Ohio mate, Danny Robison, hit Las Vegas like a whirlwind in 1973 (they were known as the Gold Dust Kids before Robison succumbed to drink and drugs), has been in the big game for over thirty years. He is low profile, rarely seen on television, and thus is able to wander around the Rio at the time of the World Series virtually unrecognized. He's not in it for fame, just the money, and he's won plenty of that. He's a wealthy man. If you ignore the killer eyes, he's a real charmer, an operator, one of the best at attracting "producers" to the game, making them feel at home, then taking their money—*all of it*; he doesn't back off when he's winning—he is a man without mercy. He prefers cash games; his tournament record is relatively modest for such a class act, just two World Series gold bracelets before the H.O.R.S.E. victory in 2006. It took the challenge of the H.O.R.S.E. and the million-dollar first prize to bring out his best. Reese, a highly intelligent man, is renowned for his ability to remain calm at the table no matter what is happening. No one ever recalls him going on tilt or "steaming" when he's losing. Mike Sexton says, "I never have seen him criticize an opponent, moan about a bad beat, throw cards, or blame the dealer when he loses a pot. His behavior is impeccable. He is the epitome of class."

Next to Reese is the sixty-six-year-old billionaire *Lyle Berman*. He came to poker with a substantial bankroll from business. He sold the family's leather-goods company in 1979 for $10 million, decided to buy it back in 1987 for $99 million, and then sold it a year later for $220 million. He built up and sold Grand Casinos, and did the same with the Rainforest Café Group, and was the key investor when the *World Poker Tour* was launched. Berman is no fish at the poker table—he began playing in Las Vegas about 1983. He has since won three World Series gold bracelets and has held his own in the big game for over twenty years.

Facing these veterans across the table, there are those who span the third and fourth ages of poker, beginning with *Jennifer Harman*, who was born in Reno and took up poker in her father's home games. At twenty-one, she decided to abandon plans to become a doctor and instead took up poker professionally, specializing in limit Texas hold'em. She has won two World Series gold bracelets but is mainly a high-stakes cash-game player. The recipient of a kidney transplant, this small, volatile woman is both liked and feared by all the big-game players—liked for her courage and upfront candor, feared because, on her night, she can wipe out the best.

Beside her is *Sam Farha*. With black hair brushed back, unlit cigarette hanging from the corner of his mouth, and a face like Humphrey Bogart, he looks like you expect a gambler to look. He left Beirut for the US when civil war broke out in Lebanon in the '70s, then went to the University of Kansas and then to Houston, where he began to play poker regularly. He's another who prefers the action of cash games to the grind of tournaments, but he won a World Series gold bracelet in 1996. In 2003 he lost a huge pot on the second day of the World Series main event and was considering abandoning his few remaining chips and leaving the game, but Barry Greenstein persuaded him to stay. He went on to win $1.3 million as runner-up to Chris Moneymaker.

His neighbor at the table, *Barry Greenstein*, is a small, slight, bearded fifty-year-old, known as the Robin Hood of poker because he donates the bulk of his tournament winnings to charity, including several million dollars to an organization called

Children Inc. A mathematician, it's often said in the poker world that he made a fortune in the computer industry before becoming a poker pro, but this is not true; his considerable wealth and the fabulous house on the ocean in Rancho Palos Verdes in California come from poker. Between 2000 and 2005 he won over $20 million playing poker, probably more than anyone else on the planet during that period. As well as playing in the big game in Vegas, he is a regular in Larry Flynt's game at the Hustler casino in Los Angeles. For years he was involved with a leading woman player, Mimi Tran, the deal being that he would teach her to be a better player while she taught him Vietnamese. He is, at the time of writing, now accompanied everywhere by another young woman player. He made a lot of friends in poker when in his book, *Aces in the Hole*, he stressed the importance of sex as a way of relaxing before a big game. Many a young gun has quoted it while pressing his case in a Las Vegas nightclub late at night . . .

Alongside Greenstein are the young guns, the twenty-first-century stars. The young black guy, often called the Tiger Woods of poker, that is *Phil Ivey*, one of the few top players to have emerged from the card rooms of Atlantic City, where he began playing with a fake ID when he was eighteen. He used the name Jerome. When he reached twenty-one, he walked into the poker room at the Tropicana and announced his name was really Phil. He first came to the World Series that year and made two final tables and won a gold bracelet. Later, in 2002, he won three gold bracelets in one year. He is another with an impressive strike rate in tournaments but who prefers high-stakes cash games. No one is more respected by Brunson and the other veterans for his skill, or by the poker world as a whole for the way he handles himself. He plays seventy to ninety hours of poker a week and is famous for his expressionless stare. He's a big, big winner . . . but he has to be—he finds it difficult to pass a craps table (he once lost $1 million in one session) and rivals the great Brunson himself when it comes to betting on golf.

His neighbor at the table is *Gus Hansen*, previously a top backgammon player. He made the big time when he won three *World Poker Tour* events in quick succession. His latest big win has been the 2007 Aussie Millions. One of the more aggressive players, capable of playing any two cards, he built up a substantial bankroll by founding an online poker site and then selling it two years later. Utterly fearless, he tends to either win big or lose big in the Bellagio game: there appears to be no room for compromise. He has admitted to losing over a million dollars in a night in Bobby's Room. In 2006 he won a monster $575,000 pot in a televised high-stakes game when he landed four-of-a-kind to Daniel Negreanu's full house.

Daniel Negreanu is, in fact, sitting next to him. A slim, young Canadian with a ready smile, he is a poker superstar, in fact the 2004 Player of the Year. He is one of the most popular of the young guns, an immensely likeable and talented thirty-three-year-old with tournament winnings of more than $10 million and three World Series gold bracelets. For a while the Wynn casino hired him as its resident star. While there he offered to play anyone at any game, heads-up for $500,000. Responsible for a prolific outpouring of poker columns and online activity, his advice and opinions are always worthwhile. He describes himself as "a poker fan first and a player second" and gives a lot back to the game.

There are some regulars missing tonight, including *Todd Brunson*, son of Doyle, bearded, burly, former boyfriend of Jennifer Harman and a man who becomes distinctly prickly if you mention his father, not because they don't get along but because he wants to be recognized as a star performer in his own right. He once said, "I'm the Rodney Dangerfield of poker—I get no respect." Actually he does—at least in the big game. They know from experience that as well as winning 12 tournaments, including a World Series event, he has become as competitive a high-stakes cash-game player as anyone around.

Also missing is *Eli Elezra*, a former Israeli commando who has made a fortune in business and plays poker in the big game as—would you believe it?—a hobby. Even so, he is good enough to have won the *World Poker Tour* title and $1 million prize in 2004. *Patrik Antonius*, from Finland, the youngest of the regulars in the big game, is also absent tonight. He made his name as a high-stakes player online, usually playing $200–$400 no-limit. He took Europe by storm in 2005, when he won the Scandinavian Open and a European Poker Tour event in Baden-Baden and came third in a similar event in Barcelona. What is extraordinary about the Baden-Baden event is that he arrived five hours late and half his chips had been blinded away. He ended that year with a $1 million second place in a *World Poker Tour* event in Las Vegas, where he now lives. In 2006 he cashed five times at the World Series.

The only other regular I know of who is missing tonight is former pool hustler *John Hennigan*. Another low-profile operator, he has won nearly $3 million in tournaments, including two World Series bracelets, but is primarily a cash-game player.

Every one of these players is world class. They have to be. A bad decision can cost $100,000 . . . a bad night over a million.

And what is extraordinary about them—*really extraordinary*—is that they all look as if they're having a good time.

Who is losing in there? Who is down $300,000 . . . or $500,000 . . . or even a million?

There's no telling.

As I keep half an eye on my own dwindling pile of chips on the $5–$10 table and watch Brunson, Reese, and the others chatting and laughing and tossing $10,000 chips into the pot, I wonder whether these players with their own room and their pictures on the wall are the highest stakes players of all time.

I decide to investigate.

The size of a bet is, of course, relative. For some recreational players, $10 bets mean they're playing for high stakes. In the history of poker some have made bets for stakes that, in terms of their importance to the "other life" of the player, are worth more than money. Cowboy Wolford, the famed rodeo star as well as poker player, once lost his priceless horse in a poker game (he won another horse in a game the following day). One man tabled his false teeth, only to lose the hand—exactly what value they were to the winner I do not know, but he took them anyway . . . after all, poker is poker and a win is a win.

Herbert O. Yardley described some of the dramas that occurred during poker games at his haunt, Monty's Place in Indiana:

> I saw . . . a poor weather-beaten corn farmer bet the last of his farm . . . only to die three minutes later, his cards clutched in his hands—a winner.
>
> I saw . . . a travelling shoe salesman lose 10 trunks of shoes . . . a bank teller trapped with marked money he had stolen from the bank . . .
>
> Horses, cattle, hogs, wagons, buggies—all sold to play poker.[1]

I am still unable to work out whether the stories of Eugene Edwards are true or a figment of his (or others') imagination, but, if they are true, no one could have played for higher stakes than a German hotel keeper called Stein, who was married to a flirtatious woman called Lena. When travelling professional poker player Dick Bradley came to town and established a liaison with Lena, Stein, who had to this point been relatively tolerant of her flirtations, finally lost patience and burst into the card room where Bradley was playing. At this point Edwards takes up the story:

"Look here, Bradley," Stein said in his broken English, "I must settle things with you. I have talked over things with my wife, Lena, already, and she says she will go away with you. If she goes this world is no good to me anymore, and you and I must settle if she goes or if she stays. I would kill you, but I'm not a fighting man and you always carry a gun. Now, what shall we do?"

To Bradley, the answer was obvious: a game of poker. He would put up $1,000 and Stein would put up Lena.

Edwards claims Stein said, "No, I will not play my wife against your money, but I will play you a freeze-out for $1,000, my money against yours, and if you lose, you will go away. And if I lose, I will go away, and she may do what she likes."

Watched closely by the other players to ensure that Bradley, who was, when all is said and done, a professional card sharp, was not cheating, the two began to play.

After about 20 minutes Bradley tabled a flush only to find himself staring at Stein's full house. There was a moment's silence and then Bradley said . . . "Well, I've lost, and I'll leave town on the morning train. That'll do, I suppose, won't it?"

"Yes, that'll do," said Stein gravely.

Bradley did take the morning train, but Lena followed a day or two later. Stein drank himself to death.[2]

Now that's high-stakes poker.

But if money is to be the deciding factor, then where better to start than Nick the Greek? Nicholas Dandolos was born in a small village in Crete. His father made carpets. His biographer, Cy Rice, described the locals as "scratching out a living from the rocky soil and raising small herds of goats and sheep. In some of the neighboring houses livestock occupied the first floor of a dirt-floored dwelling, the people living on the second."[3] I went there in the spring of 2007, hoping to find some trace of Nick. The place had not changed that much, but no one I met had heard of him.

But then Nick was not destined to be a peasant; he had gamble in him, and a lot of it. He travelled to America when he was eighteen and in an amazingly short time had a nationwide reputation for betting for high stakes. He won and lost huge sums over a period of forty years. Unusually, his reputation was based on the stakes he played for, not his winnings. He did, of course, pull off some spectacular wins—but he suffered some equally spectacular setbacks. Apart from poker, he once lost $1,600,000 in twelve days in a New York floating craps game. Stud poker was the game he played best and he's said to have won over $6 million at it . . . including $550,000 from one game in Hot Springs, Arkansas.

Cy Rice tells a story that sums Nick up. He was playing in Hot Springs and patiently ignoring the insults of a local lawyer. When he had won forty-five of fifty hands and broken the loudmouth, Nick stood up to leave. The lawyer called after him: "Hey, Greek . . . do you always run away as soon as you win a score?"

Rice writes:

The room grew deathly quiet. No one moved. Nick wheeled, headed for the table, his eyes fastened on the lawyer, who half rose from his chair, not knowing what to expect. Nick picked up the deck of cards, riffled the pack eight times, cut twice, and spread them face down in front of the lawyer.

"Pull one," he said, "high card wins $500,000."

Silently the lawyer settled into his seat. The only sound in the room was breathing . . . the lawyer's face, drained of color, was ghost-white. His entire body seemed frozen stiff, his eyes abnormally dilated, staring agonizingly at the cards.

When it became obvious the lawyer was in some sort of trauma, Nick walked away.[4]

A clash between him and the equally famous Arnold Rothstein was inevitable. The two men were in many ways poles apart. Gambler he may have been, but Nick was a gentleman, always well dressed, generous, a man of honor. And gambling was all he did. Rothstein lacked the same class and would do whatever he had to do to make money: he was involved in casinos, horse racing, real estate, show business—you name it. According to Rice, they once had this conversation:

> Nick: "Arnold, the basic difference in our gambling is that you gamble for greed and I gamble for thrills."
>
> Rothstein: "But you can't eat thrills."
>
> Nick: "True, but neither can you replace them with anything."

When they eventually met in a game of five-card stud, they ended up in a pot of $797,000, and Rothstein won it with a diamond flush.

Despite that setback Nick was undisputed king of the gambling world from 1920 through the '50s, often backed by syndicates with faith in his talents. Then he suffered another crushing blow at poker, losing $550,000 over fifteen daily sessions of two-handed lowball played at the Thunderbird in Las Vegas. He never fully recovered from that and later complained he had been cheated. He went downhill from there, ending up broke, borrowing and playing in small-limit games in Gardena. He played his last game there in 1966. It's said that he was bluffed out of a pot by a little old lady and rose and said, "Goodnight . . . it's time I quit." He died shortly after, on Christmas Day. He was eighty-three.

For the past thirty-five years or so the place to turn to for seriously high-stakes poker has been the big game in Las Vegas. This may have been played in various card rooms and by a changing list of players, but it has its constants, one of them, of course, being Doyle Brunson.

There were—and still are—rumors about the whole Las Vegas poker scene in its earlier days. It is said there was cheating. Former World Series director Eric Drache, who was a key mover and shaker in poker in Las Vegas for many years, says that the cheating has been exaggerated, but he admits it was there. Apart from what he calls the "petty larceny" of dealers stealing from the pot, he says there were known cheats playing in the cash games, but there was no conspiracy by the well-known players in the big game to cheat the producers they attracted. Drache says that the worst they would do is observe someone cheating and not speak up—there was apparently an extraordinary code that, if you identified a cheat, you would respect his "rights" and either quietly tell him to move on or alternatively vacate the game yourself.

There were also rumors about collusion between some of the bigger names. Undoubtedly some of the regulars, including Doyle Brunson, Billy Baxter, and Chip Reese, played off the same bankroll, but, as in Texas, there was never evidence that Brunson and partners colluded to win hands. If they colluded, it was in attracting the producers to the game, often big casino or hotel owners, or men playing with proceeds from crime. (Often the producers needed no enticing: they would press for a game, build it around themselves.) The skills of the big-game regulars in those days went beyond card play—they included the ability to boost egos, charm the outsiders, and persuade them that even when they were losing a fortune they were still good players and were having a good time.

The big-game regulars would argue that they could count on beating a producer with their experience and skill—they didn't have to cheat. But there is no doubt they *would* connive: first, if a producer developed too much skill at one form of poker, the group would switch the game. One of their

strengths was their versatility. They could play them all—
hold'em, stud, draw, razz, low ball, and so on. While switching the game represented a conspiracy to disadvantage the
producer, it was not, strictly speaking, cheating. After all,
the producer knew he was playing the best in the business—
that is what excited him about playing. And he did not have
to play a particular game. (Incidentally one victim of this
strategy was, of all people, Johnny Moss; he remained a top-
class hold'em player but was enticed into a lot of games he
was less skilled at and lost consistently.)

Also the producer was often disadvantaged because he had
not learned to play Las Vegas-style high-stakes poker. In this,
patience was not a virtue. The antes and blinds were so high
that players just could not sit there and wait for a premium
hand. If they did, they could lose a fortune without playing
their cards and, of course, when they entered a pot everyone
immediately folded. The big-game group shared a crucial
skill—the ability to win a hand without having winning cards.
It was power play that was often beyond the outsider's experience. It was ruthless. But it was not cheating.

In the earlier days of the big game in Las Vegas one of the big
producers was the drug dealer Jimmy Chagra. By the time he
came to town, he knew he was headed for trial and prison so
he didn't care how much he lost. Brunson, Pearson, Baxter,
Straus, and company feasted on this fish. Billy Baxter has described winning $100,000 in one game with Chagra (worth
near a million today). Chagra, who would make crazy blind
bets—sometimes as much as $20,000—also lost substantial
sums playing golf. Baxter says, "He owed me some money
from golf and he asked me to call at his house to collect it. It
was clear to me he was hoping to hustle me out of it in some
way and, sure enough, he had a pool table in his living room
and asked for a chance to get even. Well, you wouldn't believe

it—he didn't know what he was doing at that either. I won $350,000 off him before he gave up."

Doyle Brunson was once asked what was the most he ever won in one session of poker and he replied $770,000. Asked who it was from, he replied, "It was back in the late '60s and early '70s. There were some drug dealers in town who were throwing money around like crazy . . . and some of the hotel owners back in the early days of Las Vegas, they all played poker." It's not unreasonable to assume that either Chagra or Major Riddle (about whom more later) was the big loser on that occasion—quite likely they were both in the game. (Incidentally the judge in the Chagra case was murdered by Charles Harrelson while Chagra was playing in a game with Brunson and Drache at the Silverbird. "The only thing we knew for sure was that Chagra didn't shoot him," Drache said later. [Harrelson died in prison in 2007.])

Another high-stakes player of that era was a multimillionaire who came from Paris to play. He was known to the others in the big game as the Frenchman. He would play in two spells, one in the early hours of the morning and one in the afternoon. The poker writer Peter Alson witnessed him playing thus over five days with Johnny Chan and described him as wearing a charcoal suit and bearing a striking resemblance to Yves Montand. The Frenchman, he said, was driven by ego; he believed he could beat Chan and the others in the game—including Brunson and Reese. At times there was nearly $1 million in cash and chips on the table. For two or three days the Frenchman won, but Chan eventually prevailed, winning $250,000. One time the big-game group actually went to Paris to play him. This was a mistake. They lost.

Brunson, Reese, and company were not always the winners. In the early 1990s a Greek called Archie Karas came to Las Vegas. He demolished Bobby Baldwin at both pool and poker and then became involved in a big heads-up game with Chip

Reese. They played razz and seven-card stud and Reese was reported as losing over $2 million. Stu Ungar then took him on and lost $900,000. Doyle Brunson had a go and at least broke even. The only man to beat Karas, at least while he was on this winning streak, was Johnny Chan—after losing to him three times. Altogether it was reckoned, while the run lasted, that Karas won $7 million and beat fifteen world-class players.

In the late 1990s a new high-stakes poker player created a rival big game in California. He was not a professional but a recreational player, with the bankroll to do serious damage to anyone who made a mistake. This was the wheelchair-bound Larry Flynt, founder of *Hustler* magazine, subject of the film *The People vs. Larry Flynt*, and now owner of the Hustler casino in Gardena. Flynt, who will play blackjack for $15,000 a hand and in 1998 won $4 million in a session of blackjack in Las Vegas, established his own home poker game. His speciality was seven-card stud and, with a minimum buy-in of $200,000 and limits of $4,000 and $8,000, this became the biggest seven-card stud game in the world. All the top pros wanted to play in it. For some time not even Doyle Brunson and Chip Reese could talk their way in. When the Hustler casino opened, the game transferred to table 55, in the corner of the poker room, and it is still played there today. Regulars include Barry Greenstein, Ted Forrest, and Phil Ivey. Cyndy Violette (who began as a dealer in Atlantic City) is one of the few women chosen to play. Eric Drache was for a number of years Flynt's poker advisor and gate-keeper for the game; his skill was knowing just how much professional talent to have in the game and how many amateurs, to give Flynt a greater chance of winning from time to time. Not that Flynt is any slouch. Over the years he has become a top performer at seven-card stud and in 2000 he made the final table in the $5,000 buy-in event at the World Series. As recently as February 2007 he won $1.1 million in one night, probably the biggest seven-card-stud win ever.

However, the big game in Bobby's Room has established a unique position on the front line of high-stakes poker. There may be occasional bigger one-off games in other places, but this is the biggest *day-by-day* game in the world . . . the biggest regular game ever.

And the biggest one-off game? Well, now it's time to meet Andy Beal.

In March 2001 Andy Beal was forty-nine years old and immensely wealthy. He had made his first millions in real estate and, then, building on the ruins of the Savings and Loan business, he established his own bank. By the year 2000 he was making profits of over $100 million a year from the Beal Bank and other dealings. This was a man with unlimited supplies of money, but he was in no way ostentatiously wealthy; he eschewed publicity and lived relatively modestly in Dallas, Texas. What he wanted, however, was a fresh challenge, a test of his mental, mathematical, and man-management talents, and the test he chose was to take on the world's best poker players and beat them at their own game.

Encouraged by a few days in Las Vegas and by winning over $100,000 from Doyle Brunson and friends in a game, he walked into the Bellagio in March 2001 and announced he wanted to play the best, one by one, heads-up, with $20,000–$40,000 limits on bets. What was to develop from this became the biggest game in the history of poker and one that may never be equalled.

There were to be three stars of this drama. First was Beal. Second was what became known as "the Corporation"—a team, drawn mainly from the big game, led by Brunson. Third was Michael Craig.

Michael is a talkative former Chicago lawyer who, having made some money there, decided that he and his family would live better if they moved to Arizona. The town of

Scottsdale, where they settled, was also an acceptable distance from Las Vegas and Michael liked to play poker. While there he heard about the Beal game. Exactly how he succeeded is a mystery, but, one by one, Michael won over the usually secretive players, then Beal himself, to the point where he became a trusted confidant and ultimately the only one they would allow to sit at the table. In effect he became the game's official chronicler, and his book, *The Professor, the Banker and the Suicide King—Inside the Richest Poker Game of All Time*, was recognized as a classic from the day it hit the bookshelves. In fact Michael at one point became a crucial link between Beal and the players; without him the final phase of the game may never have been played. How did he pull it off? How did he persuade suspicious poker players to allow him this access? The answer is that this man is unguardedly and unquestionably honorable. Put simply, you just know he can be trusted. And trust him they did.

As with all accounts of the Beal game, what follows is based on Michael's research, supplemented by my cross-examination of him while one day we drove for six hours across the Arizona desert.

So back to March 2001, and Andy Beal was in Las Vegas looking for a high-stakes game that had to be heads-up. Beal's plan was threefold: (1) play for sums of money that, while enormous, he could easily afford, but the top pros could not (in other words, take them out of their comfort zone); (2) play in the daytime, beginning in the morning (he knew most of the pros only begin to function in late afternoon); (3) put the players who were essentially loners, and played better that way, under the pressure of being responsible to a group.

Doyle Brunson conducted the negotiations for the players, insisting that the stakes be $10,000–$20,000 and that he should put together a team, each of whom would contribute to a bankroll of $1 million. Brunson then contacted his players—nearly all were from the big game, including his old business partner Chip Reese, plus Jennifer Harman, Chau Giang, and David Grey. (Grey was a low-profile player in the big game for many years and a famous proposition gambler. He once bet Howard Lederer, who is a vegetarian, $10,000 that he wouldn't dare eat a hamburger. For that money, Lederer would! He and a partner also bet former world poker champion Huck Seed $35,000 [or thereabouts] that he couldn't play four rounds of golf in a day, without a cart, breaking one hundred each time and playing with only three clubs. Incredibly, Seed could!)

Unfortunately no one could find Ted Forrest, one of the world's best all-round players, with five World Series gold bracelets in five versions of poker and a world heads-up title. Apparently he was in Los Angeles at the time. (Ted is also a proposition gambler, taking huge bets on things like whether he could run a marathon on the hottest day of the year. He could!) Ted eventually heard there was a big game at the Bellagio and turned up to find Beal playing Reese. The rules of the card room are that if there's an empty seat, a player is entitled to take it, and Forrest, not knowing of the heads-up deal, sat down and joined in. He promptly lost $400,000 in twenty minutes but then hit form and, with Reese keeping his head down and out of the way, took Beal apart, winning over a million dollars. That night Doyle Brunson asked Forrest to join the Corporation.

The next day Beal and Ted Forrest met heads-up, with Beal insisting that the stakes be doubled. Forrest, now playing with the Corporation's bankroll, was all for this and won another $2 million, this time for the team. Jennifer Harman then took over and won a million dollars too. Now it was the turn of Howard Lederer.

Lederer was one of Brunson's first choices for the Corporation. He towers over most of the other players of his generation and not only because he's six and a half feet tall; he's an intellectual giant too, known as the Professor because of his studious approach to the game. He took up poker in New York in his late teens and, after a hard couple of years (he, for some time, cleaned a card room in return for being allowed to sleep on the couch), became a familiar face at the Mayfair Club, where he mixed with such world-class players as Dan Harrington (1995 world champion), Erik Seidel, and Jay Heimowitz. He came to the World Series for the first time in 1987 and became the youngest-ever player to make the main event final table, coming in fifth to Johnny Chan. He eventually won the first of his two gold bracelets in 2000 and then confirmed his place at the top of the game by winning two *World Poker Tour* events. He had been a top player for more than ten years when he was fielded in the Beal game. Within an hour he had won the Corporation another million dollars. Beal left town, having lost $5 million.

Did Beal conclude he was out of his depth? He did not. Within three weeks the Dallas banker was back at the Bellagio and unexpectedly chose to play in a $10,000–$20,000 side game with a table full of players. In this game he broke even, because the professionals, perhaps uncharacteristically forgetting who the fish was supposed to be, became engaged in a battle between themselves that led to even a player of Chip Reese's caliber losing $800,000. The big winner was Ted Forrest. Of him Michael Craig writes:

> Ted Forrest won $1,055,000 . . . It capped what may have been (at that time) the best month in high-stakes poker . . . Ted also won $2 million for the team against Andy Beal on March 10. With his share of the team's win, the two $1 million scores, and several other great sessions, Ted Forrest won $4.4 million at poker in March 2001, and over $6.7 million for the first three months of the year.[5]

Beal went back to Texas and returned to the Bellagio in December. He had put in a lot of homework and began well. Over four days he took a considerable sum from the Corporation stars, who now fielded Todd Brunson, who had not been part of the team to this point. Todd proceeded to lose $1 million in one hand.

In this monumental hand, both had poor pocket cards, Todd six-four and Andy Beal ten-five. The flop was ten-three-two. Todd now had an inside straight draw and Andy a pair of tens. The pot increased and Todd then picked up a five on the turn for a straight. Andy had two pairs, tens and fives. Andy bet and Todd raised, and they then launched themselves on what can only be described as a raise and re-raise frenzy. There were about twenty raises. Finally all Todd's chips were in the pot and the river card was a five, giving Andy a full house and a $1 million pot.

Altogether Andy Beal won $5.3 million in five days and it was really hurting. Some of the Corporation were running out of funds. There was panic in the ranks. According to Michael Craig, Brunson said to Beal: "Congratulations, Andy. We're broke. Go back to Texas." But Beal still had some fuel in the tank and by early Sunday morning he was playing Ted Forrest, who had the Corporation's last $1.2 million. They played $20,000–$40,000. Craig writes:

> The usual strategy for heads-up poker, especially among the pros, was to play as aggressively as possible. If an opponent showed just a bit of weakness, the aggressive pro could run all over them . . . but Beal was not backing down on this trip. That meant they were playing showdown poker for a couple of hundred thousand dollars a hand. Where did their edge in skill and experience go? When it was just aggression v. aggression it was just a coin flip who had the better cards. Beal's deeper bankroll (especially now that he had most of *their* bankroll) gave him the best of that confrontation.[6]

So Forrest decided to alter the approach and play relatively passively, allowing Andy to win more pots but using his superior skill and experience to get away from the weaker hands and win most of the big pots. Doing this he won back a staggering $3.4 million of the Corporation's money, taking their bankroll back to $4.6 million. They were still each down $200,000, but this was a fantastic fightback. Forrest, tired now, shared the strategy with Howard Lederer, who now took over and won the remainder back.

Beal eventually left Las Vegas a loser. Did that persuade him to drop the challenge? It did not. He was back at the Bellagio in April 2003. This was going to be *the* big one—starting with stakes of $30,000–$60,000. The Corporation's bankroll was to be around $10 million and the team consisted of Doyle and Todd Brunson, Jennifer Harman, Howard Lederer, Ted Forrest, Chau Giang, David Grey, Barry Greenstein, and Lyle Berman (who only played four hands and lost $900,000).

Everyone noticed that Beal had improved his game. Forrest could no longer dominate him; Lederer and Greenstein lost, too. But fortunately for the Corporation they had a star player—Jennifer Harman. On top form, three times she played Beal and three times she made a profit of $3 million . . . a stunning $9 million one-woman win. It was enough to send him back to Dallas beaten.

Did this finally convince him he could never beat the pros? It did not. With his bank's fortunes growing and no problems about a bankroll, Beal spent the summer "training" for a return and in September 2003 he was back. The deal, worked out with Doyle Brunson, was $30,000–$60,000 stakes and the Corporation could field who they wanted and change players when they wanted. But Todd Brunson and Jennifer Harman were out; Beal didn't want to play them.

After a few days of ups and downs Beal became determined to discomfort the professionals; he began a campaign for $50,000–$100,000 stakes and $10 million to be tabled by each side, winner takes all. This was undoubtedly the highest-stakes poker game in history. As part of the deal, Jennifer Harman was back in, but she lost $3 million and Todd Brunson $1 million, and once more the Corporation started to panic. None of them were poverty stricken, but $10 million would hurt like hell. They all now knew that Beal had come back to the Bellagio a competitor of real quality, with the confidence of knowing that the $10 million was only 4 percent of his bank's profits that year. It was at this point that Todd Brunson proved beyond a shadow of a doubt that he was a player equal to his famous father. Over two days he won the Corporation's money back and pounded Beal, hand after hand, until he had won all of Beal's $10 million.

Was Beal at last a beaten man? No, he was not. Back he came in May 2004. Gus Hansen and Phil Ivey joined the Corporation team, which didn't look at all happy when Chau Giang lost $1.3 million on the opening day but were greatly relieved to see Lederer back on form the next. He won $6.3 million to put the Corporation $5 million ahead. And then Beal insisted on the stakes being raised to $50,000–$100,000. Each side had to put up $10 million and Beal insisted that Howard Lederer be excluded. He knew that in the Professor he had met his match. One man he was not afraid of was the highly respected Chip Reese, and Beal now proceeded to win over $8 million from him to put himself back in front. Gus Hansen lost some more, and a desperate Corporation called in Jennifer Harman, who was seriously ill. Even so she won back $5 million in half an hour.

The pace was now frantic, the stakes incredibly high, the pressure on the professionals intense. For Beal this was not about money, this was just about winning. The stakes reached $100,000–$200,000. By now he had succeeded in his objective— the pros were out of their comfort zone. He proceeded to win a staggering $11.7 million in one day, making a profit for the four days of nearly $6 million. The world's top professionals—for the first time knowing real fear at the poker table—had lost $300,000 each.

At last Beal knew that on his day he could beat them all. This was the time to drop it, honor satisfied. Did he do this? He did not. He was back within a matter of days. It was a mistake, especially as, full of confidence, he did not insist that Todd Brunson and Howard Lederer be kept out of the game. On the first day, with the stakes at $30,000–$60,000, Brunson won $5 million; on the second day Lederer won $9.3 million. Beal lost every dollar he had previously won. He announced he had had enough. He was finished—forever.

So it was over? No, it was not. Some 619 days later he was back. In February 2006 he lost $3.2 million in five days playing $50,000–$100,000 and then hit an incredible run of form, winning $10 million in four days, the Corporation's entire bankroll. Once more, they were hurting. Had Andy Beal left then, satisfied that he had proved his point, having shown that he could beat the best, what a story he would have had to tell. But as Michael Craig wrote in a magazine article:

At 12:32 Andy Beal had won the last of his opponents' $10 million. By 12:45 I knew he was destined to lose it back . . . If Andy had been trying to "get poker out of his system" or "prove to himself" that he could play with the best in the world, this convincing four-day win gave him the opportunity for closure. But when he offered to follow the pros to LA, where they had a World Poker Tour event starting the next day, I knew the game had to go on until he lost enough money to become disgusted with poker.

The Corporation had an asset they had only briefly employed to date: Phil Ivey. He had not performed outstandingly well in the 2004 encounters, but he now came to the game in a highly aggressive mood, raising every hand on the button, keeping Beal under immense pressure, drawing him into huge million-dollar pots. Finally he broke the banker, winning the last $4 million in twenty-seven minutes. Beal had lost the whole $10 million he had won from the Corporation and more.

After more than 5,000 hands over twelve days of play, he rose, shook Ivey's hand, and said, "Good job, Phil. I'm heading back to Dallas."

And so far that is where he has stayed.

The game between Beal and the Corporation was the biggest ever in terms of the money that at one time or another was actually on the table; Michael Craig estimated that in one five-day spell alone they contested pots totalling $600 million. But did Beal suffer the biggest loss ever?

More likely that honor goes to Major Riddle, one-time majority shareholder of the Dunes hotel and casino. Riddle (Major was his name, not a military rank), a well-groomed, immaculately dressed man with equally impeccable manners, loved to play poker, especially deuce to the seven low ball, a form of draw poker where the lowest hand wins, and he loved to play with the best; his problem was that he was not in their league. In the 1960s he was the fish at (or on) the table and all who were there admit to devouring him, bones and all. Doyle Brunson was at the feast, as was Billy Baxter. "We did a good job on him," Baxter tells me. Crandell Addington was there, too.

Poor old Major Riddle didn't stand a chance. Once he lost for thirty days in a row. Yet he wasn't a fool; he knew he was being beaten and just didn't seem to care. Once when he was called to a board meeting while playing, he begged the others to wait for him to come back—so that he could lose some more. Some asked whether he was being cheated, as night after night he lost a fortune. But the players say there was no need for that; Riddle was just a bad player. One who spotted a tell was Billy Baxter, who says, "If he had a bad hand, he'd toss his chips in—just kinda flip them. If he found himself with a good hand, he would place his bet on the table. And if he drew a face card, he would look at it and look at it."

No one knows exactly how much Riddle lost. The lowest estimate I've been given is $40 million, but Crandell Addington puts it much higher. Whatever, no one involved denies it was a colossal sum, probably over $100 million in today's terms, forcing Riddle to sell his ownership-share in the Dunes.

There was a difference between Andy Beal and Major Riddle.

Beal had his winning days. And eventually he lost all he wanted to lose. He remains a billionaire.

Riddle just lost and lost until he lost it all. He died virtually broke.

Major Riddle was probably the greatest poker loser of all time.

The fourth age of poker

The twenty-first-century phenomenon

ten

Poker takes off
Card rooms in cyberspace

Mike Sexton has seen many of his peers temporarily wiped out by sports betting at one time or another. So, when he hit a bad patch and went broke himself just before Christmas 2000, he wasn't too downhearted. After all, he had been a winning poker player for thirty years, two-thirds of them in Las Vegas. He had a World Series gold bracelet. He knew that he could re-build his fortunes at the table.

Not that it would be easy. As he says, "Poker can be a hard game when you *need* to win, because then you're not just *play-ing* poker, you're working. It's always when you *need* to win that the worst bad beats seem to come. That's why to live by playing poker . . . Well, it's tough . . . you have to really love the game."

And Mike Sexton does. In fact, he's a romantic about it.

He also loved gymnastics when he was a kid in Dayton, Ohio, in the 1960s—and won a sports scholarship to college. He loved ballroom dancing—and became a professional teacher. He loved baseball—and became a popular coach of junior league teams.

But poker became a passion. He began playing as a thirteen-year-old. That's when he learned about going broke. He lost every week to a friend called Danny Robison, who was two years older.

"I would come home on Fridays with my paper-route money and he would be waiting for me on the porch. He would shuffle the cards and beat me out of every cent I had earned. That happened to me every Friday. I would come in with my head down and my mother would scold me and tell me not to play Danny, that he was better than me . . . And the next Friday, there he would be, and it would happen all over.

"Then I went to college and played other students and found I was way better than anyone else. I began to think that the kid I had been playing in Dayton was exceptional, and it turned out that so he was—he became one of the best players in the world." (Before he succumbed to drink and drugs, Danny was considered by many to be the best seven-card-stud player in the world. Like Bobby Hoff, he now plays mostly at the Commerce in Los Angeles.)

After a spell in the army, Mike found himself in North Carolina and ran a home game there, and when he travelled to Las Vegas for the World Series he stayed with Reese and Robison. He was persuaded by them, and by the action there, to move to Las Vegas in 1985 and over two decades effortlessly established himself at the heart of the professional game. His sunny disposition, generosity, and impeccable manners at the table made him one of the most popular and trusted players in town. And he had time for everybody. He stuck by and, from time to time, rescued Stu Ungar when drugs drove him into the sewer . . . Often he was the only man there for him when others turned their backs.

If I had been disposed to have a chapter in this book entitled "The Godfather—Part III," then Mike would have been the man, because his meteoric rise from that low point at Christmas 2000 to become the multimillionaire of worldwide fame he is today has relevance far beyond him alone; it both explains and epitomizes the poker revolution of the twenty-first century.

Mike had always been a bit of a visionary; he would often talk of poker's potential to become hugely popular—an "industry." Someone must have been listening, because just at the moment in 2000 when even poker was closing down for the festivities, he was contacted by a San Francisco lawyer named Ruth Parasol. This attractive woman in her thirties had made a small fortune in the *un*attractive business of processing money for online porn sites. She had also co-founded an online gaming company, later to become Party Gaming. She and her partners were minded to launch a poker site and needed someone to teach the game to the software guys in India. She asked Mike Sexton if he would do it. He needed the money and he needed a change—so within seven days, by New Year 2001, he was at work in a steamy, overcrowded office in Hyderabad, the center of a flourishing IT industry, known as the Silicon Valley of India.

After helping create the poker software in India, he went to the Dominican Republic to work with the customer support team assembled there. By now, Mike, being Mike, was fully engaged. He began to influence the key decisions. It was he who insisted the site be called *Party Poker* when everyone else preferred other names. It was he who had the idea of launching it with satellites for a *Party Poker* Million, the final to be played on a poker cruise. And it was he who urged the team to do what had never been done before, and advertise poker on television.

All three of these decisions proved crucial: *Party Poker* became an immediate success, quickly overhauling the two poker sites already out there, *Paradise Poker* and *Planet Poker*. Party Gaming eventually floated on the London Stock Exchange for *$9 billion*. Mike's small percentage of the company was now worth many millions. (Actually, for technical reasons, Mike was persuaded to sell back his share in the company before the flotation but on a deal that set him up for life.)

Nor did the rise and rise of Mike Sexton end there. He was now on a roll.

While Mike had been in limbo before Christmas 2000, a filmmaker called Steve Lipscomb was developing a plan for a television series built around a number of major $10,000-entry tournaments. His idea was that the players would buy their own way in, or qualify via online satellites, so there would be no fees for him to pay; instead, the stars of the show would be paying to appear. The venues would come free, too; top card rooms across America, from Foxwoods in Connecticut to the Commerce in Los Angeles, would be persuaded to host the events for the television publicity. As for television viewers, Lipscomb believed millions would be drawn to the game because of the specially designed cameras that would enable them to see the players' pocket cards and thus become fully immersed in the decision making and the drama of each hand.

In 2001, he took the idea to Lyle Berman—he of the Bobby's Room crowd—who liked it. Over dinner in a steakhouse, Berman offered to share the deal with Jack Binion, Doyle Brunson, and Chip Reese, all of whom turned it down, a response that cost each of them a fortune.

One decision remained: who was to present it and become, in effect, the face of poker?

They chose Mike Sexton.

World Poker Tour was launched in 2003 and, like the website *Party Poker*, it was an immediate success, quickly building an audience of over 25 million and becoming the Travel Channel's most popular program.

Now, Mike was everywhere. He was fronting a television series that, with constant repeats, was shown all over the world. He was starring in the *Party Poker* commercials. He was producing countless magazine articles. He was publishing a book. And he was playing in some of the other emerging television shows, including *Poker Superstars*. His peers presented him with an Ambassador of Poker award; it was well deserved because while he no longer had a bankroll problem, in other respects he hadn't changed. He was, and still is, accessible, modest, and generous. Typically, when he won a major event on the eve of the 2006 World Series, he handed half of his million-dollar prize money to charity.

But it was not only Mike who was thriving; so was poker. After a century and a half in the shadows, the game of the cowboy, the riverboat card mechanic, and the Texan road gambler was being exposed to the sun and flourishing in its light; in just over five years, it has become the fastest-growing recreational activity on earth. The explosion in its popularity is a twenty-first-century phenomenon.

Between that fateful Christmas 2000 and the World Series in mid-summer 2007, the numbers playing regularly have increased to an estimated 80 million worldwide; their spending on Internet poker alone has reached $100 million *a day* . . . that's *$36,500,000,000 a year*. And no one believes it will stop there. Poker has, as Mike Sexton foresaw, become an "industry," its irrepressible growth fueled by the interaction between the two overwhelming cultural influences of our time, television and the Internet.

With *World Poker Tour* in the US and *Late Night Poker* in Britain proving surprise hits, others have quickly followed, including *Ultimate Poker Challenge* and *High Stakes Poker*, with ESPN providing extensive coverage of the World Series of Poker. It is now not unusual for late-night viewers on both sides of the Atlantic to have a choice of four or five competing poker programs, screened simultaneously. The UK has two poker channels, *Poker Zone* and *The Poker Channel*. *World Poker Tour* has been followed by *European Poker Tour*, well developed by a former Poker Million winner, John Duthie, and this in turn has been televised across Europe. As the popular British publication *Time Out* enthused: "Few would have guessed that poker could be so entertaining . . . Viewers become mesmerized by the subtlety of the game and the intensity of the players."

Like the cast of characters of a vast television epic, the top players have come out from their previously private world to become stars, each finding their place in the show, their once-secret skills now admired by millions, their earning capacity now beyond their wildest dreams. It could have been constructed as a sweeping western series, *Bonanza Reborn*, with Doyle Brunson as the patriarchal head; T. J. Cloutier, Billy Baxter, and Chip Reese as rival ranchers; Mike Sexton, Eric Seidel, Johnny Chan, and Dan Harrington as their trusted foremen; Phil Ivey, Phil Hellmuth, Gus Hansen, and Daniel Negreanu as the "young guns"; and Jennifer Harman, Cyndy Violette, Annie Duke, and Kathy Liebert keeping the men's pulses racing in the gaming saloons.

Some players, like Phil Hellmuth, have become one-man industries, commentating and writing magazine articles, producing books and DVDs, selling posters and caps, and even organizing instructional "boot camps."

But television has done much more than create stars; it has, with the help of the Internet, drawn millions of new players into the game . . . by switching their focus from the television screen to the computer screen, they can play poker online, in their own home, any time of the day or night. Card playing in cyberspace has taken off and the battle for the loyalty of players has become as fierce as the battle between television companies for viewers.

Party Poker's main competitor, *Poker Stars*, has been greatly assisted by Chris Moneymaker and Greg Raymer winning the World Series main event in successive years after qualifying on its site; when the 2005 winner Joe Hatchem also signed up for *Poker Stars* the site could legitimately describe itself as "the home of champions." *Ultimate Bet* has fielded Hellmuth and top female player Annie Duke in its publicity; *Full Tilt*, launched by a number of the top television poker pros, including Howard Lederer, Chris Ferguson, Andy Bloch, and Phil Ivey, has spent vast sums on advertising; *Doyle's Room* has leaned heavily on the bulldog face of the one and only Brunson. And these are just a few of the scores of online sites that have been competing for players.

As poker sites have proliferated, the top European bookmakers have joined the action, with *Ladbrokespoker.com* emerging as the front-runner, helped by its annual Poker Million, its Poker Cruise, and its participation in the World Series, with one hundred on-site qualifiers called Team Ladbrokes.

A whole industry has developed around these online poker rooms. An array of full-color poker magazines has been launched, funded by the sites' advertising. The number of poker books has increased tenfold: Howard Schwartz, boss of the renowned Gambler's Book Shop, says that at the beginning of the 1980s he had thirty poker books on sale; he now has over 300 titles, a third of them on Texas hold'em, and many of these specifically about the subtleties of online play. Additionally, there are now thousands of other websites providing opportunities for communication, education, and information on the game. It is no coincidence that the latest James Bond film, *Casino Royale*, centers on a poker game, and a number of other poker films are in production, including bio-movies on the lives of Phil Hellmuth and Amarillo Slim.

Tournaments have transformed poker, making it more like a highly competitive sport. Players love them because they are great value: the fixed buy-in controls how much they can lose, and this relatively small outlay provides hours of competitive poker and the chance to win big money. They are also enjoyable social events that have helped to create local, national, and international poker "communities."

Poker players now criss-cross the globe to play in million-dollar-plus events. In 2005, the World Series main event was won for the first time by an Australian, the likeable Joe Hatchem, and in 2007 the Aussie Million event was won by Gus Hansen, the Dane who plays mainly in America. Two of the better-known British stars, Dave "Devilfish" Ulliott and

John Gale, have won both World Series and World Poker Tour gold bracelets. Poker has developed its own global village. It has become particularly popular in Scandinavia. As the young have discovered this alternative to drink and sex as a way of whiling away the twenty-four-hour winter nights, groups of Scandinavians have descended upon events all over Europe, as popular for their enthusiasm as they are feared for their aggression and skill.

As the live tournaments have become larger, they have generated prize money beyond the older pros' wildest dreams; one tournament win can be a life-changing event. But how many can afford buy-ins of $10,000, or even more, for the really major events? This is where the online poker rooms really score, attracting players by offering relatively inexpensive satellites to live tournaments. And, of course, the real importance of Chris Moneymaker is that he proved their value—all over the world, young players told themselves, "If he can do it, I can do it."

The Moneymaker effect and the dramatic growth in the game is reflected in the way entries in the main event at the World Series have increased:

2000—512 entries
2003—839 entries (Moneymaker's year)
2004—2,576 entries
2005—5,619 entries

All this reached a peak in 2006 when the main event at the World Series attracted 8,773 players, at least 75 percent of them online qualifiers. The prize pool was just short of $90 million.

But it is not only the number of players that has changed; it is also their nature.

There has been a changing of the guard.

A few old hands, led by Doyle Brunson and T. J. Cloutier, are still there, but the game's leadership has passed to a new generation. One can argue over exactly when this occurred, but I believe that (apart from 1989, when Phil Hellmuth became the youngest champion ever at twenty-four and laid down a marker for what was to follow) the key year was 2000, when Chris Jesus Ferguson beat T. J. Cloutier in the heads-up of the World Series main event. It was perhaps the last great clash of the poker generations and the younger won.

The changing face of poker was further confirmed in 2003, the year the World Poker Tour arrived, making stars out of even younger players such as Hansen, Ivey, and Negreanu.

The older guys were still around, still popular, still influential, still making money in cash games and every once in a while still winning a noteworthy event, but the truth is they were rarely at the final table any more. Poker was in new and brilliant hands.

Some of the characters now emerging would match any of the colorful personalities of the game's past.

Three of them have been described as "the mad, the bad, and the ugly."

Actually, *Chris Jesus Ferguson* is not mad, just eccentric. He is so named because, with his pale face, shoulder-length hair and beard, he personifies the popular image of Christ. It has to be said, however, that the Messiah was never pictured wearing a black Stetson and wraparound shades. He is a devotee of swing dancing and has also developed a talent for throwing cards so fast they can cut an apple in half. All this helps to cover up the fact that he has a brilliant brain. The son of an academic who lectures on games theory, Chris has a PhD in computer science. He developed his own poker software to explore strategies and applies sophisticated mathematical calculations to his game. All of these are contained in a series of black folders; he doesn't have to worry about security—Andy Bloch is probably the only other poker star who would understand them (the two of them created the software used by the *Full Tilt* site). Anyway, it all works: after winning the World Series main event in 2000, he was twice runner-up in the World Heads-Up Championship, losing to Phil Hellmuth and Ted Forrest in successive years, and his winnings in live events now exceed $6 million.

If Chris is not really mad, then Men *"The Master" Nguyen* is not really bad . . . there are just a few rumors, but I'll come to that. Men was one of the Vietnamese boat people, escaping with eighty-seven others, spending five days at sea with only handfuls of rice and sips of water to sustain them until they eventually reached freedom in Malaysia. From there, he travelled to the US, where he was given political asylum, worked in a tool-manufacturing factory, and married, becoming the father of eight children. Amazingly, three of his daughters were born on the same day, December 22, but in separate years. He became known for the school of players—a cartel—all Vietnamese, who have achieved considerable success. He is their hero, their leader, their master—hence his nickname, Men "The Master." He lays down the rules and he takes 50 percent of their winnings. It is about this group that rumors of collusion surface from time to time. They have never been confirmed and Men denies them, but the question mark always seems to be there. Undoubtedly, he does not need the extra money; he is a phenomenal poker player. He has been *Card Player* magazine's Player of the Year four times, has cashed 120 times in major events and has won more than seventy-five tournaments. He has five World Series gold bracelets. And, to balance the suspicions, it is worth noting that he has been quietly donating to projects in Vietnam. He has raised the funds to build two schools there.

Chris may not be mad and Men may not be bad, but *Mike "The Mouth" Matusow* really *can* turn ugly. He's called "The Mouth" because of his constant trashing of the other players. He is frequently suspended during major events for swearing at the table. He is at all times a disaster waiting to happen, capable of playing beautifully for days and then blowing the whole event with one catastrophic mistake. For that reason, he is also known as Mike Meltdown. That's a shame because on his day he's another great player. He has made the final table of the World Series twice—in 2001, when he came sixth to Carlos Mortensen, and in 2005, when he finished ninth out of 5,619 players, winning a million dollars. That same year he won the *World Poker Tour* Tournament of Champions and another million. (One of his biggest wins came when he didn't play; in 1998, he paid a third of Scotty Nguyen's buy-in for the World Series main event and scooped a third of the million-dollar prize money when Nguyen won.) After some wild years under the influence of drugs, Matusow was arrested at his house in Henderson, Nevada, in September 2003 and charged with "selling and trafficking controlled substances." While he swears to this day it was a set-up, he spent eight months in prison. Phil Hellmuth loaned him $5,000 so that he could return to the poker table. Now a member of the *Full Tilt* team, he is always a force to be reckoned with—and possibly, just possibly, is beginning to get himself under the kind of control necessary to win a World Series. Then again . . .

Two others who bridge the gap between the veterans and the younger whiz kids both played with Howard Lederer at New York's famous Mayfair Club.

Erik Seidel, a tall, slightly gawky figure, especially when wearing his *Full Tilt* jersey, achieved notoriety beyond poker because the hand he lost to Johnny Chan in the heads-up of the 1988 World Series main event was shown in the film *Rounders*. A former New York trader who was wiped out in the October 1987 stock market crash, he became a backgammon professional and then a winning poker player. He went on from the Mayfair to Vegas, and seven WSOP bracelets and winnings of $6 million.

Dan Harrington, now in his sixties but still a serious contender, is instantly recognizable in the poker world by his green Boston Red Sox cap. Dan has been a champion at both backgammon and chess and, despite his nickname, "Action Dan," is a conservative, thoughtful player. He won the World Series main event and a million dollars in 1995, and went on to make three main event final tables, including in consecutive years (2003, 2004), an exceptional achievement. In 1995, when he won, he proposed to all nine players on the final table that they make a deal there and then. He explained that if they all took the money they had won and invested it, they could all be rich. They all declined. Later, after some had been knocked out, he repeated the proposition. The survivors still declined. So he went on to win the whole million. Harrington has recently become a giant in the game for another reason: he has co-authored a set of three instructional books, *Harrington on Hold'em*, that have taken the poker world by storm.

A second feature of the past decade has been the emergence as top-level competitors of a number of women players. The poker room—traditional preserve of the macho male—is under attack.

Just over a hundred years back, Eugene Edwards in his book *Jackpots* felt safe to tackle a question that in today's politically correct world would have him run out of town. "Can women play poker?" he asked. And his reply, "No, they cannot."

Women, he said, were too nervous and did not have the physical strength. "There isn't one woman in 100,000 that could sit down at a poker table at eight in the evening and play until daylight broke . . . She would faint or have hysterics."

Then there was their vanity. "She would see it as a personal insult if she was reproached for being slow or making a misdeal."

He also claimed women were poor losers and, worse, they were cheats: "No one who has ever watched a woman play cards will dispute that assertion. She will renege, she will hold out cards and violate all the rules of the game, trusting to her sex to be excused."

Fortunately for him, Mr. Edwards is buried deep enough that it's unlikely even a determined and furious Annie Duke can find him!

If women still rarely feature at poker's top table, it's because they're still vastly outnumbered. When they do, they owe respect to no man. Jennifer Harman does not turn up at Bobby's Room daily to risk losing a million dollars of some man's money; her bankroll has been earned *by her*, playing poker for high stakes with the best in the world. And few men enjoy playing Annie Duke, especially her brother Howard Lederer, who, in 2004, was ruthlessly knocked out of four World Series events by his sister. As for Kathy Liebert, in 2004 she made the second-last table of the World Series main event, where she faced the writer Jim McManus, who later described her "maneuvring her $300,000 stack like some cute Vegas Rommel, blitzkrieging antes and blinds, setting us all in if we even think about drawing against her."

None of these three will even play in the ladies' gold bracelet event at the World Series. Annie Duke feels particularly strongly about it. "I think a separate women's event is so insulting to women, so insulting. It's like saying, 'We know you can't beat the boys, so we're going to give you your own events, where you have hopes of actually winning a bracelet.' We don't need that."

All three have real achievement to back them up.

Kathy Liebert won a $1 million event in 2002, Annie Duke won the $2 million Tournament of Champions in 2004, and the two of them came in seventeenth and tenth respectively in the 2000 World Series main event. Annie, who has cashed over thirty times at the World Series, was just one away from the final table that year. Even more impressively, in 2006 she came in eighty-first out of more than 8,500 competitors. As for Jennifer Harman, she is not only a big cash-game winner but has two World Series gold bracelets.

Another major coup came in the UK in 2006, when a popular woman in her early thirties, poker player, commentator, and writer *Vicky Coren*, became the first-ever winner of a European Poker Tour event, pocketing nearly a million dollars in front of a cheering crowd at her own home card room, London's famous Vic.

One of the first women to take on the top men pros—and the first to win a World Series event, in 1982—was *Vera Richmond*, wealthy daughter of Alfred Neiman of Neiman Marcus. The first woman to play in the main event was *Barbara Freer*, back in 1978. But the first woman to be accepted *by the men* as a real class act was *Betty Carey*. She played with the best in Vegas in the late '70s and early '80s, then her career ended abruptly after she became involved in a private heads-up match with a well-known casino boss. She was wiped out and claimed around town that she had been cheated. Those in the know say her complaints were justified, but it was explained to her that if she didn't shut up, serious things would happen to her. So she disappeared and was last heard of living in Wyoming.

The honor of being the first (and still the only) woman to make the World Series final table fell to *Barbara Enright* in 1995, the year Dan Harrington won. Barbara was a hairdresser from California who began playing regularly at the Monterey in Gardena. She started at the lowest possible level, $1–$2 draw poker, and worked her way up to the point where she could compete professionally and cashed five times in the World Series. She came to the 1995 final table as the crowd's favorite, and played brilliantly, but went out on a bad beat. There were five people left, and she raised the pot with a pair of eights and was surprisingly called by Brent Carter of Illinois with a six-three of diamonds; he overcame the odds to make two pair.

Another popular woman player of the 1990s was *Susie Isaacs*. It's said that she started when she was four years old in Nashville, Tennessee, by acting as a lookout while her older brothers played. She sold her comic books to enter the game and quickly proved a winner. She won a World Series ladies' seven-card-stud event two years running and altogether won over $300K at the game. She just missed the main event final table in 1998, coming in tenth.

Marsha Waggoner has cashed at the World Series thirteen times, and seventy-two times in tournaments. Marsha was born in Australia, where she worked as a blackjack and poker dealer before she started to play. She moved to the United States in the early 1970s, and in California built a reputation as a poker pro and became executive host at the Hollywood Park casino in Los Angeles. It was there she met her husband, Kenna James, another high-profile player. Their first encounter was not promising; Marsha accused him of cheating. Fortunately, he not only proved his innocence but also won her heart. She has cashed seventy-two times in tournaments and her career winnings exceed $500K. Marsha's motto is "Be nice"—and she is.

Beyond the US, the pioneer female player was Britain's *Lucy Rokach*, an aggressive Midlander who in 2003 was given a lifetime achievement award by the European poker community and has bruised more male egos than any other woman in the European game; she is still in poker's list of top ten woman money earners.

If it were not ungentlemanly, one would describe these as old-school women players. Over the past decade, they have had to make way at the top for a new and formidable generation.

Annie Duke and her brother, Howard Lederer, were raised in New Hampshire, where her father was an academic. She herself double-majored in English and psychology and was destined to become a professor, but, after five years of study, she left just four weeks before she would have qualified for her PhD, took off for Montana, and married a man who had never even been her boyfriend. To help pay their costs, she borrowed some money from Howard and began to play poker in the card rooms of Billings, Montana, and went from there to become the most successful woman player of all time.

She first entered the World Series in 1994 and placed thirteenth in her first tournament and third in her second, and then cashed in the main event, unseating Howard in the process. Her biggest win to date has been at the 2005 WSOP Tournament of Champions, an invitation-only event, where she took the $2 million first prize, beating Phil Hellmuth in a heads-up. Prior to the 2007 World Series, she had won $3.2 million in live tournaments. With Hellmuth, she is one of the front-people for Ultimatepoker.com, and with Howard does tutorials and group camps. She is an outstanding teacher. In early 2004, she took on film actor Ben Affleck as a pupil and he went on to win the California State Championship that year.

She's one of the toughest players in the game, does not suffer fools gladly, and is a woman of strong opinions who is not afraid to express them.

"I don't think your job as a poker player is to get respect from people. Your job as a poker player is to win. If that means that some people don't respect you at the table and that helps you win, then you should be happy with that . . . I don't need anybody to think I'm a good player. I really don't. I just don't care what people think of me. They can say whatever they want. I know how much money I've made . . . As a woman, one of the things you have going for you is you tend to get less respect and can use that to your advantage."

We have already met *Jennifer Harman* in Bobby's Room. The fact that she can hold her own in such company and at those stakes says it all. As a poker player, she's a natural. This was demonstrated when, in the year 2000, she won her first WSOP gold bracelet at a game she had never played before—no-limit deuce to seven lowball. Five minutes before the event, she asked Howard Lederer how the game was played—that was the only tutoring she had. She subsequently won another gold bracelet at limit hold'em in 2002. Coming into the 2007 WSOP, her tournament winnings had exceeded $1.7 million, but who knows how much she has won in cash games.

Her skills at limit hold'em are such that Doyle Brunson asked her to write the chapter in *Super System 2* on that subject.

She's extremely close to Doyle Brunson, who she describes as a second father, partly because she spent six years as a girlfriend of Todd Brunson. She's now married to Marco Traniello, who decided that if he couldn't beat her he might as well join her and is rapidly becoming a classy poker player in his own right. She operates within a circle of close friends and supporters, notably Carlos Mortensen, Erick Lindgren, and, above all, Daniel Negreanu, who she credits with being a major influence on her game.

Cyndy Violette began as a blackjack dealer in Las Vegas in the early '80s and then started to play poker. After some ups and downs, she ended up in Atlantic City and made a lot of money playing $75–$100 seven-card stud and moving on to stakes of $2,000–$4,000. A friendly looking woman with a warm smile, she is a health freak. Michael Caplan describes her playing at the final table in the 2004 World Series seven-card-stud high-low tournament and returning during the dinner break to her room at the Golden Nugget, which "she had transformed into a temple of tranquillity, complete with scented candles, cones of incense, a portrait of serene-looking Brigid, Celtic goddess of the sun, and a fridge full of health food." In one interview, she described herself as "a macrobiotic vegetarian, a dedicated astrologist and aromatherapy junkie."

Cyndy just looks too nice to be a tough poker player, but the results say otherwise: thirty-three cashes in major events, total tournament winnings of just under $1 million, a World Series bracelet and a reputation in cash games. In 2005, she cashed in six World Series events, including three final tables, and in 2006 she cashed in seven.

Kathy Liebert is the first woman to win a tournament with a buy-in of $5,000 or more, and the first woman to win $1 million in tournament poker at the inaugural Party Poker Million in 2002. She won a World Series gold bracelet in a hold'em shoot-out event at 2004 and has two second-place finishes. She grew up in New York, obtained a Bachelor's degree in business and finance, and worked for Dun & Bradstreet as an analyst. She made some money on the stock market and began to travel. While living in Colorado, she began to play $5 limit poker at a couple of local resorts and became a proposition player. This experience equipped her for an assault on Las Vegas, where she won $34,000 in her first two events. She has since won $4 million. Her million-dollar win in the 2000 Party Poker Million really put her on the map and she went on to win a World Series gold bracelet in 2004 and the series *Poker Royale: Battle of the Sexes* on television in 2005. If ever there was a woman capable of looking after herself in what was for so many years a man's world, it is Kathy Liebert—she has a blue belt in karate.

These brief stories do not, of course, tell the full story. These women are not only exceptional players but they also lead exceptional lives—or is the right word "eccentric"? In Vegas, I talked to the thirty-one-year-old French-Canadian poker pro *Isabelle Mercier*.

I was struck by the fact that she has no home. She lives out of two suitcases and has done so for four years.

It's hard to imagine. No place to look forward to returning to, nowhere to chill out at or hide away in. No pile of books and records. No bits and pieces picked up in journeys around the world. No shelf with framed pictures of family or friends.

She lives in hotels with vacancies. Her home is the Hotel Vacancy.

What kind of personality is this? Introverted? Socially dysfunctional? Manic depressive? Not at all. She's bright, friendly, self-possessed, happy . . . if she *had* a home, she could be the girl next door. Except that she has a passion for being free. And she is totally focused on what she's doing. She has no desire or reason to "clutter it up" with an address or possessions.

It was to be free that she gave up being a commercial lawyer (this woman is seriously clever, gaining a degree at the University of Montreal and a Master's at the Sorbonne in Paris) and began to travel . . . and to be free that she became a card dealer, because it would enable her to work anywhere. She ended up dealing at the Aviation Club (ACF) in Paris, where the famous French player and promoter of the club, Bruno Fitoussi, saw her potential and made her poker-room manager within two weeks.

She worked there for four years. In that time, she took up playing the game and her passion for being free was replaced by a passion for poker. She picked up the nickname "No Mercy" Mercier because of her aggressive play and intimidating stare.

Like many players, she can have a dark few hours if she has lost. She's probably more merciless on herself than she is on her opponents. Consider this story:

"I hadn't had a result for six months and I was really starting to feel like 'loser of the year' . . . I didn't feel good at all and something crazy happened.

"I had read a book called *Ask and You Shall Receive*. The author is from Québec . . . in fact, this was a book that encouraged me to turn pro in the first place . . . but I didn't know the author.

"And the day before one event, I was in the middle of a crisis and I was crying and it was four in the morning and I was thinking I was the loser of the year and I cannot win and this is pointless and I'm going to play tomorrow and I'm just going to bust out in the first hour. And I was really super negative and really down.

"And I was looking for an answer because, I didn't know what was going wrong now. And I went to bed and woke up the day after and opened my computer to look at my emails and this author had written to me.

"He didn't know me, but he heard about me playing poker—I had started to be well known in Québec—and he had written to me personally and said, 'Hello, Isabelle, I hear of what you do and am very proud of you and I'd like to work with you because I think poker is about bluff and intuition and it's part of my research.'

"I couldn't believe it. So when I arrived at the tournament, it was, like, 'Get out of my way people, because he believes in me.' I was on fire and I made it to the final. This was a major day of my life. So, since that day, I have worked with him and he is like my spiritual mentor . . . he's behind me."

It's a story that tells a lot about being alone, of vulnerability, of a passion to succeed and the pressure it creates . . . and it's all told with a captivating honesty and lack of guile. There may not be much in the suitcases, but there's a hell of a lot going on in her head.

She first appeared on the international scorecard in 2002, winning over 50,000 euros for coming second in a no-limit hold'em event in Amsterdam, but she achieved her first major success in September 2004 when she won the Ladies Night Out—WPT Invitational in Los Angeles, beating players of the caliber of Cyndy Violette. The victory and television publicity mattered a lot more than the relatively modest $25,000. It was then that Mike Sexton dubbed her "No Mercy" and the nickname has stuck. It also led to her signing as a *Poker Stars* player, with all of the benefits that come with it.

With her confidence boosted, she went back to Europe and cashed five times that November and continued to play well into 2005.

She arrived in Monte Carlo in March that year with her eye on the European Poker Tour Grand Final. She suffered a bad beat and came in tenth. That night, her friend Gus Hansen spent an hour or so with her. He patiently talked to her about the importance of playing position, of how to play her blinds— good, solid poker talk that put her in the right frame of mind to storm back the following day and play another event at the same festival and win it.

She cashed three times at the 2005 WSOP and in 2006 achieved her best World Series result and highest payday, coming in fifth in the $5,000 no-limit hold'em event and winning $175,000.

She tells me she is working on her aggression—not to control it but to increase it. "Men are more aggressive and competitive and take risks more easily, so we have to work on that, because without aggression you can't win. Men like Phil Hellmuth and Marcel Luske are monsters at the table and there are no women monsters yet . . . but I'm aiming to be as big a monster as those guys and scare everybody."

The third change in the profile of poker players has been the emergence of the Internet kids. The old-style pros could not have imagined this in their worst nightmares: a new breed of utterly fearless players, in their early twenties, respecting no reputation, wearing website caps and T-shirts, listening to music on iPods . . . young players who have experienced countless hands of poker online and had access to books, CDs, and tutorials that were not dreamed of in the old days . . . competitors who can pick up in a few weeks what the old-time pros took a lifetime to learn.

Because online players use an alias, we don't always know who the best are. Some of them never come out into the live poker scene; why should they—they're quietly making a fortune at home.

In late 2006, a young gun in his mid-twenties from Norway called Johnny Lodden played a heads-up with someone with the alias "Fast Freddie." They ended up with over a million dollars on the table and what is believed to be a record online pot of over $465,000. A poker magazine reported that on another occasion Lodden was being abused online by an American player and challenged him to play a heads-up for his whole bankroll. The American defiantly posted $190,000, no doubt hoping to intimidate Lodden, but the young Scandinavian's answer was to post a current balance in his poker account of $5.9 million. The American disappeared.

Given the enthusiasm for the game in Scandinavia, it is perhaps not surprising that another young phenomenon also comes from Norway. Playing under the name *Annette–15*, she is, in fact, Annette Obrestad, who is eighteen and almost unbeatable. In the first five months of 2007, she won over $300,000. She is believed to have been devastating opponents since she was fifteen. She claims to have never put money into an online account; she won first in a free-roll event, reinvested the winnings, and has never looked back. What terrifies her elders is that she is still three years short of the age when she can enter a live card room; who knows what she will achieve when she can.

And she is not the only one who threatens the status quo. For a while the Internet players stayed within their cyberspace preserve and the older professionals reaped the benefit of the fresh money that was pouring into live poker. But now the online players are emerging, hungry for the fame and fortune achievable from events like the World Series and playing an aggressive brand of poker that takes no prisoners.

They're so young it's frightening. In Vegas, I find myself having a hamburger with Jeff Madsen, clean-cut, cooperative, friendly; every American mom's dream of what her son will grow up to be. Except, of course, it's unlikely they would dream that he would slip off to Las Vegas on his holidays and win around $1.5 million.

He comes from near the beach in Santa Monica. His parents are in their fifties and his sister is twenty-three, a couple of years older than Jeff. The family is comfortably off and his teenage years were relatively uneventful . . . hanging around with his friends, skateboarding, that kind of thing. His dream was to be someone in the film industry, hardly surprising with Hollywood just down the road, so he enrolled as a student at UC Santa Barbara, studying every aspect of film production, his ambition to be a writer or director. He also played a few home games of poker with his friends and, from there, began playing in the card room of a nearby Indian reservation casino, where he started at the lowest levels, $1–$2 limit, and then found he could beat most of those who were there. He won a couple of $2,000 tournaments. He couldn't, however, play at the Bicycle or the Commerce, the top Los Angeles poker rooms, because he was under twenty-one. So he started playing on the Internet and reading about poker instead.

He read Brunson's *Super System*, Harrington's books, and one by T. J. Cloutier and Tom McAvoy. And he watched poker on television, especially his hero, Phil Ivey. And then, just a few weeks after his twenty-first, he set off in summer 2006 for Las Vegas, quietly confident that he could cash in a WSOP tournament or two. He *really believed that*, partly because twenty-one-year-olds don't see why they shouldn't do whatever they want to, and partly because he just knew he was a good poker player.

No one particularly noticed when he came third in an Omaha high-low event, picking up $97,552. For this, he earned just a paragraph in Nolan Dalla's daily report. Dalla, a renowned observer, admits, "I thought he was just one of those played-out-of-their-skin World Series stories—that afterwards he would just disappear."

Then, a few days later, Madsen stunned everyone by winning a $2,000 no-limit hold'em tournament, involving 1,579 players and paying a first prize of over $660,000. He was the youngest gold bracelet winner in history.

Another one-off? Still just a lucky kid from California?

Move on a few days and he wins another one, this time a $5,000 no-limit hold'em event with 507 players and a first prize of $643,381. Some of the world's top players were left lying injured in his path. Erick Lindgren came second.

As Nolan Dalla commented: "No player has ever skyrocketed to the top of the poker world so quickly, so effortlessly. Not Stu

Ungar. Not Johnny Chan. Not Phil Hellmuth. At twenty-one, Ungar was still hustling gin games in New York. Chan was washing dishes in his parents' restaurant. Hellmuth was a University of Wisconsin student, playing in $20 buy-in hold'em games."

And Jeff still wasn't finished. Back he came to take third place in a $1,000 seven-card-stud hi-low split event, winning another $65,971.

This took his winnings to nearly $1.5 million and made him the number one player at the 2006 World Series.

By this time, no one could entertain the slightest doubt that luck wasn't a factor here; we were seeing the emergence of a sensational poker player.

And the extraordinary thing when you talk to him is that he doesn't think he's extraordinary. When you say to him, "but this performance is amazing," he just says, "I know," and then looks at you as if to say, "*You* tell me how I did it."

And what now? Now, he sounds like a twenty-one-year-old: "Well, I have not got a car. So, I guess I'll buy one."

In my 2006 book, *Swimming with the Devilfish*, I described what was happening at that time:

> Just as they [the veteran professionals] become "respectable" for the first time in their lives . . . with the chance to win more than they ever dreamed of . . . we see them threatened by a wave of cash-hungry, unsentimental, new-generation players who, because of the speed of Internet play, can accumulate more experience in twenty weeks than they have in twenty years . . .
>
> Now they're fighting to hold their own in the race for the first-ever poker sponsorships, the television fees and the million dollar prizes.
>
> Can they maintain their control of the game, cling on to their transformed territory?
>
> This is the drama currently being enacted in the card rooms and on the television screens . . . it's the "old school" v. the Internet kids, and no-holds-barred.

All of this has, of course, only served to make the newly emerged poker world more exciting.

So, when one wondered at the end of the 2006 World Series what lay ahead, the answer appeared to be: blue sky.

Or was it? In fact, there was a cloud approaching. And soon after that World Series came to its climax, it burst . . .

The cause of the crisis was a man who hoped to be President of the United States until he learned that he had to be more than a household name in his own household. This was William Harrison (Bill) Frist, a fifty-four-year-old physician who was a two-term US Senator for Tennessee and briefly Senate Majority Leader before retiring in 2006. In 1998, he was the nearest doctor when a man shot two police officers inside the Capitol building; it is ironic that he saved the assassin but the police officers died. A multimillionaire from his share in a health-care company founded by his father and brother, he became a respected specialist in heart surgery and, in politics, concentrated on health-care policy. As he began to dream of the White House, so he began to cater to the far-right, opposing same-sex marriages and abortion, and supporting the death penalty. In 2006, he fastened onto Internet gambling as an issue and helped promote a piece of legislation called the Unlawful Internet Gambling and Enforcement Act.

As time was running out before the House closed shop for the 2006 elections, it was clear to Frist that the Act wasn't going to make it. So he waited until the very last minutes of the last night the Senate was in session, September 30, 2006, and attached it to an entirely different measure—one to do with the security of the country's ports. It was passed at midnight. It was never debated and most Senators didn't even know what they were voting for. It was a shocking abuse of the democratic process.

The following Monday, *The Guardian* newspaper was one of many to discover what had happened. Under the headline

"Washington's weekend ambush wipes $4 billion off the value of on-line gaming shares," it reported the panic that had swept through the poker world.

> The industry's bet that America's legislators would never get round to outlawing Internet games such as poker went spectacularly wrong yesterday. An estimated $4 billion was wiped off the sector's value as share prices crashed after a weekend ambush in Washington . . . Party Gaming and 888 Holdings both admitted they will have to suspend their operations in the lucrative US market . . . The disaster for the sector, which had made London its financial home after a flurry of flotations in 2005, was being compared with the collapse of the dotcom boom.

Many at first thought that online poker had been banned by law, but Frist had realized that wouldn't work . . . so he concentrated on the mechanism whereby players bet and receive their winnings. To put it in a nutshell, the online sites could no longer transfer funds to banks and credit-card companies, and vice versa.

Not all the online sites caved in. The ones that did were public-listed, fearing prosecution and with responsibilities to shareholders. Thus *Party Poker, 888, Pacific Poker,* and *Paradise Poker* were all forced to turn away their US players. But other privately owned sites, led by *Poker Stars, Ultimate Bet,* and *Full Tilt,* have decided that the law is open to challenge and have kept in business, and at least initially profited as the number of players on these sites increased. The Sunday after *Party Poker* said goodbye to its American players, *Poker Stars* achieved a record entry for their weekly $1 million-guaranteed event— more than 6,100 players, creating a prize pool of $1,231,400.

One of the companies that backed away was Harrah's, the World Series promoter. It announced that it would not accept players paid for by the online sites. The sites responded by saying they would pay the $10,000 buy in to the players' bank accounts and that they could buy in themselves. (The one exception to all this was the UK firm Ladbrokes; because it had never admitted US players, it was unaffected by the law and was allowed to send its team of over one hundred qualifiers in the usual way.) Many feared, however, that the temptation to pocket the $10,000 rather than travel to Las Vegas would be too great for many.

As I write, the poker world is still trying to fully understand what has happened, what the full effects will be, and what it can do.

But as it stands, in one brief moment, late on a September night, when no one was watching, by the cynical behavior of one man, the poker revolution—the amazing advance of the game over just a few years—had been, if not crushed, at least temporarily stopped in its tracks.

Is poker a game of chance or a game of skill? This is what this is all about. The anti-poker forces believe poker to be gambling—a game of chance. From this, they believe, the innocent should be protected. The poker world believes—indeed, *knows*—that it is a game of chance *and* skill but, above all, it is a game of skill.

Somehow this question has to be independently and properly addressed. Poker has become too popular for this matter to be decided by the talents of an advocate or the prejudices of a judge in some obscure court—let alone by the machinations of opportunistic politicians. The poker world will not fear any serious inquiry.

Of course, luck *is* a factor; every poker player has experienced bad beats . . . devastating, shocking upsets when an opponent lands a card that is in breathtaking defiance of the odds. In hold'em, you can cleverly position yourself to win, you can correctly back the probabilities, but you cannot deal yourself the card you need to clinch it. Sometimes you can have an appalling run of bad luck, for hours, days, weeks. It's not just about poor cards; when you find yourself with a potentially winning hand, someone always lands a better one . . . or alternatively you get a 100 percent winner but no one on the table has a decent hand and they all fold, leaving you with no profit on a chance you've waited for all day. Oh, it can be cruel. (Think back to T. J. Cloutier in 2000; at last on the brink of being world champion—probably his last chance—and on the last card of the last hour of the last of many days of play there are only three cards in the pack—three out of forty-three—that can deny him . . . and one of them comes to end the dream. That's a bad beat.)

No poker player will deny that on any given day, in any given game, anyone can win. The cards fall his or her way so favorably that even incompetence or inexperience cannot stop them winning. Oh yes, luck has its day.

BUT—and this is the point—over time the luck evens out and skill takes over. Furthermore, with skill you can minimize the luck factor and also minimize how much you lose when you do lose. You can play a hundred hands, lose twenty and win one but still be a winner because of your ability to get away from potential disasters and maximize the income from that one success. Keeping out of trouble is one of the most valuable skills a poker player can have: keep control of events and the bad days are not *too* bad.

But, oh, there is so much that experience and knowledge and skill bring to the game. In hold'em, there's choosing the right starting hands to play, reading what the community cards tell you, correctly assessing by their behavior and betting what other players are likely to do, betting to either control a potential loss or maximize a win. You need mathematical skills to work out the odds of a hand winning and the value that lies in playing a hand, the concentration to take the correct decisions at each point, the psychological skills to judge what other players will do or can be made to do, the discipline to do the sensible thing (and that often means folding a hand you desperately want to play because the odds don't favor it). And then there's heart—the courage to make a bold play that will decide the issue . . . to put all your chips or even the whole tournament on the line to back your instincts and judgment.

If it were not a game of skill, how could there be so many books on how to play and win? What point is there in a book telling you how to be lucky? I defy any judge or any politician to read the set of three books by Dan Harrington and then say poker is a game of luck. They will find revealed in them a game of extraordinary complexity, requiring a remarkable range of qualities. No cliché is truer than that hold'em *takes a minute to learn and a lifetime to master*.

If it were not a game of skill, why would we see the emergence of a number of players who achieve consistent success? The big names, the stars, have not reached the pinnacle of the game over many years by losing. So, what are they? Just lucky? Of course not; they're great players. They are not only equipped with natural talent (as all champions have to be), but they have also worked and studied. They have proved that, over time, skill can and does prevail.

How ironic that America, a country that will ask many of its young men and women to give their lives in the cause of "freedom and democracy," should seek to deny them the right to play a game so popular that it has become known as "the American pastime," while in Russia, of all places, they have defined it as a sport, their Federal Agency of Physical Culture and Sports stating it has become convinced that "poker requires analytical talents, tenacity, training, and skills in order to win . . . and is very different from a game of chance."

The problem with poker players is that, on the whole, all they like to do is play poker. Playing *politics* does not appeal. But this is what they have to do. They have to get their act together and fight their corner . . . and as I write—at the time of the 2007 World Series—they are beginning to.

The 100,000-member Poker Players Alliance has hired Capitol Hill veteran Alfonse D'Amato to spearhead a campaign to reverse the Frist legislation. Representative Shelley Berkley is drafting a bill calling for a year-long study to identify the "proper response" to the game's popularity, and Barney Frank, chairman of the House financial services committee, is promoting a bill to make Internet betting lawful. He envisages a properly run industry with safeguards for compulsive gamblers and children, and fair taxation of profits.

So, the dark cloud that has cast such a shadow over the game during 2006–2007 may be slowly lifting. There is hope.

As I write, I do not know what the outcome will be.

What I do know is that poker was born outside the law, flourished outside the law, and will not be stopped by the law . . . any more than Prohibition stopped people drinking. There are only two options: either to make the game "legitimate" and then better regulated—and even more effectively taxed, to the benefit of both the poker world and the community as a whole—or to drive it back underground.

In the meantime, spare a thought for Doyle Brunson, who has conceded at least partial defeat and, with his fellow directors, sold the list of American players on *Doyle's Room* to *Full Tilt*.

The wheel has turned full circle for the Godfather. From outlaw to respected citizen back to outlaw. Well, of course that is over-simplifying but, as he sees his dream of a flotation of *Doyle's Room* for millions of dollars recede, that must be what it feels like to him.

So to mid-2007, and I am near the end of a journey across boundaries of time and place. It has taken me as far north as the Black Hills of Dakota and south to the Mexican border, east to Connecticut and west to California—and to other countries too. It has spanned over 130 years, from the days of the Mississippi steamboats, Wild Bill's Deadwood, and Doc Holliday's

Tombstone . . . and the thirty-eight years since the World Series began.

The one constant has been poker. Some of its mysteries I have solved; others, I suspect, may never be. Some of the controversies I may have freshly stirred; others I have laid to rest. Some of poker's ghosts I have found wanting; others are revealed as men and women of exceptional character and skill.

My message is that the game endures, and remains as challenging and compelling as ever; it has adapted to, and recruited to its purposes, the passions and technologies of our times.

So, where and when do I end my travels?

How do I conclude my story?

There can be only one answer: the Olympic Games of poker . . . the 38th World Series.

Hopefully, there in July 2007, I can answer the residual questions:

What has been the real impact of the political assault on poker?

Have the old-style poker pros been finally swept away forever by the ambition and sheer numbers of the Internet kids? Who is winning the battle of the generations?

And how does it feel? How does it feel to sit where the ghosts once sat and compete for the same title they aspired to . . . world champion? And to know that to win is . . . well, just possible . . . and that it could change one's life forever?

Fortunately, one factor separates this game from nearly all others: its democratic nature. Anyone can play in any event . . . including me. All you have to do is put your money on the table and your self-confidence on the line.

So I will end my journey at the World Series.

I will enter the main event.

I will be a player.

eleven

Ghosts and guardians at the 2007 World Series

I am at Table 48, Seat 9. It's on the rails, so I will have an audience. I like that—what is the point of playing in the World Series main event if no one sees me?

But, of course, I am being watched anyway . . . the ghosts are watching . . . Johnny Moss, Stu Ungar, Sailor Roberts, Jack Straus, and the others . . . they're there, way up under the ceiling, in huge black-and-white photographs, looking down at me and 1,300 others as we begin play on Day One.

All day, I sense their presence in the room, just as I can see the living guardians of their legacy—Amarillo Slim, in cowboy apparel at a table to my left, and Doyle "Dolly" Brunson, wearing his Stetson, farther up the room. Bobby Baldwin is two tables away. Billy Baxter and Bobby Hoff are there, too. So are Chip Reese and Tom McEvoy, T. J. Cloutier and Johnny Chan.

Ghosts and guardians . . . what do they make of this spectacle: 1,300 players and 130 dealers at 130 tables . . . the color, the chatter, the click of 26 million chips . . . the television cameras, the crowd on the rails?

As I wait for someone to cry "Shuffle up and deal," I wonder, too, what they would have felt if they had been with me just a few hours back, at the old Horseshoe, now known simply as Binion's.

I went to the old Horseshoe, as I always do, to see the pictures on the wall. But they were not there . . . all that remained was a patch of faded wallpaper.

I eventually found them . . . at least some of them. They had been moved to a stand-alone board near the poker room, one that you could easily miss. And some *were* missing.

How could they do this?

These were not just pictures on a wall. They were *a place* . . . a gallery of the ghosts and the guardians, and they had been there for years. They should never have been moved.

One set of pictures was all there was to the Hall of Fame. No gallery, no Hall. A second set of pictures called the Gallery of Champions contained all the winners of the World Series main event.

These players became famous at the old Horseshoe. They reached the climax of their careers, the summit of their ambitions, there. They have always been honored in that space, visited and revisited by all who care about the history of the game.

And now they had been moved.

I was told it was because too many came to see them—that if they were moved it would be possible to fit in a few more craps tables, or a few more slot machines.

It was a *business* decision.

Well, of course it was.

I fear the ghosts and guardians will be unimpressed by the modesty of my ambition: it is to get through the first day. I know it sounds weak, but I'm a realist . . . if I do that, it will be a real achievement . . . I will have played with the best in the world under intense pressure for over sixteen hours and survived—and by the time the first day is over (it is actually spread over four days, there are so many entries) I will have left in my wake nearly two-thirds of the field—over 4,000 players.

And, I tell myself, if I do get through, my objective will be revised: then it's kill or be killed, all the way to the summit!

My first hand is seven-four. I fold it . . . and relax. This isn't too bad. It may be the World Series, but it's still just poker. I think: I can do this.

After nine minutes, the first player is knocked out. For me and 1,299 others, this is good news: we can no longer be humiliated by being first out.

Now I have two queens. I bet aggressively and win 1,500 chips. I've won a hand in the main event. I can do this.

Before it seems possible, two hours have passed. We are at the end of Level One. Time for a break. And I'm still here.

I think: Yes, I can do this. I really can.

On the way out, I pass Phil Hellmuth, who yesterday I saw inducted into the Hall of Fame. This was well deserved. By winning his eleventh gold bracelet and breaking one or two other records at this World Series, he's become the talk of world poker . . . *the man.*

He turned up to accept the honor in his now standard outfit—black cap, black jacket buttoned up to the neck, black shades—and he came late (he always does). He also clearly felt his honor was overdue. But there was humility, too—he came with his family, Mom and Dad as well as wife, and he paid a genuine tribute to Brunson. With Phil, Poker Brat is always in conflict with Poker Nice Guy, and on this day the latter won.

But while Phil has this week confirmed his place as a towering presence in the game, Doyle Brunson, without the *Doyle's Room* promotional machine of last year to support him (the online sites have been banned from marketing themselves at the Rio), seems a little diminished. He made the final table in the $10,000 buy-in Omaha event and for a while everyone became excited, thinking maybe he had it in him to challenge Phil's record; but he faded quickly on the last day. A lot of the time he looks world-weary. Truth is, he probably is. But he knows how to behave the elder statesman. He turned up with Johnny Chan to present Hellmuth with his eleventh gold bracelet. And he was one of the few players who came to see him inducted into the Hall of Fame. He knows he is the ultimate guardian of the legacy of the old-timers and he makes the effort and it's admirable.

But, oh, what are we to do with the Hall of Fame? Phil's name is clumsily announced by two men in suits—Messrs Nameless and Nameless, presumably executives of Harrah's, who clearly believe they purchased the Hall of Fame when they purchased the World Series . . . but who are these men and what do they know about poker?

The Hall of Fame needs reform. It has no home, especially now it has lost its piece of wall at the old Horseshoe. It does not have a recognizable and authoritative ownership. And there are names on the list that should not be there.

The Hall of Fame is another of Benny's legacies, and not a bad one in principle. The criteria were (are) impressive: you need to have played consistently well for high stakes with top competitors, maintaining all the while the respect of your peers. And you must have "passed the test of time, maintaining a high standard of excellence over the years."

Based on these criteria, many in the Hall of Fame clearly deserve the accolade. But what about Edmond Hoyle and Wild Bill Hickok, both honored posthumously? Hoyle never played poker; in fact, he died in 1769, decades before the game was invented. As for Wild Bill, he doesn't measure up either. Of course he loved the game, but all available research indicates that he was not a great player. Henry Chafetz sums it up: "Bill had been a fanatic about draw poker, but he was not the shrewdest of gamblers and often came out on the short end."[1] Nick the Greek is another questionable member; he played for high stakes, but he was not a consistent winner. And there are others who are there because they were Benny's friends, not on merit.

The Hall of Fame needs a proper home and to be run by the players and its members voted in by the players.

Back in the Rio, I now have 23,200 chips but am becoming increasingly aware of a player on my right. He's about forty, of Asian appearance, with thick, black hair sticking up at the front. His eyes are hidden behind dark glasses. He does not join in any chat, is concentrating intensely. And he is already quietly amassing a pile of chips. His name, I discover, is Tuan Lam.

I am playing a hand badly . . . I make the mistake of playing ace-jack. This is a weaker hand than it may appear and one I seem unable to throw away. When a jack comes on the flop, I decide to raise Tuan's 1,500 bet with a further 1,500, thinking I can scare him off. Instead he calls, then when a queen comes on the turn, he bets 3,000. I have to concede that ace-jack has let me down for the umpteenth time and fold, and I am back under 20,000.

Level Two ends on that note. We have been playing four hours.

Is poker surviving the political attack from Washington, D.C.? On the evidence of this World Series, it has been wounded, but by no means fatally.

Its main effect has been to reduce the entry for this main event. At 6,358, it's nearly 2,000 less than last year, but there is a simple explanation: the online sites have not been able to buy in their satellite winners directly. Instead, they sent the $10,000 in cash to their homes. For many, this will have been the biggest sum of money they have ever seen and, not surprisingly, some will have decided to stay at home and use the money for other things . . . or boost their bankroll for playing locally or online.

But in every other sense, this 2007 World Series has broken records: 54,000 registrations for 55 events; a record 3,151 players on one day during the preliminaries; an overall prize pool of $160 million, including $60 million for the main event. These are figures no other recreational activity can match.

I'm still in . . . *It's Level Three and I score a few minor victories, but it is one step forward, one step back . . . I still can't get away from the 20,000 mark. How come Tuan Lam is building a huge stack and I am standing still?*

I wait patiently. In the meantime, 400 players have gone out. Then another disaster. I know I should not be chasing connectors, but I have nine-ten and I call a Tuan raise and the flop has jack-queen. Tuan checks and I think, "Time to be aggressive," so I fire off a 5,000 semi-bluff and to my horror he calls. This should not be happening: if he checked, why is he calling such a big bet? The last card is no help to me, and he appears to instinctively know that because he now seizes the initiative and bets, and I have to fold. Tuan strikes again. Who is this man?

My stack of chips is dwindling fast and there are ten hours to go. My heart sinks. I so wanted to get through the first day and now, I fear, the end is in sight.

Then comes the most dramatic hand I have played in my life . . . I have ace-ten of hearts and, for some reason I cannot explain, I feel really good about it. I hear a voice say, "All-in."

Poker gods forgive me, the voice is mine.

One player calls my bet.

I can't believe I've done this. All my chips are in the middle. My tournament is on the line. A humiliating debacle stares me in the face. I should have waited for a better hand.

When this happens, the dealers telegraph the drama by crying out, "All-in with a caller." As far as I'm concerned, my dealer may just as well have been calling out "Man about to die." The nearby spectators close in to form a small crowd on the rail. A TV camera arrives. They sense blood—mine!

I turn over my ace-ten of hearts and the other guy turns over ace-king. The odds are with him.

I rise unsteadily to my feet, ready to leave, only to see it get worse. The flop comes king-king-seven . . . he has three kings. It's the end.

But then I notice that two of the community cards are hearts.
One more heart and I have a flush. Please God . . . a heart.
The turn card comes. No help—it's a club.
Then the river card . . . and, would you believe it? . . . It's a heart.
I have pulled off a miracle flush. I've won the hand. And I've doubled up. There's a collective gasp from the others at the table and a roar from the spectators on the rails.

I've seen scenes like this on television. Now I know what it's like.
If every poker player is due fifteen minutes of fame, this is mine.
I turn to smile at the television camera.
But it's gone.
It doesn't care about me winning. It's not in the business of smiles. It only wants to be there at the death—so it's followed the loser from the table. My fifteen minutes of fame have become five seconds.
Still, who cares? It's an unforgettable moment.
And what does it all add up to?
I'm back to 20,000, where I began nearly six hours ago.

Jamie Gold is out. This is the man who in 2006 won the main event and $12 million but became one of the most controversial and unpopular world champions ever. Whether he deserved this is another matter.

Gold, who was thirty-seven in 2006, was a Hollywood television producer and also represented actors. Johnny Chan mentored Gold as a player while developing a show with him, and Gold came to Las Vegas having cashed in a number of events in LA. He proceeded to play his way to the final table, arriving there with more chips than all of his opponents combined and, to his credit, never looked like losing them.

It all began to fall apart within hours of winning. He had a "friend" with whom he had made a business deal and to whom he had promised to share any winnings in the main event 50/50. The friend became concerned when Gold seemed in no hurry to share the $12 million. Gold claims that he was confused over the tax implications and wanted to sort it all out before keeping his word, but the friend called in his lawyers and the dispute entered the public arena. It has always been a tradition of poker that deals are made on a handshake and always kept, so many in the game reacted badly to Gold, feeling their new world champion had let the game down. He was viciously attacked in poker magazines and online.

The matter was finally settled privately and Gold now admits he handled it badly.

Then it turned out that Gold had broken some small rule while playing in the event. The organizers cleared him, but it didn't help his image. Nor did it help that his subsequent performances in televised poker were unimpressive. There was a feeling that he was lucky to win, and that he was rather sleazy.

At the 2007 World Series, he has done much to rehabilitate his reputation. He has discussed his mistakes openly. He handled the press conference well. He went out of the main event with good humor. At the end of a tough year that also saw his father die and his mother having to cope with a tumor, he has begun to win back a few friends.

Level Four *comes and goes. They announce that 180 players have fallen in the 120 minutes of the level. I am landing no playable cards; I'm virtually a spectator. But I'm still here.*

We've now been at it for eight hours—ten, if you include the breaks . . . and there are still two levels to go. This is longer than I have ever played non-stop before and I'm beginning to tire. There is no respite from the pressure. Poker is about decision-making; relax for a moment, make one bad decision, and you're gone. But it's becoming harder to concentrate. This is becoming as much a test of endurance as it is a trial of our poker skills.

But not for Tuan. He looks calm and relaxed. And his stack grows.

By now, over 500 have gone. Heads are rolling—famous heads. Four former world champions are out, including Doyle Brunson.

Who, I wonder, can win this? While I pay my blinds and antes and watch the others play, I consider who, on form, could win the main event this year.

One is *Gus Hansen*, who is already on a big stack and looking very determined.

Four others are Carlos "The Matador" Mortensen, Allen Cunningham, J. C. Tran, and John Juanda, all in-form players on the US circuit. *Carlos Mortensen* (thirty-five) has made history by becoming the first player ever to win both the WSOP main event (2001) and the World Poker Tour world championship (2007). Quietly spoken and calm, he is nevertheless capable of audacious bluffs. He has lifetime winnings of $8,350,000. *J.C. Tran* (thirty), yet another Vietnamese-American, leads the 2007 Player of the Year standings, helped by three World Poker Tour final table appearances. His lifetime tally is over $5,500,000. *Allen Cunningham* (thirty), who made the main event final table last year and won a gold bracelet this year, has won well over $6 million and has the game to outstay most players in the world over this distance. *John Juanda* (thirty-six) was born in Indonesia, lives in California, and was a high-school track star. At one time, he earned a living by selling Bibles door to door. He is rated exceptionally highly by his fellow pros and no doubt by his bank manager: he has won $6,600,000 so far.

Finally, both the 2004 and 2005 main event winners, forty-three-year-old former corporate attorney *Greg Raymer* and forty-two-year-old Australian and former chiropractor *Joe Hachem*, cannot be ruled out . . . they know what it takes to beat a massive field and have maintained their form well.

Of course, there's one other threat. He is sitting two feet away from me. *Tuan Lam*. I sense there's something about this man, but who is he? In the break, I follow him outside for a breath of the warm summer air. We chat for a few minutes. In a quietly spoken but impressive way, he tells me he was born in Vietnam and after a hard childhood escaped that sad country in a small boat with a few others, sailing stormy seas for three days until they reached an island in Indonesia. After living there a while, he persuaded the Canadian authorities to accept him and worked there in a form of slave labor until he was employed as a dealer in a casino. He learned to play poker and began to play on the Internet. Over the past four years, he has won a million dollars and, in addition to a home in Canada, has built five houses for his family in Vietnam. The World Series was his first experience of playing live. He says that if he wins a lot of money, he is going to spend some of it helping his family's village in Vietnam.

I think, well, if he makes the final table, at least my chips will be put to good use!

Level Five *and at last I get a hand . . . two aces on the big blind— the best hand in the best position, because I am the last man to play pre-flop and that's where I intend to take the hand down. But they all fold to me. It's almost as if they can see the aces. All I get are the blinds and the antes. This is disappointing.*

I go nearly two more hours without a hand and then on the last one before the break I get ten-ten. I bet 2,000 and get two callers. The flop comes king-queen-nine and I bet 4,000. They both fold and I end the level at 21,000.

After all this time, I've increased my stack by 1,000.

But I'm still in.

I look at the clock. It's 1:30 a.m. We've been at it thirteen and a half hours and we now have a break—and then another two hours.

I am exhausted now. And I'm disappointed not to have won more chips. I find myself fighting the temptation to throw them all in the middle on any minimally playable hand. To hell with it, double up or die.

Tuan Lam, on the other hand, looks as if the break—what for me is a desperately needed break—is for him a totally unnecessary interruption.

So absorbed do we become in our own individual battle for survival that we forget that there have been 1,300 individual dramas taking place in this room on Day 1A . . . for many, this is not just the main event of the 2007 World Series but the main event of their poker lives . . . maybe their whole lives.

Let me tell you about Kate. A woman in, I would say, her late thirties, she came to my table with only twenty minutes of the first day left. Her husband followed her on the rail, but soon had to leave as they ushered the spectators out for the closing minutes. We spoke and I discovered she was from Wales. She had only five yellow 1,000 chips in her hand and was toying with them in a way that suggested she was about to throw them in.

"Going to hang on for tomorrow?" I asked, hoping this would come across as a good idea. But she said, "No, I want to double up."

I thought this was a mistake for two reasons: she was putting unnecessary pressure on herself to find a big hand in the last ten or so we would play. And her chances of recovery being minimal, it seemed sad she could not leave Las Vegas with at least the achievement of making it through the first day.

Then came the very last hand and the very last minute of a very long day and Kate got two queens. In she went with her chips, was called and was knocked out by kings.

One moment her face was full of hope, the next utter despair. She was devastated. As she began to walk unsteadily away, she looked back, as if still hoping that somehow she could be saved, but she couldn't.

I went after her, shook her hand and told her how brilliantly she had done to get so far. Which she had. But I don't think she heard me or saw me.

It will be a long time before I forget her.

There were many similar stories lived out in that room that day. Every departure from the main event is a crushing blow . . . the end of a dream . . .

But, speaking of dreams, back to my own.

It's two *in the morning. I still have 21,000 chips . . . but they are simply not enough. After a day of unplayable cards, I have to somehow win another 13,500 chips just to withstand the tyranny of the blinds, now up to 400–800, and the antes, now up to fifty, and have a fighting chance on Day Two.*

But, above all, I want to get through.

I desperately want to get through.

I HAVE TO GET THROUGH!

I get ace-king. Tuan—of course—bets 2,500. I call. There's an ace on the flop. He checks. I bet 5,000. He folds.

Gotcha!

Up to 23,500.

I then summon up the nerve to steal the blinds and antes.

Two hours become one hour . . . and my stack is being decimated by the same blinds and antes—1,700 a round.

With my brain no longer working properly and my eyes half-closed, I am still trying to do the math in my head—keeping track of how many chips I need to survive. I separate them into piles. On the right, enough for the remaining blinds and the antes, and on my left what I could carry over to the second day. It could be over 10,000.

I know now that, unless I lose my head, I can get through.

Pitiful, I know . . . but better a realistic ambition achieved than an impossible dream denied.

Then, on the second-to-last hand, I get jack-jack. Do I want to get involved now? I do. I bet 3,000 . . . and thankfully no one calls, not even the impassive Tuan, and I pick up the blinds and antes and have 12,200 to take into Day Two.

It's five to four in the morning, just five minutes short of sixteen hours since we began, and I've made it.

In a daze, I put my chips into a bag, I write my name on it, and I am allocated a table for Day Two.

It's Table 13!

I'm one of the first out of the room. I walk alone up the "avenue" between the card room and the hotel with tears in my eyes . . . tears of exhaustion—I'm feeling every minute of that sixteen hours now—but also tears of elation and relief.

I can't wait to get to my room and my computer and get the message out.

I'M THROUGH.

It is an extraordinary spectacle: the parade of players from the Rio casino to the poker room for the start of the second day. All 6,358 players have had their chance; 4,000 are out. We who are left are an army of survivors. As we march in our hundreds down the lengthy "avenue," I'm reminded of those old Crusader films—armies of infantry, lined up with spears and shields, marching stoically towards the enemy, each of them knowing they will probably die that day.

We, the poker infantry, may not have suits of armor, but we have our uniform: the jeans and T-shirts, the shades and baseball hats. However, for us, the enemy is not only in front but also at our side—we are *each other's* enemy. No one is our friend—even our friends are not our friends.

I often, when watching those films of ancient battles, wonder why anyone in their right mind would actually choose to be in the front line. I mean, why not hide away at the back? Today, in the poker war, I am on the front line—but not by choice. We who have the short stacks *are* the front line . . . the spear carriers in the drama, the "people of poker," the providers of the prize pool we will never share. But we are not fantasists; we know the odds. As we march onwards, most of us know there will be a massacre today . . . hopes and dreams will be shot to pieces . . . the overwhelming probability is that we'll never come back.

Yet we know, too, that if this is the end, it is an honorable one: we've put up a fight, survived a whole day of battle, avoided the carnage.

As we march, we walk over the dead bodies of some of the most famous names in the game—for once the Officers and Generals are going down too, and in numbers—the veterans Doyle Brunson, Amarillo Slim, Chip Reese, Mike Sexton . . . the World Series specialists Phil Hellmuth and Johnny Chan . . . the big twenty-first-century money winners Phil Ivey and Howard Lederer . . . the current champion Jamie Gold . . . and the top Brits— the Devilfish, El Blondie, and three of the Hendon Mob . . . these are some of the best in poker, but their rank did not save them . . . they didn't do what we did—they didn't get through.

So it is with pride, not fear that we march on . . . all resolved that if we are going to die the poker death, then we're going to go down fighting, not fade away at the dictate of the blinds.

We will not be blinded out; no matter what the hand, we'll play it now.

With 12,200 *chips left and blinds of 500–1,000 and antes of 100, I have five rounds before I go broke.*

But in reality I have about twenty hands maximum to make my move and it really should be sooner . . .

And it comes sooner than I expect—the very first hand.

I have ace-three in fifth position and I go all-in. Once more, my World Series is on the line.

But they all fold and I am 2,500 up. Whew!

I then have a really poor run of cards—there is simply no opportunity to act until the small blind calls my big blind. I decide this is a weak act on his part and bravely go all-in a second time with only ten-five. He quickly folds.

The poor cards continue and I now know the truth—luck is not going to help me today. The poker gods are looking elsewhere.

I test that belief soon after . . . I get king-seven suited in late position and go all-in for a third time, but this time the big blind calls.

As soon as he does, I know the game is up. He would not do this without a big hand. Resigned, I rise to my feet.

He has jack-jack, so I need a king to survive and I just know it's not going to come.

On a lucky day, it would come. But I already know that today is not that day.

I am out after thirty-five minutes.

It's a bit anticlimactic. No one seems to notice or care.

I pick up my bag and walk away.

No point in looking to the other players for sympathy. Within a minute of my departure they will have forgotten I was ever there.

They have other hands to play.

That, I'm afraid, is poker.

As I walk from the hall, I pass Tuan Lam, playing at another table. He has a huge stack of chips, some of them mine.

I find myself hoping he makes the final table.

If I cannot be there, why not the man I had stayed with for 16 hours and helped send on his way?

Now I can concentrate on discovering who is winning the generational war . . . the tried-and-tested pros or the "Internet kids"?

The "kids" made a flying start to this World Series. Six players in their twenties—three of them twenty-one-year-olds—won gold bracelets in quick succession, one of them, Steve Billirakis from Chicago, at twenty-one years and eleven days, replacing Jeff Madsen as the youngest World Series gold bracelet winner ever. The six shared prize money in excess of $3 million. How the old hands must have gritted their teeth.

But then the older pros made a comeback. The veteran Freddie Deeb won the H.O.R.S.E. and by the time it came to the main event it looked as if the older generation were holding the line.

But then, in the main event, the youngsters really struck.

By the end of Day Two, the talk of the Rio was a twenty-two-year-old Italian called Dario Minieri, already famous in Europe for playing for high stakes online. (He made so much money that he could use one poker site's frequent player points to buy a Porsche!) He now took the World Series finale by the scruff of the neck and built a lead of over a million chips with an aggressive approach that left opponents quaking. By raising and re-raising virtually every hand, he raced to nearly two and a half million chips. Was he to be a runaway winner?

No, he wasn't. The following day he self-destructed and went out surprisingly quickly—only to be replaced by a twenty-one-year-old Norwegian, who now seized the lead with a similar exhibition of aggression and nerve. But on Day Three he, too, self-destructed.

Sunday, July 15 was perhaps the biggest day in poker history, for while the main event was building towards the final table, there was a lot else happening.

For a start, just up the road in a room overlooking the famous Bellagio fountains, a prestigious *World Poker Tour* event was reaching its climax with a heads-up between Mike Matusow and Kevin Saul, a young pro from Chicago. The latter won and took $1,342,320.

(Incidentally, earlier, a quiet, elderly looking man with the appearance of a university professor left one of the tables, knocked out in twenty-third place. He picked up $30,985 and headed for the airport. Hardly anyone in the room knew who he was. It was Bobby Hoff.)

Meanwhile, on the same day, there were a whole series of huge events on the Internet. One, with a buy-in of only $11, attracted a massive 17,501 players, with the winner taking $19,285. At the other end of the scale, there was a $10,000 buy-in no-limit heads-up tournament limited to only sixteen entrants. The winner collected over $100,000. Simultaneously, on another site, a $200,000 guaranteed prize pool attracted 998 entrants and paid $45,000 to the winner, and on yet another a $100,000 guaranteed tournament drew 903 entrants and paid the winner $25,000. But all these were dwarfed by two with a million dollars guaranteed prize money. The first of these attracted 7,054 entrants, generating $1,410,800 worth of prizes, with the winner getting $198,923. The other had a buy-in of $500 and attracted 2,321 players. The winner got $212,894.

I doubt if there has been a day in poker history when so many people have been playing in major events and when there was so much money on the table—especially when you add to the above the $60 million prize money for the World Series main event, including the $8 million first prize.

It is on this Sunday night that we finally discover who will play on the final table.

I do not really care who wins. They've all lasted ten days and outplayed 6,350 others—they are all deserving. And they will all become rich.

It's the composition of the final table that fascinates me, for it answers a lot of questions.

First, we can now see the extent to which poker has become a worldwide game. This is the most international final table ever, with four Americans (one born in Laos), one Vietnamese-Canadian, one South African, one Dane, one Russian, and one Englishman.

The Russian, while well known on the European circuit, is the first from his country to make the World Series final table; the South African is the first from the continent of Africa.

Second, it clarifies where we are in the battle between the Internet kids and the older pros. The kids have provided the fireworks of this World Series but often it is they who have been burned. While demonstrating with some spectacular performances that they can, at least for a time, leave everyone else standing, they have in many cases proved to be sprinters rather than marathon runners, with a tendency to build up an intimidating stack and then self-destruct.

However, one of them has made it. He's a twenty-two-year-old New Yorker, an online poker pro who has become famous under the name of RaiNKhaN, and in 2006 he became highly controversial when his name began to appear in a lot of tournaments—up to twenty-eight—at the same time. It was suspected that he was using a computer program that automatically plays hands to a pre-determined strategy. These are illegal in online poker rooms. Finally, one online site looked into it. RaiNKhaN was cleared after claiming he could play over forty tournaments at a time and providing a video of himself playing more than twenty-five tournaments simultaneously on a single seventeen-inch monitor. To someone like me who struggles to win playing just one, this is simply beyond my imagination.

With this twenty-two-year-old now on the World Series final table and a sixty-two-year-old (the South African) playing, they make it one-all in the generational battle (the others are all in their thirties—or, in the case of one, forty).

BUT if the younger players have not taken over, Internet players generally are proving a point: four of the final table are either Internet professionals or play most of their poker online. Their success adds to the evidence that players can switch without difficulty from online to live poker.

So, altogether, it's a final table that reflects the state of the game . . . an international game, a game that unites the generations, a game that can be played to the highest standards both online and live . . . and a game being played with a skill and subtlety that even the ghosts and the guardians would admire.

As they look down on it from their place near the ceiling, or in a few cases from the rail, they can be happy that the game they helped build into, first, the great American pastime and, then, the world's most popular game is in good shape and in good hands.

Oh, and one other thing . . .

. . . the Vietnamese-Canadian on the list of nine is Tuan Lam.

After ten exhausting and exhilarating days, Tuan *and my chips* have made it to the final table.

The World Series of Poker $10,000 buy-in main event 2007

1. Jerry Yang (USA) $8,250,000
2. Tuan Lam (Canada) $4,840,981
3. Raymond Rahme (South Africa) $3,048,025
4. Alex Kravchenko (Russia) $1,852,721
5. Jon Kalmar (England) $1,255,069
6. Hevad "Rain" Khan (USA) $956,243
7. Lee Childs (USA) $705,229
8. Lee Watkinson (USA) $585,699
9. Philip Hilm (Denmark) $525,934

Stop Press

Since this book was written, the poker world has become more optimistic about its chances of overturning the Unlawful Internet Gaming Enforcement Act (see pages 293–295). The Poker Players Alliance, now backed by more than 800,000 players, has made its presence felt in Washington, D.C. and has been winning support for its proposal that the online game should be subject to regulation and taxation instead of being effectively shut down as a result of the legislation.

Annette Obredstad (see page 290) has justified expectations triggered by her early online success and pulled off a sensational win in the first World Series of Poker Europe event, defeating an impressive line-up of world class players and winning nearly $2 million. At eighteen years and 364 days she became the youngest-ever winner of a WSOP gold bracelet.

Finally, the poker world was shocked and saddened by the death of Chip Reese in December 2007. The first winner of the World Series H.O.R.S.E. event and one of the best poker players in history, Reese died in his sleep. He was 56.

My thanks to . . .

- Mike Sexton, Nolan Dalla, Tom McEvoy, T. J. Cloutier, and Carl McKelvey . . . your friendship and support has been inspirational.
- Crandell Addington, Doyle Brunson, Bobby Baldwin, Billy Baxter, Thomas "Amarillo Slim" Preston, Bobby Hoff, Eric Drache, Noel Furlong, George McKeever, Padraig Parkinson, Isabelle Mercier, and Jeff Madsen . . . for your time and memories.
- Michael Craig, Tony Holden, David Schwartz, Dana Smith, Joseph Rosa, Liam Flood, Jim Sherer (and his team at the Kansas Heritage Center in Dodge City), Arlette Hansen and Kathy Toscanas (both in Deadwood), Linda Urbaniak, Jeff Banks, Steven Richards, Patsy Scarbrough, Melanie Thatcher, Gary W. Sleeper, Joe Saumarez-Smith, Jennifer Synder, and Steve Delaney . . . all of you gave me more helpful advice and/or practical assistance than I can ever adequately acknowledge.
- Howard Schwartz and all at the Gambler's Book Shop in Las Vegas, for friendship and many favors.

Finally, special thanks to:

- Ladbrokespoker.com, Colin Cole-Johnson, and Cieran O'Brien, and the whole poker team, for your generous and much-appreciated support. You made this book possible.
- Jane . . . for support (and sacrifice) way beyond the call of duty.

Des Wilson,
April 2008

Photography

Gathering the pictures for this book proved difficult. While they have all been supplied by the reputable sources listed below, all of whom have assured me they have the authority to allow publication, these sources could not in every case identify the actual photographer so that proper credit could be given. I apologize to any photographer who, as a result, is not properly credited for his/her work and will be pleased to make suitable acknowledgment in later editions.

To these sources, I owe special thanks:

Ulvis Alberts

Ulvis Alberts is probably the greatest of all poker photographers and I thank him for permission to use some of his pictures.

If you wish to contact Ulvis and find out more about his work, his email address is: AmberCprod@aol.com.

Poker Images

I thank *Poker Images* for supplying a number of pictures and for obtaining the permission of the photographers to publish their work.

The University of Las Vegas Special Collection

I thank David Schwartz, director of the UNLV Special Collection, for providing pictures from the university's Special Collection and for his permission to publish them.

Howard Schwartz and the Gambler's Book Shop

Howard Schwartz has a collection of photographs taken by himself and others, and I thank him for providing some and allowing me to publish them.

The Gambler's Book Shop is an outstanding source of publications on poker and gambling generally and details can be found on their website: www.gamblersbook.com.

Michael Vu

Michael took a number of pictures for me at the 2007 World Series of Poker and I thank him for his outstanding work.

Michael Vu's website and email address are pokerazzo.com and michaelvu@mac.com.

Tom McEvoy

Tom McEvoy is another who helpfully provided pictures.

Finally, the front-jacket picture I took myself at the World Series of Poker in 2006; I am also responsible for the Tombstone pictures and that of Amarillo Slim.

Des Wilson,
October 2007

A simple guide to Texas hold'em

Texas hold'em can be played head-to-head (or *heads-up*, as it's known) by two players but is usually played at tables of six, or nine or ten.

Let's assume you are one of those players.

You are dealt two cards, face-down. Only you can see these two "pocket" cards. They are, for you, *the* key cards. Their potential to develop into a winning hand, when joined by the *community* (shared) *cards* yet to be dealt, will decide whether you play the hand and if, and how much, you bet. The first round of betting is based on these two cards.

Two players, those to the left of the dealer (identified by a button that moves clockwise round the table—hence the term *on the button*), have no option—they *have* to start the process with compulsory bets. Because these bets are made before the players have seen their pocket cards, they're called *blind bets*. The first is the *small blind* and the second, usually double in size, is the *big blind*.

The purpose of the blinds is to get the game going by getting some money in the pot.

Assuming you are not one of the blinds, you have at this point just three options:

1. If it's weak, you can *fold* your hand at no cost.
2. You can *call* the bet by matching the big blind.
3. You can *raise* the bet. The other players now have to match your bet or fold.

When this round of betting is complete (sometimes with further raises—or re-raises—by other players), three community cards are dealt, this time face-up for all to see. These are called *the flop*.

You—and also the other players—now link them to your two face-down cards and judge whether the chances of a winning hand have been strengthened or weakened. You will then decide whether to fold your hand now, or participate in a second round of betting.

When that round is concluded, a further community card is dealt. This is called the *turn* card—or *4th Street*.

Another round of betting takes place.

Finally, one more community card—the fifth—is dealt. This is called *the river*.

So, if you're still in the hand, you will now have your own two pocket cards and five community cards from which to make up the five-card hand that you can now either (1) discard by folding or (2) bet it's the strongest hand at the table.

And that's what it's all about—either avoiding losing money with a weak hand or, preferably, winning money with the strongest hand. (There is one other option: you can *bluff* the other players out of the hand by convincing them you have the strongest hand. Bluffing is a big part of Texas hold'em.)

Notes

Chapter One

1. Joseph Rosa, *Wild Bill Hickok: The Man and his Myth* (University Press of Kansas, 1996)
2. Thadd Turner, *Wild Bill Hickok—Deadwood City, End of the Trail* (Old West Alive Publishing, 2001)
3. Turner, as above
4. John Ames, *The Real Deadwood* (Chamberlain Brothers, 2004)
5. Harry "Sam" Young, *Hard Knocks* (South Dakota State Historical Society Press, 2005)

Chapter Two

1. Roger A. Bruns, *Desert Honky-Tonk—the Story of Tombstone's Bird Cage Theater* (Fulcrum Publishing, 2000)
2. Bruns, as above
3. Herbert Asbury, *Sucker's Progress* (Dodd, Mead and Company, 1938)
4. Eugene Edwards, *Jack Pot* (Chicago, 1900)
5. Town of Ellsworth official website, William G. Cutler
6. Robert K. DeArment, *Knights of the Green Cloth* (University of Oklahoma Press, 1982)
7. Asbury, as above
8. Edwards, as above
9. DeArment, as above
10. Casey Tefertiller, *Wyatt Earp; the Life Behind the Legend* (John Wiley and Sons, 1997)
11. Sherry Monahan, *The Wicked West: Boozers, Cruisers, Gamblers, and More* (2006)
12. Tefertiller, as above
13. Bob Boze Bell, *The Illustrated Life and Times of Doc Holliday* (Tristar, 1995)

Chapter Three

1. Herbert Asbury, *Sucker's Progress* (Dodd, Mead and Company, 1938)

2 to 6. George H. Devol, *Forty Years a Gambler on the Mississippi* (first published by Devol and Haines, 1847; reprinted in 1955 by Applewood Books)

7. Eugene Edwards, *Jack Pot* (Chicago, 1900)

Chapter Four

1 to 3. Byron "Cowboy" Wolford with Dana Smith, *Cowboys, Gamblers and Hustlers* (Cardoza Publishing, 2002)

4. Herbert Asbury, *Sucker's Progress* (Dodd, Mead and Company, 1938)

5. Paula Mitchell Marks, *And Die in the West* (Touchstone, 1989)

6. Don Jenkins, *Johnny Moss* (JM Publishing, 1981)

7. Cowboy Wolford, as above

8 to 9. Jenkins, as above

Chapter Five

1. Ed Reid and Ovid Demaris, *The Green Felt Jungle* (The Trident Press, 1963)

2. Al Alvarez, *The Biggest Game in Town* (Houghton Mifflin, 1983)

3. Sally Denton and Roger Morris, *The Money and the Power—the Making of Las Vegas and its Hold on America* (Vintage, 2002)

4. A. D. Hopkins and K. J. Evans (eds), *The first 100: the Men and Women who Shaped Las Vegas* (Huntington Press, 1999)

5. John L. Smith, *Sharks in the Desert* (Barricade Books, 2005)

6. Gary W. Sleeper, *I'll Do My Own Damn Killin'* (Barricade Books, 2006)

7 to 8. Reid and Demaris, as above

9. Jim Gatewood, *Benny Binion* (Mullaney Corporation, 2002)

10. Sleeper, as above

11. Reid and Demaris, as above

12 to 13. Michelle Ferrari and Stephen Ives, *Las Vegas* (Bulfinch Press, 2005)

14 to 15. Benny Binion recording, Oral History Program, University of Nevada, 1976

16. Denton and Morris, as above

17. Benny Binion recording, as above

18. Andy Bellin, *Poker Nation* (Yellow Jersey, 2003)
19. Denton and Morris, as above
20. Benny Binion recording, as above

Chapter Six

1 to 3. Doyle Brunson, *Super System* (Cardoza, 1978)

Chapter Seven

1. Anthony Holden, *Bigger Deal* (Little, Brown, 2007)
2. Michael Craig's website, 2007
3. Cy Rice, *Nick the Greek, King of the Gamblers* (Funk and Wagnalls, 1969)
4. Stephen Longstreet, *Win or Lose* (Bobbs-Merrill, 1977)
5. Al Alvarez, *The Biggest Game in Town* (Houghton Mifflin, 1983)
6. David Spanier, *Total Poker* (High Stakes Publishing, 1977)
7. Michael Kaplan and Brad Reagan, *Aces and Kings* (Wenner, 2005)
8. Nolan Dalla and Peter Alson, *One of a Kind* (Atria, 2005)
9. Phil Hellmuth, *Bad Beats and Lucky Draws* (Harper Resource, 2004)
10. Chris Moneymaker, *Moneymaker* (Harper Entertainment, 2005)

Chapter Eight

1. Rex Jones, *The Railbird* (Gambling Times, 1984)

Chapter Nine

1. Herbert O. Yardley, *The Education of a Poker Player* (High Stakes, 1959)
2. Eugene Edwards, *Jack Pot* (Chicago, 1900)
3. Cy Rice, *Nick the Greek, King of the Gamblers* (Funk and Wagnalls, 1969)
4. Cy Rice, as above
5 to 6. Michael Craig, *The Professor, the Banker and the Suicide King* (Warner Books, 2005)

Chapter Eleven

1. Henry Chafetz, *Play the Devil—A History of Gambling in the United States from 1492 to 1955* (Clarkson N. Potter, 1960)

Additional reading

In addition to books already referred to, the following were helpful:

Bradshaw, Jon (ed.), *Fast Company* (High Stakes, 2003)

Curtis, David A., *Stand Pat* (LC Page and Co., 1906)

Dowling, Allen, *The Great American Pastime* (AS Barnes and Co. Inc., 1970)

Gamblers of the Old West (Time Life Books, 1978)

Grotenstein, Jonathan and Storms Reback, *All In* (Thomas Dunne Books, 2005)

Lessinger, Matt, *The Book of Bluffs* (Warner Books, 2005)

Lewis, Jerry D. (ed.), *The World's Great Poker Stories* (AS Barnes and Co. Inc., 1962)

May, Jesse, *Shut up and Deal* (Harpenden—No Exit Press, 1999)

McDonald, Glenn, *Deal Me In* (Sybex Inc., 2005)

McManus, James, *Positively Fifth Street* (Picador, 2003)

Schwartz, David G., *Roll the Bones: The History of Gambling* (Gotham Books, 2006)

Sheehan, Jack (ed.), *The Players—the Men who made Las Vegas* (University of Nevada Press, 1997)

Slim, Amarillo with Greg Dinkin, *Amarillo Slim in a World Full of Fat People* (Harpers and also Yellow Jersey Press, 2003)

Sparks, Richard, *Diary of a Mad Poker Player* (Russell Enterprises, 2005)

Index